BEYOND 911

BEYOND 911

A New Era for Policing

MALCOLM K. SPARROW

MARK H. MOORE

DAVID M. KENNEDY

BasicBooks
A Division of HarperCollins*Publishers*

Sparrow, Malcolm K.
    Beyond 911 : A new era for policing/Malcolm K. Sparrow,
Mark H. Moore, and David M. Kennedy.
        p. cm.
    Includes bibliographical references and index.
    ISBN 0–465–00675–2 (cloth)
    ISBN 0–465–00676–0 (paper)
    1. Police. 2. Police—United States—Case studies. 3.
Police—Great   Britian—Case   studies. I. Moore,   Mark
Harrison.
    II. Kennedy, David M., 1958- . III. Title. IV. Title:
Beyond nine-one-one.
HV7921.S657   1990
363.2—dc20   90-80239
                                                                    CIP

        95 96 97 RRD 10 9 8 7 6 5 4

Contents

■

v

Part II   Reconstituting the Police

Introduction

This is a book about the plight of the cities and what the police can do to help. It is a hopeful book, for we believe that policing can do far more than most would credit. Policing can fight crime (even the devastating and seemingly invincible drug trade) with unexpected effectiveness. It can act against the amorphous fear that grips and paralyzes so many of our neighborhoods. It can make a major contribution to improving and maintaining the quality of urban life. And—most important of all—policing can do all these things in ways entirely worthy of a democratic society.

We believe these things, as these pages will show, for a number of reasons. Partly we believe them because we have seen it happen: drug-infested neighborhoods reclaimed for families and children at play; simmering racial tensions dissolved; crumbling housing projects pulled back from the brink. Partly we believe them because we have come to view current, mainstream policing as hobbled by its own history and habits, and we no longer accept that what are now so evidently the limits of police performance are really limits at all. But more than anything else, we believe them because of the work of a new, innovative breed of police chiefs, who—in their desire to discover and redefine the potential of their agencies—have dared to ask fundamental questions about the role of the police. Many of these chiefs have already found new ways to use the police, not only to fight crime but also to serve other important social needs, and to do so in ways that stand up to public scrutiny. To varying extents, and in different ways, they have sought a fundamental reordering of the relationships between the police and the community and other government agencies, and between police managers and their officers. They have had the courage to begin to rethink their basic mission, their operational methods, and their organizational structures.

Such challenges to police orthodoxy present enormous opportunities. It is these opportunities that we explore in this book. Policing today has a chance to forge new attitudes of mind and structures of relationships that will help it produce high-quality solutions to society's problems—not just one problem but many problems; not just now but in the future—whatever the issues and constraints. That is why we have not written a book specifically about fighting the drug trade, or inner-city decay, or racial tensions, although all those issues appear in these pages. Similarly, we have avoided dwelling on specific managerial issues, such as patrol allocation or criminal information management. Rather, our goal has been to make a modest but broader contribution to the fashioning of police departments as healthy democratic institutions: effective, responsive, and dependable.

This aspiration has been given special point over the last few months, as we have been busy sewing up the seams of this book, by the extraordinary emergence of Eastern Europe from the tyranny of totalitarianism, a tyranny that was enforced (to different degrees in different countries) by police and secret police. Such events, quite apart from their broader significance and their place in world history, give us good reason to pause once again and consider the wide range of functions, styles, strategies, and philosophies that fall under the name *policing*.

In some societies policing has been a method of imposing the will of a small but powerful minority on a fearful, and often silent, majority; in others policing has helped the majority keep minorities in check. At other times, and in other places, where national government has lost its grip on law and order, policing has acted as a kind of corrupt local power brokerage, striking constantly shifting and unstable balances between competing political enterprises.

But in the free world, at least, policing has been ordained an instrument of democracy itself, an instrument by and through which the pressing concerns of all can be heard, their safety guaranteed, their crises addressed, their conflicts interrupted or resolved, all subject to law. And the challenge of democracy for policing demands more than a fair, thoughtful, and effective response to crime and conflict; it also demands that the fairness, thoughtfulness, and effectiveness be visible, even transparent, and open to public review.

This is a noble aspiration, and policing, so constructed and regulated, can be a noble calling. If policing has sometimes fallen short, if society has sometimes failed to demand so much—and both are all too true—it is democracy's and society's loss. Both can do better. This book, we hope, will help.

This book falls into two parts. The first, chapters 1 through 4, is descriptive. Chapter 1 offers grounds for hope. It tells the stories of three pathbreaking police departments: how they have departed from conventional policing and the good they have been able to do. Chapter 2 offers history, showing what the contemporary police are, how they got to be that way, and why their current form and beliefs stand in the way of progress. Chapter 3 emphasizes the significance of executive leadership in overcoming those constraints by tracing the work of seven pioneering police chiefs who have, in different ways, pointed the way forward. Chapter 4 interprets these leaders' experience, and in doing so explores the most important issues facing contemporary policing.

The second part of the book, chapters 5 through 8, is prescriptive. Here we make our case for how society, police managers, and police officers must change their attitudes and behavior toward one another. We do not present any particular model of how policing should be done; it is far too early to know just what the future form of policing should be, an answer that will in any case probably differ from one place to another. We present, instead, a vision of a different set of working relationships: the relationship between the police and the public through which the police and their missions are shaped and controlled; the relationship between the police and the public, and the police and other government agencies, through which those missions are accomplished; and the relationship between police managers and police officers through which discipline is maintained and performance helped or hindered. We recommend changes in these relationships that will both work an immediate transformation in police operations and keep police departments open to additional changes in the future.

Chapter 5 addresses the role of values in shaping policing's external relations and internal management. We argue that both are currently dysfunctional and propose changes based on new values and a new attention to values. Chapter 6 addresses the relationships through which police policies and operations are guided and evaluated by the public. We describe those relationships in their currently quite troubled form and propose a new kind of openness and accountability for police agencies. Chapter 7 addresses partnerships between the police and the public and other parts of government. We believe that the police cannot do the job traditionally defined as theirs without a great deal of help, making the formation of close, productive, and just alliances of the utmost importance. Finally, in chapter 8, we reveal why we remain so firmly optimistic about the future of policing. We pay tribute to the character, inventiveness, and energy of the majority of police officers and to the innovative chiefs who are finding safe ways to allow those qualities free expression. We argue that changing officers' professional environment, redefining their responsibilities, and restructuring their incentives can make them, and policing, flourish.

We know that the kinds of change we argue for in this book rarely come quickly or easily. But they are happening, as we shall show, in enough departments and cities to give genuine grounds for optimism. It is on this basis that we invite all those concerned with the quality of life in our cities—mayors, officials, police, community leaders, and residents—to take another look at policing: to reexamine with us what the police are, how they got to be what they are, what their role is, and what their role should be.

PART I

■

Modern Policing:
Crisis and Renewal

CHAPTER 1

■

The Cities and the Police

WILSHIRE, A BLIGHTED section of Watts in south central Los Angeles. Crime rules. Street dealers peddling cocaine duel for turf with submachine guns, and hookers do daylight business in abandoned cars. Wary Los Angeles police officers move through the streets by fours. Ordinary people live under siege. Drug dealers take over front lawns to do business with passing cars; in some places the foot traffic is so heavy it wears the yards down to dirt. To keep residents inside and out of the way, dealers fire guns in the air, urinate on houses, stage pit-bull fights. "I knew an old woman and her husband," says one Wilshire officer, "when they'd leave home together, the woman went out and got in the car first, laid down in the backseat while the car was in the garage. The old man would leave the radio and the lights on in the house, and he'd come out and get in the car and drive out with her in the backseat covered up. Once they left that area she'd sit up, but they could not let the dope dealers know they were leaving the house unattended. If they did, it wouldn't be there when they got back." The police seem helpless. They know where the worst problems are, but they're so busy responding to 911 calls that there's nothing more they can do. "We have no time for extra patrol," one officer says. "You never have a chance to really go out and concentrate on a problem."

Shattered, sprawling New Briarfield Apartments, Newport News, Virginia, federally subsidized home to hundreds of black single mothers. Fear rules. Collapsed walls and splintered doors invite break-ins; vacant apartments attract junkies, drunks, and gangs of kids; piles of trash and pools of fetid water breed rats. Cowed, New Briarfield's residents lock themselves in their apartments: many are afraid to go anywhere on the grounds even in broad daylight, and most refuse to go out at night even by car. Fearful of their neighbors, they stay home alone. The police seem helpless. Time after time they are called to emergencies at the apartments, and time after time they arrive too late.

Link Valley, a six-block open-air cocaine bazaar in the heart of Houston. Drugs rule. Once a pleasant apartment development, Link Valley now has more in common with Beirut or Medellín than with the calm, landscaped residential neighborhoods that surround it. Dealers operating on the streets and from vacant apartments service a drive-through clientele that comes from all over Houston and surrounding areas to make quick, easy purchases and dash back home. Most of the residents have fled, leaving empty buildings soon stripped of plumbing, wiring, and appliances. Trash is everywhere. Landlords trying to make improvements or board up empty structures are driven off by cocaine traffickers. Fences and walls are holed or leveled to ease access and escape. From the first of the year through mid-December 1988, the Houston police log 825 emergency calls, hundreds of narcotics arrests, and at least six murders in Link Valley; officers call it "Death Valley." The drug trade is so robust that one operation in a ramshackle apartment building needs flashlight wands to manage its traffic flow.

THE PLIGHT OF THE CITIES

Most Americans now live in cities, in increasingly uncivilized circumstances.[1] There is no question that many of the problems they confront are deep and structural: the cities' fragile economic bases, their crumbling infrastructures, their diminishing stocks of middle-class jobs and neighborhoods, their troubled schools, their deepening ethnic rivalries, the changing and possibly worsening social and moral habits of their populations. These are the issues generally looked to as the root causes of urban troubles. It is not always necessary to look so far afield, however. Some of the cities' most urgent problems are much more immediate. Crime, fear, drugs, and disorder can devastate not only individual lives but also the lives of communities.[2] When streets and parks are dangerous, the quality of community life suffers. When they are dangerous enough, all who can—usually the white, the better off, the better educated—flee.[3] The poor and powerless are left behind to suffer ever more dire straits. Residents, banks, and public agencies are discouraged from investment and maintenance; merchants move their businesses; racial and ethnic tensions deepen. The harm can be grievous.

The police encounter this spiral of crime and decline every day, in legions of Wilshires, New Briarfields, and Link Valleys across the country. They see, as well, every day in every city, masses of other problems that mean a great deal to those cities and the people who live in them. Between the poles of root causes and serious crime lies a vast world of mundane friction and hurt. Disorder and neglect—aggressive, drunken panhandlers, threatening youths, walls sullied by gang graffiti—often seem to signal that an area has been abandoned to the forces of decline, and can be an even stronger trigger for fear than crime itself.[4] Disputes—inside families, between landlords and tenants, employers and employees, black and white neighborhood basketball teams, delivery drivers and other road users—can cut at the fabric of social and community life and often develop into assaults and other crimes. Social and medical emergencies—runaways, the homeless, the dangerously ill clothed and ill fed—are serious on their own merits and frequently lead to victimization and crime.

5

This is where the police operate—endless, tedious, and grinding though it may be. In most cities police departments are large, powerful organizations, staffed by well-trained, resourceful people, available twenty-four hours a day for the price of a phone call. How well they perform is an absolutely crucial matter. It can mean the difference between a city in which neighborhoods are lost to drugs and one in which they are not; between a city in which the streets look and feel secure and one in which they do not; between a city in which domestic disputes are quelled before wives are killed, and runaways housed before pimps reel them in, and one in which both are lost to violence and degradation. As the crack epidemic has shown in cities like Detroit and Washington, DC—where frustrated residents have turned to driving out drug dealers by main force—it can even mean the difference between the rule of law and vigilante violence.[5]

Insofar, then, as the control of crime, fear, and disorder is important to cities' well-being—that is, to a very considerable degree—urban conditions are police business. The police have tried to handle that business, in modern times, in clear and well-defined ways. Their end has been to control crime, especially murder, rape, robbery, and the like. Their means has been to enforce the criminal law: by patrolling in cars, answering emergency 911 calls, and investigating crimes after they've occurred. Most police, and most of the public, believe fervently in this end and these means. The idea of a police force that fights crime vigorously, answers calls promptly, and investigates cleverly draws nearly universal support. Most people can't imagine anything else the police could possibly do.

The trouble—as Wilshire, New Briarfield, and Link Valley attest, as all the many Wilshires across the country attest—is that traditional police goals and methods are often too narrow and ineffectual to help troubled cities win back the ground they have lost. Even in less dire circumstances, traditional policing often cannot lend cities and neighborhoods all the support it might. Crime fighting, rapid response, and the like offer neither police nor residents much of a handle when it comes to addressing—far less preventing—such diffuse problems as fear and community tension.

There is, happily, reason to hope for better. In the United States,

England, Australia, and elsewhere, police departments are beginning to break the frame of their past approaches to policing cities.[6] They sense the necessity and the capacity to engage the problems of cities on a broader front and to develop new methods for dealing with crime, fear, drugs, and urban decay. They see the challenge of policing not simply as controlling robbery, burglary, and assault but as helping create and maintain communities in which citizens are safe, secure, and tolerant. Their departures harbor the germs of a significantly different and more effective role for policing.

The times, to these departments, have seemed to demand no less. Los Angeles, Newport News, and Houston—three such innovators—had model modern police departments. They patrolled purposefully, answered emergency calls promptly, investigated crimes systematically. They got nowhere. Wilshire's and Link Valley's dealers and prostitutes and New Briarfield's drunks and burglars simply melted away when patrol cars drove into sight. (Wilshire police lore has it that the area's street peddlers were so bold that the Los Angeles chief of police, inspecting the area in an unmarked car, was repeatedly stopped and pressed to buy cocaine.) Officers flying to answer 911 calls usually arrived, sirens and flashing lights notwithstanding, to find the TV already stolen, the shots already fired, the dope already sold. For all that, the departments were busy, too busy to pay any constructive attention to less serious matters, like a project full of poor tenants living in constant fear or the near siege of an old couple's home.

In most police departments that would have been the end of it, for in most departments patrol, emergency response, and investigation *are* police work. When they fail there is nothing else to turn to. Los Angeles, Newport News, and Houston had other ideas. In Los Angeles the department created a new, vital relationship with the neighborhoods of Wilshire, then brought the combined energies of community and police to bear against crime and disorder. In Newport News the department expanded its focus on crimes and emergency calls—the endless incidents of police work—to include the problems and situations that gave rise to those incidents, and found ways to mitigate the causes. In Houston the police reconsidered their basic goal—putting bad guys in jail—and came up with a

7

new idea of what their job was and a new partnership with the community to get it done. We tell their stories here as particularly vivid examples of approaches many of the departments we will describe in this book have essayed, with considerable promise. This is not more policing, but better policing, not tougher policing, but smarter policing. If there is hope that better police work can markedly improve the safety and quality of life in troubled communities—and there is—it lies down these paths.

COMMUNITY POLICING IN WILSHIRE: THE POWER OF PARTNERSHIPS

Late in 1984 senior officers in the Los Angeles Police Department's Wilshire Area (the LAPD calls its precincts "areas") found themselves in a peculiar position.[7] According to the Parker Center, LAPD headquarters, they were doing a pretty good job. Wilshire's reported crime was declining, and its response time—the average time it takes a patrol car to get to the scene of a 911 call—was excellent. These routine accounting measures were the LAPD's—and almost every other major police department's—key indexes for the performance of its patrol force, so area commanders could rest assured that as long as these measures were favorable, and as long as they presided over no major scandals or malfeasance, their performance would be judged positively.

Wilshire's captain and his senior staff didn't feel nearly so good about their performance. Statistics aside, their area was a mess, and they were frustrated that they couldn't do more about it. Street drug dealing was rampant; there were drunks everywhere; major streets had been all but taken over by prostitutes. The area seemed dangerous and uninviting, and Wilshire's respectable residents clamored constantly for increased police presence and attention. Many of Wilshire Area's patrol officers were frustrated too. Virtually all they did was answer 911 calls, many to situations that though indisputably important were not even remotely emergencies—scenes of stolen cars or burglaries many hours old—and they felt they were wasting their time.

Officers who'd been with the department for some time felt particularly frustrated because they could remember when things had been different. Back in 1970 the LAPD had created a special patrol rank—senior lead officer, or SLO—to pursue crime prevention and keep in touch with the city's ordinary citizens.[8] Senior lead officers were responsible not only for patrolling and answering calls but for listening to, educating, and mobilizing the residents on their beats. They held neighborhood meetings in schools and police stations, organized crime watches, and taught crime prevention and earthquake safety classes. Sometimes they heard about and organized a police response to problems that otherwise would have gone unnoticed; sometimes they could alert a neighborhood that a burglar or rapist was active locally. Sometimes their contacts in the community even knew, and said, where suspects in major crimes had gone to ground. Residents and police alike favored the new role.

Officers found it hard to do the extra work, though, especially as the department's call load got heavier through the seventies and eighties (as did that of every major police department). "When I was working swing shift, four to midnight, if you were to drive out there and make yourself available for calls, you wouldn't be available one minute that night for anything else," Joe Ciancanelli, an SLO in Rampart Area, said recently. "There wouldn't be a dull moment, no time for anything. Day watch is pretty much the same." By 1984 many of the LAPD's SLOs had largely given up on their community contacts and crime prevention work. In busy Wilshire, says one SLO, "SLOs weren't accountable for anything. People would call in with complaints, and we'd say, 'OK, ma'am, we'll get you some extra patrol.' That was the end of it."

Early in 1985 Wilshire Area's senior officers decided they'd had their priorities backward. Launching the Wilshire Community Mobilization Project, they took all eight of the area's SLOs off patrol duty entirely and set them to work. "We made them the department's representative for *everything*," says Ernest Curtsinger, Wilshire Area's captain. They were expected to figure out what the people of Wilshire wanted, and they were held accountable for seeing that they got it, even if that meant spending time on drunk patrol and hauling abandoned cars rather than answering emergency calls. Crime, Wilshire's captain decreed—against the tide not only of his own department but of more than forty years of police thinking—was no longer his only priority.

His mind had been changed in part by his personal frustration with Wilshire's condition and in part by a 1982 *Atlantic Monthly* article written by two prominent students of police behavior, James Q. Wilson and George L. Kelling.[9] In "Broken Windows," Wilson and Kelling framed a simple argument that struck at the heart of modern policing's mission. Police departments that focus solely or even primarily on serious crime—as virtually all do—will not, they said, be of much help to a community struggling to keep its head above water. There are often clear signals, they pointed out, that marginal neighborhoods are going downhill, signals like broken windows, trash, or street prostitution and drug dealing. Such disorder, while often too minor and resilient to warrant much attention from police, attracts miscreants and breeds fear in communities; fearful people avoid one another, and the deterioration accelerates. Alienation and hopelessness eat away at security and civility. Fighting crime, Wilson and Kelling said, is important. Fighting fear and disorder is essential.

"Broken Windows" struck a deep chord in Wilshire Area's command staff. "We have long since passed the point where we can stick with catching bad guys, chasing people, recovering stolen property," says Curtsinger. "The job is much more than that, and probably always was. We just didn't, I think, pick up on it fast enough." Wilson and Kelling's ideas rang just as true to Wilshire's patrol officers. "People in the neighborhoods were not necessarily concerned with what our department's mainly concerned about: robberies, burglaries, theft of motor vehicles," says one. "What they were concerned about was a group of winos that they'd been calling about for years and years that are loitering on this corner down here, the prostitutes along Washington Boulevard, the graffiti on the walls that's getting worse and worse, day after day after day, that no one is doing anything about." Wilshire Area decided to figure out some way to give the people what they wanted.

The SLOs printed newsletters introducing themselves, handed

out business cards, went to block meetings, met with the city council representatives for their areas, got their own station-house phone numbers and answering machines. The more they circulated in the community, the more convinced they were that they were on the right track. "The citizens out there are concerned about nuisance problems," says a Community Mobilization Project SLO. "They expect to be burglarized in their lifetime, sometime, OK? They know it's going to happen. But the nuisance problems, like for instance drunks on the corner, this is a problem they want corrected."

Wilshire's SLOs discovered, to their delight, that nuisances such as drunks on corners were something they could deal with. "Before, a radio car would pass by, yell, 'Hey guys, get out of here'—two minutes' worth of work and they're on their way to the next five calls they're holding," one SLO says. "What we'll do is we'll send a 318, a vice investigation, to our vice unit, to start an investigation of the liquor store for selling to the drunks in the first place. We'll go down to the location three, four, five times a day. Every time we see someone we can take to jail for drinking in public, we'll take him to jail. We'll do a constant, constant patrol until the problem doesn't exist. It might take a week, it might take two months, but we just keep hitting: and we do that with all the problems that come our way."

A lot of the problems that came their way were not, by any stretch of the imagination, traditional police issues. "People will call the police department for *everything*," Curtsinger says. Normally police departments try to shrug off the vast volume of—to their minds—nuisance calls that come their way. Under the Community Mobilization Project, Wilshire Area handled them. "The SLO is now, basically, the conduit for all city government services," Curtsinger says. "We have intersections where the trees have grown over the stop signs. People feel helpless on their own to get the city to come out and trim the trees so people won't keep running those stop signs and having accidents. So they call their local SLO, who in turn calls the city council, whoever he has to contact. And guess what? The tree gets trimmed! Street maintenance is the same way; that's the kind of response nobody has ever been able to get. It's a big city, there are a lot of players, and if you don't know what everybody does and who to call, all you do is get referred to somebody else. Now they only have one person to call."

The LAPD, the people of Wilshire soon discovered, could be hell on nuisances. The SLOs got abandoned cars towed, got local businesses to donate paint and organized graffiti paint-outs, got broken streetlights fixed. Out of their patrol cars, able to take a moment when they wanted to talk to people, they started to know people, and people started to know them.

As those bonds formed, it became clear that SLOs in close contact with their neighborhoods can be very effective against crime. Neighborhood bonds mean information, and information is power.[10] The day after a shooting in SLO Jimmy Ross's area, a man Ross had met on the street came into the police station. "The guy said, 'Give me a little time and I can get some information for you on this guy you are looking for,' " an SLO says. "Boom, they went out and picked him up." The information had always been out there. "If there's a rock house in an area, everybody on the block knows what's going on," says one SLO. "But to get someone to stand forward . . ." The more Wilshire's SLOs circulated, the more streetlights they got fixed, the more people came forward. "I had a guy call me last week who had a rock house directly across the street from his house," the SLO says. "He had eighteen license numbers, different luxury cars—they came in limousines and whatnot. Well, this guy says, 'Hey, I want you to come during the day when they can see you. I want them to know I'm not afraid of them.' He pointed out several suspects to me, and the next day Narcotics Division picked up one of the guys who was holding, and he in turn gave them information leading to several other arrests. If you can't get them to believe in you, if you can't get them to go out there and do a little extra, you really don't have anything. You have to make those people believe that there's something that can be done in that particular neighborhood."

People in Wilshire did begin to believe that there was something they could do to salvage their community. The Community Mobilization Project, says Roderick Sites, a Wilshire resident for twenty-three years, "has been greatly effective in giving the people here in the community a feeling of hope, a feeling of being able to relate to the police department, which a lot of people hadn't been able to do." Before the project, Sites's neighborhood had felt pretty much on its own. With CMP, besieged residents and the LAPD made a close alliance. Crime watches in Sites's neighborhood, organized by SLO J. D. Allen, went to great lengths to get the goods on the local villains. One resident and her neighbor kept tabs on a woman living up the street who was wholesaling drugs to the street retailers. "I saw her coming over here in her car delivering drugs, and I called Ellen up and say this is what's happening," the resident says. "She can watch all the way up in one direction; I can see over on my side. They usually come down here, and turn and go straight over past her house. So Ellen will say, 'Who is that? Isn't that so-and-so?' And I'll drop the phone, go over here where I can see it. 'Yep, that's so-and-so.' So we know that. Or she'll get half the license number, I'll get the other half. I went and got the make of the car; it was a Mitsubishi." As time went on the neighborhood watches grew increasingly savvy and extraordinarily active. "When the time comes to actually make an arrest, it takes a lot of surveillance," one member says. "We're getting tuned in to making sure our information is accurate, in case things change a little bit. So our people are getting information all the way down to how dealers are traveling over the fences and things like that. Where we can catch them, what they're wearing today, how they come and go."

And as time went on, the neighborhood started to recover. "A year ago if I had seen some gang members in my yard, I would have went in the house, hid the kids under the bed, and that's it," says one woman. "I see them now in front of somebody else's house and I go, 'Hey, don't do that,' or 'Take your butts to school,' or something like that. And they respect you. You find out they'll call us bitches, they'll talk about us, but none of them will hurt us." There was a strong feeling that the community had, somewhere along the way, turned an important corner. "We don't have half the problems that we had before," one of Sites's friends says. "It's unreal, the improvement. You have kids playing out in the street again."

Thus, in less than two years, Wilshire's police had discovered, to their great and unexpected pleasure, that they did not have to watch helplessly as their area fell apart. The people of Wilshire Area knew what they wanted, and if the LAPD helped them get it, they in turn would help with business the police had traditionally insisted on keeping to themselves. Captain Curtsinger has no doubt whatsoever about the lesson to be drawn. "If we are going to have any impact on the crime problem," he says, "we have got to get more involved in community-oriented policing. Adding policemen in the field is not the answer. Number one, we can't afford it. And I don't care if they got another $25 million set aside, $25 million is not enough. It's too costly and it doesn't even work. So what we got to do, is we got to start dealing in the community. That's what these SLOs are doing. It *really* works."

PROBLEM SOLVING IN NEWPORT NEWS: THE POWER OF THOUGHT

The Newport News police, facing the New Briarfield morass—and a host of other problems, seemingly as intractable—also found an approach that works.[11] They had different sources of inspiration, different thoughts, different methods than did the police in Wilshire, but they shared completely Ernest Curtsinger's sense that the old ways were no longer the best ways. Once, says Darrel Stephens, the thoughtful, soft-spoken man who was Newport News's chief of police in 1985, when the department finally came to grips with New Briarfield, "my solutions to problems were traditional: more patrol, more investigations." Stephens came instead to believe that more was not enough, could never be enough. Traditional methods, he thought, were in large measure *why* the police couldn't seem to get anywhere. There was good reason to believe, Stephens says, "that the foundation of police strategy was sand instead of rock."

Where Wilson and Kelling, in "Broken Windows," had taken aim at *what* police generally try to do—fight crime—and argued that it was the wrong end, Stephens took aim at *how* they invariably try to fight crime and argued that they used the wrong means. His targets were the heavy weapons in the police armamentarium: preventive patrol and rapid response. Neither, Stephens said, really works.

His foremost evidence came from two groundbreaking exper-

14

iments in Kansas City, Missouri. In one, in 1972, the police department tested the utility of preventive patrol by giving three areas of the city very different degrees of attention. One area got no patrol at all: officers answered emergency calls, but otherwise they stayed away. One was patrolled two to three times the normal amount; one was patrolled as usual. Hundreds of measures of crime and fear were assessed, from police statistics and neighborhood surveys, to test the effect of the variations. The results dumbfounded the police world. The variations in patrol seemed to have no appreciable impact at all. Levels of crime and fear were almost identical in all three areas, and neither the residents of the high-patrol area nor those of the no-patrol area noticed that anything had changed.[12]

Nobody was quite sure why all this was true. There were various ideas. Much crime, like loan-sharking and drug dealing, is consensual; it usually causes no real public ruckus. Much violent crime—rapes, assaults, murders—happens among friends, often inside and out of sight. Predatory muggers and burglars learn quickly to be discreet and fleet. Whatever the explanations, one of policing's most basic tenets had been seriously undercut. "Routine preventive patrol," said Kansas City's police chief, "has little value in preventing crime or making citizens feel safe."

Five years later Kansas City did much the same kind of experiment with rapid response, with equally startling results. In 1931, when policing in the United States was struggling to escape from a depth of corruption and incompetence that made the Keystone Kops as much documentary as spoof, Herbert Hoover's Wickersham Commission, a leading reform body, looked hopefully to the time when police could be anywhere on a moment's notice. "For the safety of society," the commission wrote, "the police must have not only competent men keen on the scent, but the necessary equipment, both teletype and radio, to instantly spread the intelligence of the crime and descriptions of the criminals to long distances, giving their direction and method of escape, while at the same time having equipment for pursuit more than equal to those of the criminals used in making their escape."[13]

The sentiment seemed unimpeachable, and over the next decades police executives pursued it relentlessly. They took officers off foot beat and put them in cars, equipped the cars with radios, took dispatching away from the precincts and centralized it at headquarters, set up special 911 systems. Rapid response, as the police lexicon demonstrates, became the next best thing to an end in itself: officers driving around aimlessly but available to be dispatched on a radio call are "in service," while officers who've *taken* a call and are doing something useful like chasing a criminal or soothing a frightened victim are logged "out of service."[14] The effort was extremely successful. Most departments today can deploy a car anywhere in their jurisdictions within a very few minutes.

The trouble, as Kansas City's 1977 response time study revealed, is that by the time the police start flying to the scene it's generally already far too late.[15] Many crimes—so-called discovery crimes—are revealed only when victims return to their cars or homes to find them stolen or burgled; the scene is stone cold, and rapid response is relevant only to the victim's peace of mind. For involvement crimes, with victims actually confronting the villains, rapid response should help. Generally it doesn't. In Kansas City, the chance of arresting a villain at the scene became infinitesimal if victims waited more than five minutes to call police. Unfortunately, most waited far longer. Having caught a criminal in the act, at best, or having been assaulted, at worst, most understandably took some time to look their houses over, call a friend, patch themselves up, or simply have hysterics before calling 911. By then the criminals were long gone. Only *2 percent* of the department's serious-crime calls seemed to merit a rapid response.[16] Similar studies elsewhere confirmed Kansas City's findings.[17]

For Darrel Stephens—who was a patrol officer in Kansas City during the first study—and others like him, the discouraging news about patrol and rapid response spoke volumes. The fact that the foundation of modern policing was sand, as Stephens puts it, was bad enough. Some of the implications seemed even worse. By relying on patrol to prevent crime and rapid response to catch criminals, police had backed themselves into an isolated, reactive corner. The beat officers of old had naturally seen crime on their beats in terms of patterns: they were responsible for all incidents on their turf, and a rash of burglaries or overdoses signaled a burglar or a dealer who needed to be dealt with. Modern officers, tied to their radios, saw crime as an endless string of isolated incidents. Fourteen burglaries in the same neighborhood might draw fourteen different cars. Something better, Stephens thought, was called for.

Something better was available. Herman Goldstein, a law professor at the University of Wisconsin who'd spent a lot of time in the trenches with different police departments—including Kansas City's, where he met Stephens—was inspired by just these issues to write an article in 1979 calling for a new kind of "problem-oriented policing."[18] Many seemingly distinct police incidents, Goldstein said, stem from common underlying conditions and problems. To understand the incidents, police must look to their causes; to do that they must cast a wide net for any information that might help. To address the problems—and thus the incidents—police should use not just their ultimate power of arrest but any promising (and legitimate) avenues that come to mind.

Sketched so baldly, Goldstein's thesis seems painfully obvious. In policing circles, by contrast, the theology of patrol and response was so deeply ingrained that his ideas, where they were credited at all, were nigh unto revolutionary. Their first big chance came in 1983, when Darrel Stephens took over the Newport News police department and launched its Problem-oriented Policing Project, with help from Goldstein, the National Institute of Justice, and the Police Executive Research Forum. Stephens's simplest hope for the approach was also his most heartfelt. "I wanted," he says, "police officers to have a chance to *think*."

He wanted them to think about crime. Stephens was well aware of Wilson and Kelling's broken-windows theory on fear and disorder and gave it considerable weight, but he was taking aim first and foremost at classic police problems. Patrol and rapid response might not be effective against burglary, street crime, car theft, and the like, but Stephens was convinced that something must be. It was up to his department, and the problem-oriented approach, to figure out what.

The task force of department personnel he convened to consider problems for special attention thought the same way. It nominated a host of thorny issues that had consistently resisted police efforts.

Burglaries at the New Briarfield Apartments were one; prostitution and robberies in the downtown business district were another; thefts from cars in the huge parking lots outside Newport News Shipbuilding were still another. This was crime at its most mundane, the ordinary, endless, daily grind of every police department in the world.

Tackling the New Briarfield burglaries began with a luxury almost unheard of in ordinary police work: pausing for a time to figure out just what was going on. Early in 1985 detective Tony Duke was put in charge of analyzing the New Briarfield problem, any way he wanted to. Duke turned to his task with a will.

He began with ordinary departmental information and resources. The department had recorded seventy burglaries in New Briarfield in 1984 and made a host of felony arrests in and around the apartments. Duke hoped there might be useful patterns concealed in the crime and arrest data, but no matter how he looked nothing emerged. There seemed to be no rhyme or reason to where the arrestees lived (most turned out to have been collared for assault rather than burglary anyway). The burglaries had occurred almost randomly around the apartments, and followed no apparent time pattern. Duke's hopes that it might profit to keep an eye on a few particularly industrious burglars or stake out apartments that seemed particularly likely to be hit were disappointed.

He turned instead to New Briarfield's residents. What the police did not know, they might. Stephens had freed up an enormous amount of police time by creating a headquarters unit that ultimately took 35 percent of all police reports over the phone, reducing street officers' burden greatly. Duke put some of this time to good use, organizing a team of officers who ultimately visited and talked to almost half New Briarfield's renters. They learned a number of striking things. One was that better than half the residents agreed with the police that burglary was New Briarfield's most important problem, an unsurprising consensus given that fully one-fifth of New Briarfield's families had been broken into at least once in the last six months. Thirty percent, though, were even more concerned about the apartments' disrepair. Interviewers saw truly striking sights: occupied apartments open to the weather for weeks when roofs or floors collapsed, a month-long deluge from a broken water main, a swimming pool brimming with noxious garbage. Flimsy, warped doors and windows sported huge gaps and cracks. It was no wonder New Briarfield was burglar heaven.

The survey had a profound effect on Duke and the task force. When Newport News police had handled the apartments traditionally—visiting them only, for the most part, when called in on a crime—they had tended to blame everybody who lived there for the constant trouble. Predator and prey had blurred. Now, having gone door to door, made some friends, absorbed a sense of what life in New Briarfield was like, the police began to care. They found one young mother so afraid of being burgled that she kept her food at her mother's, 3 miles away. She, and all the others like her, were clearly worth helping. Duke and his people also began to think that their burglary problem was not a thing in itself; that it was caused, at least in part, by New Briarfield's abysmal deterioration. And, given their newfound sympathy for residents, they began to think that living conditions in the apartments were themselves worthy of attention.

Like Wilshire's SLOs, the Newport News police discovered that they could be hell on nuisances. Barry Haddix, the officer who patrolled the New Briarfield area during the day, made cleaning up the apartments something of a personal crusade. He leaned on the complex's building manager to settle a feud with private garbage collectors that had prevented trash pickup for months; he had her clean out the fermenting swimming pool and dispose of a collection of dangerous abandoned refrigerators that had been dumped on New Briarfield's grounds. He mobilized city authorities to rid the area of junked cars and clean up its neglected streets. Things were beginning to happen.

Tony Duke, meanwhile, was poring through real estate records trying to figure out who was really responsible for New Briarfield. It was no easy task. The apartments had been passed for years from one hand to another, exploited for tax breaks at every turn. It took weeks for Duke to uncover the current owners. When he did, New Briarfield's dilapidated condition became a little easier to understand: the owners were more than $1.5 million in arrears and near default on a $5.3 million loan from the Department of Housing and Urban Development.

Those facts represented leverage Newport News could use. In May 1985 Darrel Stephens helped arrange a meeting of the city's redevelopment and housing, codes compliance, fire, planning, and social-service agencies to frame a plan for New Briarfield. It was the first time in the city's history that the various arms of local government had confronted such a problem together. It did so decisively. New Briarfield, the group concluded, was beyond salvation: meeting city housing codes and fitting doors and windows that might keep thieves out would cost its owners more than the complex was worth. Better to face facts and knock the place down, if new housing could be found—or built—for the current residents.

Things moved rapidly therafter. Bowing to pressure from the city, HUD foreclosed on its New Briarfield loan in July. Federal bureaucrats turned out to be more amenable to making improvements than the apartments' absentee landlords had been and soon began work that included replacing many units' floors, doors, and windows. Constant pressure from tenants—fostered by crime prevention and self-help associations, founded with police help, that by now included 90 percent of New Briarfield residents—helped keep HUD attentive. People who six months earlier wouldn't open their doors to one another were now *organizing*. At the same time Newport News opened negotiations with HUD to replace New Briarfield with new low-income apartments, a large shopping center, and an extension to the local elementary school.

Those talks were difficult and their success far from certain, but even as city officials worked to bring them to fruition, it was evident that something important had already been accomplished. Not only were New Briarfield's residents feeling much more active and optimistic, and living in much improved circumstances, but the apartments' burglary rate—the police department's core original concern—was down 35 percent.[19] Darrel Stephens, it seemed, had been right. Give officers some time to think about things, look to root causes, act against problems rather than just incidents, and the police *can* fight crime.

A FIGHT AGAINST DRUGS IN LINK VALLEY:
THE POWER OF NEW IDEAS

Link Valley shows something perhaps even more encouraging: that the police can fight even the most threatening and frightening of modern crimes—the urban drug trade—and that they can do it, if they play their cards right and have the right kind of help from the community and the city, without even putting anybody in jail. In Link Valley, which had succumbed wholly to the ravages of the cocaine blight, the police and community together fashioned a new kind of solution, aimed not at law enforcement but at crime prevention.[20] A coalition of police and community framed the strategy and assembled an extremely wide variety of resources—law enforcement, corrections, city government, neighborhood volunteers, business, and media—to carry it out. The result, a year later, was a Link Valley that was safe, clean, and, as far as residents and police can tell, drug free. More important, perhaps, the participants are convinced that what they did is replicable, even a model for others to take up.

Link Valley had not, of course, always been blighted by drugs. In the 1970s and mid-1980s Link Valley had been a nice middle-class community. Built next to a major freeway and close to the Astrodome, the Texas Medical Center, and one of Houston's major airports, it attracted, nearby residents recall, a quiet, respectable mix of medical students, athletes, airline employees, and local people. Sergeant J. W. Collins, a husky, direct twenty-five-year police veteran who runs a tactical squad out of Beechnut Station, which has responsibility for Link Valley, recalls the drug trade hitting Link Valley like wildfire in early 1986, spreading in only a few months from a few dealers hanging out at a bank of pay phones on one edge of the area to a full-blown crisis. By 1987 his unit was in Link Valley every day. Nearly everyone who lived there left, abandoning the apartments to the dealers and their drive-through clients.

"The thing that made it so bad was that it was so close to the freeway," Collins says. "Most of the consumers who went there were white, and most of them would be considered casual consumers. The drug of choice there was not crack—I don't remember making more than one or two crack arrests in that whole time—it was powdered cocaine. And a lot of them, being white, they were nervous about driving down into a black section of town. They were doing something illegal, they stood out, they were more likely to come into contact with the police, get robbed, whatever. But they didn't feel that from going to Link Valley, because they could see the freeway. And they knew that all they had to do was pull off, buy the drugs, and get back on. They would never even get out of their cars." Link Valley became so appealing a market, patrol officers say, that license plates from as far away as Louisiana were not uncommon.

The police made hundreds of arrests in Link Valley every year, to no particular avail. Houston had a serious jail-space shortage, which meant felons were less likely to land in jail and less likely to serve long sentences if they did. Midlevel dealers—those one or two rungs above the street—seemed to have little trouble replacing, in quite short order, anyone the police picked up. Making arrests in Link Valley was like shooting fish in a barrel, but there always seemed to be more fish.

In frustration, Collins turned to what seemed to him some of the underlying causes of Link Valley's intractability. Things wouldn't be nearly so bad, he reasoned, if dealers didn't have the wealth of empty buildings and apartments to work and hide in. Many of the buildings were clearly unsafe and in violation of city codes; the city had the power to board them up or even demolish them. But Collins's overtures to the Housing and Conservation Division were met, he says, with great coolness. Considerable work (enormous work, often, in the cases of out-of-state holding companies or buildings that had undergone condo conversion) was required to ascertain ownership and prove violations. Even when both had been done, long and cumbersome due process preceded any action by the city. It became clear that the city was not eager, or perhaps even willing, to work very hard to address Link Valley's gross structural problems. Collins was stymied.

He and the police might have stayed stymied if the residential neighborhoods around Link Valley had not been galvanized into action. On September 19, 1988, Glora Pastor, age sixty-six, was robbed and killed in her home north of Link Valley by young men who were found forty-five minutes later parked in her van outside a Link Valley drug den. Publicity, and local shock, was great. The heads of several local civic associations, including a trim young accountant named George Harris, formed the Stella Link Revitalization Coalition and approached the police demanding action and offering help.

The coalition wanted a crackdown. "When we first started this, naturally the drug dealer was the number one enemy in our minds," Harris says. They wanted to see arrests and long jail sentences. Beechnut's Captain William Edison and Sergeant Collins, who were responsible for the police end of things as the group's strategy emerged, could easily have used the community's newfound backing to mount a massive police push. They didn't. They determined instead to try something new.

"Enforcement, by arresting them and putting them in the criminal justice system, just wasn't working," Collins says. "So we wanted to try something different. And obviously, when you look at it, the consumer was the problem, whether it's here or in another part of town. If you don't have the consumer, then you're not going to have the dealer: the man in the McDonald's is not going to keep his McDonald's open if he doesn't sell enough burgers. So we wanted to focus on the consumers. And the only way you could do that was by keeping them out of the area long enough to force the dealer to go someplace else to sell his wares, because he had money invested in the narcotics and I'm sure he has a cash-flow problem just like everybody else and has to move his product." How they were going to focus on the consumer was another matter entirely, but the idea had taken firm hold.

Their second main notion was to get on top of the area's physical decay. "The place looked bad," Collins says. "The people who went in there presumably didn't feel as guilty about destroying the neighborhood when it already looked like it was destroyed. And we knew that when some of the owners had gone out there and tried to board up their buildings, the dealers actually ran them off, physically ran them off. So the dealer didn't want it to look better either, because he wanted people to think that this was a neighborhood lost. The

23

fastest, cheapest way to make it look different was to clean up the trash. [If we could keep the dealers away for a while,] then the owners who wanted could come in and either board up or fix their property."

Despite its initial desire to see a wave of arrests, the Stella Link coalition soon came on board, which George Harris and other participants credit in large measure to Collins's honesty and bluntness. Beechnut Station officers were no longer, if they ever had been, in the mood for the soothing platitudes so often the staple of police-community relations. "We invited [Collins] to a meeting that we held for the civic group leaders, and he got up and let us know what was going on over there," Harris says. "And he didn't pull any punches. There've been this many murders, we've made hundreds of calls for service, 200-plus drug arrests. And it's a revolving door, and the problem is open and abandoned dangerous buildings."

Once focused on prevention, the police and the coalition soon came up with a plan, with clear jobs for each party. The police were to secure the streets of Link Valley and interrupt the flow of drive-through drug buyers. Mindful of the inefficacy of their traditional buy-and-bust tactics, they decided instead to throw a perimeter around the area, to block most access points and oversee, car by car, entrance through the few remaining. Nobody, as far as they knew, had ever done anything like that before, but police lawyers became convinced that case law developed on drunk-driving roadblocks in Massachusetts offered adequate precedent. The tactic would not allow them to search drivers or vehicles for drugs, weapons, or paraphernalia, but since Collins and his cohort had become much less interested in arrests than in somehow warning people off, that didn't bother them very much. The nerve of average middle-class drug purchasers, they thought, was likely to fail if they had to pass through a line of watchful police to do their business.

The coalition was to clean up Link Valley and arrange for its battered apartment buildings to be repaired or at least physically secured by replacing locks, boarding up doors and windows, and whatever else it took to make it harder for dealers to reestablish themselves. The first part of that job was a massive volunteer cleanup to be planned and performed by the coalition. The second depended

24

on tracking down the buildings' titleholders. This was not, as Collins had found earlier, a trivial task, and the city still showed little enthusiasm for taking it on. Instead, one of the coalition's more active members, a bank officer, persuaded the company that did his bank's title searches to donate enough time to trace ownership of Link Valley's buildings, a project representing thousands of dollars' worth of work. Collins and the coalition got their list.

The Link Valley operation, though still in the planning stage, was garnering a great deal of media attention. This, participants figured, was all to the good; they wanted dealers to leave and buyers to stay away, and if publicity helped the cause so much the better. This view represented something of a sea change on the part of the police. "The media is very important on something like this," Collins says. "Before this, I may not have had the same opinion about the media. A lot of times I think policemen distrust the media. I know, personally, that there were things that, years ago, I could have told the media that would have made them a better story, and I didn't tell them unless they asked me. I was never dishonest, but I didn't volunteer anything. Now I see that wasn't the thing to do. Now I think of them as people with jobs, and I always made sure that they had what they needed." The test of this new attitude came a few days before the neighborhood cordon was to go up, when police lawyers decided that the law required prior announcement of the operation. "When I first heard that, it didn't set with me too well," Collins says. "I envisioned that, at the beginning, we were going to go out there and arrest some of these people. But then the more we thought about it, actually, that's what we wanted: we wanted to get the word out to the consumer. And how else can you get the information out to the consuming public except through the media?"

On January 27, 1989, at one o'clock in the afternoon, some one hundred police officers moved into Link Valley before setting up the perimeter and found, essentially, nothing: no drugs, no guns, no dealers, no signs of crime except shattered, bullet-pocked buildings and hundreds of discarded hypodermic needles. The publicity had driven all the villains away. No arrests were made, which sparked some critical comment from various media observers and local officials, but Sergeant Collins, Captain Edison, and company were delighted. The idea had been to move the dealers out of Link Valley, and the shift was apparently well under way.

The next day the coalition moved in for its cleanup. Harris and his fellows had succeeded beyond their wildest dreams in mobilizing both local and corporate help; Collins recalls parked cars lined up for a mile on access roads as volunteers walked in with hoes and garbage bags. People who were there still talk about the day with awe. "The cleanup was just incredible," says Sue Davis, a city council aide involved with the coalition. "Hundreds of people. Hundreds. Old people, young people, people with their kids, some guy with a landscape service showed up with some workers, a judge sent over thirty or forty probationers, it was just incredible. You walked down this several-block area and everywhere was a beehive of activity. We got some companies to loan us bulldozers, and the solid waste department had moved in these huge, huge Dumpsters the day before, and we ended up having to get more because there was so much trash we cleared out.The health department had gotten donations of little disposable boxes you put syringes in, some people brought cookies and Cokes, and one of the state reps showed up; he hadn't helped in the planning process but he showed up to work, he was out there cleaning stuff up. For most of the day they hauled trash out of the buildings, cut down weeds, cleaned garbage out of the streets: it was a horrible mess, nasty, dirty, filthy work, and they just went after it wholeheartedly. It was the most amazing thing I've ever seen in my life."

By day's end the coalition crew had cleared 250 cubic yards—ten semitrailer-sized Dumpsters—of trash out of Link Valley. If anything was going to signal a change in atmosphere, Collins figured, that would. "After the first weekend," he says, "you could drive through and know that it wasn't the same place. Maybe then the people who were destroying the neighborhood would feel a little guilty about it. I don't know if they did or they didn't, but it was an idea."

Beechnut kept the cordon (which required, after the initial cleanup, only a handful of officers) around Link Valley in place for a month. Cars that came to the police checkpoint were stopped, warned that they were entering a high-crime area, then allowed to proceed (residents were issued stickers that conveyed free passage). For the first few days traffic along the service roads into the area was heavy. "I think," says Collins, "a lot of the consumers came there to see if we were doing what we said we were going to do." Then it tapered off. Officers on the checkpoints say that almost everybody stopped said they were there to see a friend, drove into Link Valley, and promptly drove out again. As far as police could tell, drug trafficking had stopped completely. Officers issued numerous citations for minor motor vehicle violations—expired inspection stickers and the like—and made, to Collins's recollection, one firearms and two drunk-driving arrests. They didn't pick up anybody on narcotics charges. Beechnut Station lifted the perimeter late in February.

By then Collins and the coalition had been in touch with the Link Valley property owners identified by the coalition's title searches, and many had already come in to lock, board up, fence in, and otherwise secure their buildings and grounds. Twenty of the twenty-three owners involved eventually brought their buildings into compliance with city ordinances. Many did so willingly; one local bank that held title to several Link Valley properties sent a representative to take a look around and promptly razed a large apartment complex and a strip shopping center. Some required persuasion, even formal city citation, before they acted; to date three owners have been cited and sued, and one jailed, on housing code and tax violations.

In the meantime, to everybody's delight, Link Valley has stayed quiet. The police operation, the cleanup, the physical improvements, and the attendant public spotlight have apparently broken the cycle of crime and decay permanently. The police were prepared to go to special lengths to prevent the drug trade from reestablishing itself, but none were necessary. To the casual eye, Link Valley now looks like any other quiet, well-groomed middle-class residential area (overlooking the fact that more buildings than not are empty and sealed up and not a few are speckled with bullet holes). Its residents come and go, day or night, as they please, and toys and bicycles dot

27

front lawns. Collins and his squad take particular delight in the conversion of a seedy game hall, one of their first and worst trouble spots, into a newly minted storefront church.

Crime statistics bear out first impressions. Six months after the end of the operation, calls for police service in Link Valley proper were down 44 percent, and Part 1 crimes—murder, rape, robbery, assault, burglary, larceny, arson, and auto theft—were down in every surrounding neighborhood, in some places by as much as 12 percent.[21] As important, if more impressionistic, is the police department's sense that closing down Link Valley's open-air market has not meant that another has sprouted elsewhere in Houston. Collins has been unable to find any new powdered-cocaine market anywhere in the city. He doesn't really believe that Link Valley's old consumers reformed; more likely, he suspects that they started smoking crack or buying the powdered drug in bulk from lower-profile retailers. Whatever they've done, it doesn't seem to involve dragging a new neighborhood down, which he considers a major victory.

And so, of course, it is. But Link Valley is also a victory for policing as a whole, for it makes the point, in the most graphic and encouraging of ways, that policing need not be stymied by the constraints of business as usual or the weaknesses of traditional tactics. One small group of police, and one small group of activist residents, armed with the determination to crack a tough problem and the willingness to think along new lines, did what traditional policing has failed to do in city after city: they eliminated a major, entrenched open-air drug market. The problem was not lessened, or moved, or contained; it was *solved,* and apparently for good. The police and the coalition worked their magic, moreover, after years of police failure, *the very first time they tried.* In this case, their core new idea was prevention, an idea that was exactly appropriate to the problem they faced. That idea, and the tactics they used to apply it, will not necessarily work for every Link Valley, or for every other important problem the police and the cities face. Other situations and cities will call for other new thoughts and new approaches. But Link Valley shows something terribly important and enormously promising: that new ideas can transform policing.

*   *   *

Wilshire, New Briarfield, and Link Valley are three of a rare breed: policing successes that change the face of entire neighborhoods and communities. There are, as we shall see, other such successes. The evidence is accumulating that approaches like these work, or at least are well worth trying. Many have been put in place, and operated for some time, with few or no additional resources. They differ in details, rationales, inspiration, but they are alike in important ways: in focusing not just on crime but also on public order and fear of crime; not just on goals set by the police but also on goals set by the public; not just on individual incidents but also on classes and causes of incidents; not just on police resources but also on community and other government resources; not just on reacting to trouble but on preventing it. They hold the hope, where ordinary policing no longer seems to, of making a real difference in the lives of troubled cities.

They are also very much the exception. There is nothing magical about these new police approaches; they are for the most part still young and unformed, but the ideas that lie behind them are reasonably well articulated, and there are prototypes to choose from. Officers and public alike seem to take to them. Nonetheless, they are not being widely essayed. Contemporary policing believes in an idea of what the police are and what policing is that leaves little room for, and often actively discourages, the kind of creative and innovative work Wilshire, New Briarfield, and Link Valley represent.

It is no accident that the stories we have told here come from the Los Angeles, Newport News, and Houston police departments, whose chiefs, as we shall see, have made major efforts to change the way their departments think and work. The progress of policing as a field, and the possibility that it can make important new contributions to cities, neighborhoods, and communities, depends utterly on such deep institutional change: in the idea of policing, in the values and beliefs of police officers, and in the way police departments are managed. Without these changes even good ideas and promising beginnings such as we have just seen will founder on the rocks of contemporary policing. We chart these obstacles in the next chapter.

CHAPTER 2

■

The Road This Far

Policing's Origins, the Reform Model, and Barriers to Progress

NO SURVEYOR of the landscape of Anglo-American policing can fail to be struck by police departments' remarkable similarity of form and style. There are, of course, variations, sometimes significant ones, from force to force, reflecting local contexts, development, and traditions. But the essential sameness is so strong, and so accepted by both the police and the public, that it might seem that the police sprang forth fully developed in all their modern particularities: aloof, highly mobile, and deeply dedicated to the pursuit and apprehension of criminals. It is also easy to imagine that this essential sameness is proof against change: that what is now has always been, and ever shall be.

The appearance of immutability is an illusion. American policing went through a major crisis in the first half of this century that changed its character enormously, and other English-speaking forces, especially in the large cities of the British Commonwealth, have changed in ways that, though less abrupt and self-conscious, have had a similar impact.[1] The responsibilities, purposes, methods, and social support of policing have all changed. Policing as we know it today is the result of that reform and those changes, not a historical accident but certainly a historical artifact.

Without knowledge of this history, observers of the police could be forgiven for assuming that the current nature of policing was preordained. Even so, there would be another reason for skepticism. Policing is young; the police as we know them have existed for only about 150 years, since British Home Secretary Robert Peel created London's Metropolitan Police Force in 1829. American policing is younger still. The art and science of policing is in its infancy. There is no reason to think that its ends are correct and immutable, or its means effective and mature.

There is far more reason, at present, to have serious doubts on both counts. Confidence that the police are properly engaged, properly deployed, and properly organized is beginning to be undermined by discoveries about the limitations of the current approach and the surprising strengths of some alternatives. Mounting evidence—the unabated increase in levels of crime, evaluations of police tactics, signs of serious alienation between the police and the public—suggests that the model that has long dominated police thinking and led to such remarkable uniformity in thought and practice may in the long run be untenable.[2] At the same time, new insights into different ways to do police work are beginning to bear fruit; there is even reason to believe that policing is at a turning point, about to move, as it has once before, to a new understanding of what its ends, means, and form should be.

But even if, as begins to seem clear, the current model of policing cannot survive indefinitely, and even if there are better ways, it is also clear that it is not going to be easy for any police department to move away from today's model. Police history has created a strong culture, resistant to criticism and highly resistant to change. We look now to that history to illuminate the outlines and the limitations of the current approach, as well as to provide an understanding of the origins of today's powerful police culture.

31

THE ORIGINS OF THE POLICE

The modern police were born amid the wave of street violence and industrial unrest that swept Britain in the early nineteenth century.[3] Public safety in England was then pursued—where it was systematically promoted at all—by private gentry, who took turns as public watchmen, and by the military, who were called in when things really got out of hand. Against the unprecedented crime and strife that vexed, especially, Londoners, the watchman system was ineffectual and the military all too bloodily effectual. Robert Peel—after whom English police will evermore be called bobbies—introduced his Metropolitan Police Act in June 1829, and by the end of that year there were over a thousand officers in London, operating according to a model that has set the mold for all subsequent police organizations in English-speaking countries.[4] They wore uniforms, they walked beats, they worked from stations grouped into divisions, their authority to use force was carefully prescribed by law, and they were charged with controlling crime and making the streets safe.

The troubles and shortcomings of the young Met, as it soon came to be called, were also foreshadowings of those every police department yet to come would eventually struggle with. The new bobbies were immediately corrupt, they were unsuccessful in controlling crime, and they were heavily influenced by local wealthy merchants.[5] The watchmen before them had been open to bribes from keepers of the many houses of ill repute; the bribes persuaded the watchmen not to exercise their statutory powers to render such buildings uninhabitable by tearing out all the doors and windows.[6] The constables inherited this source of income, together with other miscellaneous supplements to their meager wages. Consequently supervision of the early patrolmen was strict. Police administrators fought constantly to control the cowardly, the corrupt, the lazy, and the drunk within the ranks. About a third of the constables were dismissed each year for the first few years of the Met's existence.[7]

The police's failure to control crime could not be similarly punished; nobody, on the street or at police headquarters at Scotland Yard, had any real idea how to control crime successfully. Early police administrators assumed that crime could be suppressed if officers patrolled small areas—their beats—with sufficient regularity to stand a good chance of coming on any mischief. The whole city was therefore covered by beats, each patrolled constantly. Unfortunately, the strict control exercised over constables included frequent scheduled supervisory checks, making the officer's location at any time quite predictable, much to the advantage of London's villains.

Despite the Met's shortcomings, it was a vast improvement on what had gone before, and it was the model American cities turned to when they set up their own police forces. The Americans departed in one critical regard, however: where the commissioner of the Met reported to the home secretary, a member of the British prime minister's cabinet, and was thus largely removed from the currents of London politics, in the United States control over the police was municipal—and wildly partisan. Police chiefs came and went with mayors, precincts were laid out to be contiguous with political wards, and precinct captains worked hand in hand with ward leaders. Power within departments was extremely decentralized, with precinct captains directing, hiring, and firing their men, often at the behest of local party captains (whose frequent close connections with crime bosses often meant that convicted felons ended up as police officers). When the mayoralty changed parties, it was not unusual for the entire police department to be fired and replaced by supporters of the new victors.[8]

The effect of this muncipal control, in the words of pioneering student of police history Robert Fogelson, was to make the police "adjuncts to the city political machines."[9] They were openly used to influence election results by encouraging some citizens to vote for particular candidates and dissuading others from voting at all, and they frequently assisted in manipulating ballot boxes. They remained corrupt, running protection rackets and "licensing" the vice operations—notably drugs, gambling, and prostitution—that flourished in the burgeoning immigrant sections of major American cities. The command ranks vied over particularly lucrative precincts; New York's Tenderloin, a notorious haven for misbehavior of every description, was so christened by a famous remark by a policeman named Williams, who upon being assigned there announced in delight that while he had been eating chuck steak, he would soon be eating tenderloin.[10] And even when they tried, the American police were probably no better than their English brethren at controlling crime.

Despite this somewhat black picture, the early American (and English) police forces had certain strengths. One of the foremost was that—drawn from and operating from within their communities— they enjoyed a fair degree of local support and political legitimacy. Officers usually lived in or close to the areas they patrolled. And while their closeness to the political machines and their lack of principled central direction permitted much malfeasance and abuse, it also permitted much good. With little in the way of guidance or theory as to what they ought to be doing, many police forces simply assumed responsibility for whatever emergencies and crises crossed their paths. On the principle that if it needed to be done, and nobody was doing it, they would, various forces provided ambulance services, ran soup kitchens, collected garbage, and sheltered homeless (often in police stations).[11] In a time before widespread and well-supported social work and social programs, and before municipalities had assumed many of their current routine obligations, the police often filled important vacuums.

THE REFORM ERA AND THE EMERGENCE
OF THE REFORM MODEL

It was not enough. The lawlessness of the big-city police made them a key target of the powerful movement for municipal reform that swept the country toward the turn of the century.[12] A number of groups drew a bead on police practices. Some focused on crime and saw the police as failing in their primary task of controlling it. Some sought political reform or, through it, political power, and saw the police, with their close allegiance to ward politicians, as a major obstacle. Some were concerned with the moral realm and saw the police's failure to suppress vice as the principal cause of moral pollution in their cities. Together, they mounted an attack on the police that fell into three broad areas: their purposes and responsibilities, their organizational form, and their accountability. Reformers saw the scope of police action as dangerously broad and wanted it more narrowly defined. They saw police organization as surrendering too much to political control and demanded a politically impartial and disciplined force. Above all, reformers resented the ward-level control of the police and insisted that their accountability be shifted at least to the city if not to the state level.[13]

If the reformers' motivations were diverse, their ammunition in the battle for change was not. Over and over they fired police scandals—of which there was no shortage—at the status quo. For example, in New York City a commission headed by Senator Clarence Lexow was established in 1894 to investigate serious allegations of police corruption. Despite fierce resistance from machine politicians, the commission successfully subpoenaed patrolmen, captains, and inspectors, along with judges, politicians, saloonkeepers, policy bankers, con men, gamblers, prostitutes, peddlers, storekeepers, and scores of citizens.[14] Their evidence revealed a police department rotten to the core: detectives permitted thieves and con men to go about their business in exchange for a share of the proceeds; jobs and promotions were given out as political favors; illegal activities were informally licensed; and police methods were unfair, oppressive, illegal, and frequently brutal.

Despite these revelations the commission made little impression on the department. A few officers were found guilty of criminal offenses, but their convictions were overturned by the courts and they retained their jobs.[15] It was only after another investigation into the affairs of the department that important reforms began to be made. In particular, in two strikes at the heart of the ward system, an independent commissioner of police was appointed to run the department, and the police were relieved of their responsibilities for supervising elections.

In cities all over the United States similar investigations began the serious business of probing police corruption and incompetence. Time after time the relationship between the local police and local politicians was shown to be corrupt, with both sharing power with local crime bosses. The image of the police that emerged during the period 1895–1920 was of fragmented departments that completely failed to control crime, were totally unwilling to clamp down on vice (because they shared in its proceeds), and were hopelessly out of control. Control, further, seemed impossible to impose, because the police were not answerable to anyone outside their own wards. By the turn of the century the battle for control of the police was well under way. Reformers demanded that the police be made accountable to the city rather than to the wards and that they be tightly controlled. The ward politicians, often using their considerable influence over the courts, resisted steadfastly—decrying external pressures for control as unwarranted interference in the affairs of their communities.

Nevertheless, the reformers slowly but surely gained ground. So began a gradual evolution of policing. Following the pattern set in New York, political police boards (the existing but powerless city-level authorities) were replaced with commissioners.[16] Commissioners, once it had been discovered that they could do nothing by themselves, were given capable and extensive staffs. *Departmental Headquarters* began to mean something substantial, with central staff starting to make demands on the ward captains. Precinct captains were required to report daily to headquarters, either directly or through inspectors. Recruiting procedures were codified and standardized across the city. Applicants with criminal records were barred from employment. Promotion procedures based on exams and merit became standard. Police officers were made subject to civil service regulations, which made them dismissable only for proven cause.[17] The ward politicians lost grievously. They lost the power to grant appointment to and promotion within the force. They lost the power to dismiss officers who chose not to fall into line with their whims. They largely lost the power to grant police protection to particular businesses.*

To deal with their prime concern, the problem of corruption, the new authorities forbade officers to accept rewards of any kind. They also imposed all kinds of conditions on officers' private lives, conditions designed to minimize exposure to temptation and corrupt

---

*This matter proved something of a sticking point. It was never possible to distinguish fully a general public duty to prevent crime in some particularly crime-prone place from a corrupt provision of extra police services to a friend in business. Forbidding the latter while allowing the former can best be achieved by controlling private rewards to police.

influence. These included restricting officers from living in the areas they policed, from moonlighting, from incurring debts, or from being involved in businesses in their areas, as well as requiring them to declare the business interests of their families. Some departments went so far as to curtail informal contact between their police and the general public. Instructions such as "Police Officers shall not make any unnecessary conversation with the public"* became commonplace and have in some cases survived nearly to the present day.[18]

Police reaction to the reformers' pressures was, at first, hostile. Officers were happy with their ward bosses and benefited from their intimate relationships with them; officers already owed their ward politicians a great deal. Also, it seemed to the police that the reformers were demanding the impossible in expecting them to suppress crime completely when little (if any) progress had been made in understanding crime, its causes, and what to do about it. Moreover the reformers were saying that the police role was to enforce all of the law, denying them the discretion they had always enjoyed. Strict enforcement of all laws would inevitably push police into conflict with the immigrant communities and make them unpopular with the new motoring public. In short, the reformers threatened to whisk away officers' traditional political supports while making their job more difficult, more dangerous, and very much less popular. Initially, then, the reformers met with nothing but opposition from the police.

During the latter part of the reform era, however, some in the police began to take a rather different view, as it slowly sank in that the ever-growing catalogue of police corruption and incompetence was turning them into a laughingstock. There emerged considerable internal pressure to salvage the police reputation.

The need was filled by architects of a new, "professional" police—notably August Volmer, O. W. Wilson, and William Parker, all chiefs from California police departments. They recast the reform agenda to uplift rather than denigrate policing. The reformers had argued that policing should be independent, competent, and correct.

*Some British police forces had this directive, or something similar, in their instruction books well into the 1980s.

BEYOND 911

Volmer, Wilson, and their supporters agreed: so long as independence and competence were rooted in police authority and judgment, and correctness was rooted in law. They argued that police chiefs should truly run their departments, free from political interference, and that police officers should be well educated and well trained in the skills and tools of law enforcement. Their methods and conduct should be governed by their own special expertise. The police role should be more tightly defined, with its legitimacy anchored in the law rather than in politics and its professional scope limited to law enforcement and the fight against crime (not incidentally the one area guaranteed to generate broad public support).[19]

The idea was immediately popular among top police officials, who saw a way to escape the reformers' brickbats with their authority and standing enhanced. It was popular among reformers, who began to believe that professionalization could produce the kind of police restraint and prudence that political control had so manifestly failed to secure. Rank and file support gradually emerged as a result of expectations of higher salaries and better working conditions (the idea that under police professionalism "nobody can tell a cop his job" was also rather appealing). Within a few decades this professional model—also called the reform model, the term we will use—had taken firm root in departments all over the country.

Major changes in police organization and deployment followed, chief among them the centralization of authority and a widespread shift from foot to motorized patrol. Police reformers, especially the extremely influential O. W. Wilson, took the view that the only administrative arrangement conducive to the control chiefs should exercise was a strictly disciplined paramilitary hierarchy.[20] Their exercise of that belief hastened and completed earlier reform efforts to break the back of the ward system. New operational arrangements moved even more power to headquarters. Reform chiefs saw vice control as the single most corrupting influence on police and therefore sought to remove it from the daily lives of ordinary patrol officers.[21] Many police administrators set up specialized, centrally based vice squads, supposedly under tight and direct supervision at headquarters. Frequently patrol officers were actually forbidden to make vice arrests, obliged to steer clear themselves and pass their information on to the central squads. The proliferation of centrally based squads—for everything from burglary to narcotics to crime prevention—in fact became a hallmark of the new reform depart-ments.

The wholesale shift of officers off foot patrol and into radio cars began slowly and snowballed. At first the few cars available were generally used by supervisors. As cars proliferated they were used for ferrying patrol officers to and from their beats, which they still patrolled on foot. But two factors began to work together to enhance the appeal of motorized patrol: the gradual improvement in the po-liceman's lot brought a reduction in working hours, while the bur-geoning central squads drained men to headquarters. The smaller patrol strength, coupled with the pressure to maintain patrol over the entire city, forced patrol officers to spend more and more of their time in their cars. The advent of radio communications was the final link in the chain. Now it was possible for one man (or two) in a car to cover districts of many square miles and still arrive at a trouble spot within minutes.

By 1950 radio-controlled patrol cars were universal in American cities. The fact of the change seems to have preceded the theory, but the theory soon developed, and it cemented the primacy of motorized patrol. Reformers like Wilson and Parker reasoned that a visible police presence, in the form of motorized patrol cars, would deter criminal conduct.[22] They assumed further that the more times a car passed any one point, the less chance there would be of a crime occurring at or near that point. Hence the most effective crime-prevention activity for patrol officers, when not busy on a call, was deemed to be driving about. So was born the philosophy of preven-tive patrol and rapid response, which has come to be the cornerstone of the reform strategy.

Use of motorized patrol as the dominant police tactic also helped keep patrolmen separate from the public they served, theoretically reducing the risk of corruption. Officers in cars had originally been able to patrol on foot when not responding to emergency calls. But access to police services became so easy with the introduction of 911 emergency telephone systems that the number of public calls for service increased substantially. All too soon patrolmen found themselves so busy answering calls that they were unable to spend much time on foot. The more time they spent in their cars the less contact they had with the general public.

Another important development for the reformers was the rationalization of methods used to record crime statistics, leading to the establishment of the FBI's Uniform Crime Reports.[23] These national reports, compiled from departmental figures, were by the 1960s accepted as reliable indicators of reported crime levels throughout the country. The crime rates they reported were readily adopted, by both police and public, as the single most important measure of police performance. The reform strategy painted police as waging a "war on crime," and the Uniform Crime Reports were bulletins on whether the police, or the criminals, were winning.

This focus on crime and crime rates is responsible for one of the most distinctive characteristics of the reform model: its tendency to be incident driven and reactive. What patrol officers do in a modern police department is almost wholly determined by incoming calls requesting service. What detectives do is almost wholly determined by reports of crimes. The reformers' desire to focus the police on crime, and to restrict the discretion they can exercise, has to a considerable degree been built into the very structure of modern policing.

The reform model of policing as it emerged during the first two-thirds of this century remains mostly intact. The police now deeply resent political interference. They root their legitimacy, methods, and aspirations in the ideas of law enforcement and crime control. The idea of professionalism has been reinforced through the advent of specialized police procedures and advanced forensic technologies. The reformers' accomplishment in transforming policing has been huge. The magnitude of the transition, achieved in sixty years in the face of such fierce early resistance from police and politicians, testifies to their determination and perseverance. They got, without question, what they were after. We can look, now, at what that has meant.

THE DOMINANCE OF CRIME CONTROL
AND LAW ENFORCEMENT

The reformers produced a conception of policing whose purpose has been largely focused on crime control and whose methods have been largely limited to law enforcement. Every discussion of the purpose of the police begins with crime control. For many the discussion ends there as well. Crime control is widely taken, both inside and outside the police, as the only important police function, with everything else they might do not only secondary but a dangerous and wasteful distraction. This is not in itself new; much thinking about the police has taken more or less this form for the last century. But the degree to which the reform model, especially in recent years, has narrowed the debate is unprecedented—and troubling.

The first narrowing concerns what the police count as crime. Nearly every major department focuses its main energies on and judges itself according to its success in controlling or solving the crimes included in Part 1 of the FBI's Uniform Crime Reports (known in departments across the nation simply as "Part 1 crimes"). They number eight: murder, rape, robbery, assault, burglary, larceny, arson, and auto theft.[24]

These are critical crimes, but they are not the only critical crimes. Emphasis on them slights other offenses that matter a great deal to their victims: wife battering, child abuse, sexual abuse, frauds and confidence games, white-collar crimes, protection rackets, loan-sharking. Especially importantly, it devalues crimes that are of enormous significance to the well-being of neighborhoods and communities: drug dealing, prostitution, vandalism, panhandling, public drinking, even traffic, parking, and litter violations. As officers in both Wilshire and Newport News discovered, the public often cares far more about these matters than it does about apparently more serious ones. And, of course, under the reform model the police do attend to those crimes to some degree, but such efforts never seem central or very well integrated into the overall mission of most departments.

The second narrowing concerns what the police count as valid means of crime control. The reform model leaves the police, for the most part, with one heavy weapon: arrest. Arrest is the most important activity of the police department because it triggers the process of prosecution, adjudication, and sentencing by the other elements of the criminal justice system. That process is in turn assumed to control crime through three mechanisms: the threat of arrest and punishment deters potential offenders; those who are not deterred are arrested and prevented from further misdeeds by incarceration or close supervision; and some of those incarcerated or supervised may be permanently swayed from criminal pursuits through rehabilitative training, counseling, and schooling.

For the reformers the benefits of this approach were quite clear: automatic and uniform recourse to the criminal justice system reduced the opportunity for arbitrary or corrupt police action and placed the police under more direct court supervision. Police became retrospectively accountable to prosecutors and the courts for the appropriateness and conduct of arrests. Compared with what went before, the elevation of arrest as a major police tactic was a major accomplishment.

Arrest remains unquestionably popular. Putting bad guys in jail seems to the police and the public alike a just and plausibly effective response to crime. If the police restrict their attention to verifiable and actionable offenses, society can be assured that their great powers will not be abused. But by focusing on individuals, and by doing so only after crimes have been committed—that is, by being reactive— the police cut themselves off from opportunities for crime prevention. Perhaps there are ways to resolve trouble before it escalates into crime, and ways to reach potential criminals before they cross the line into serious misbehavior. Reform police departments have pursued these thoughts to some degree, through schemes like property marking, police athletic leagues, and drug-abuse education.[25] But these programs are rarely pushed very hard, usually being relegated to specialist squads seen as peripheral by the rest of the force, and even they are often focused on ways to extend the powers of the police to apprehend and arrest. Other avenues, if there are any, are almost never explored.

The reform model's final important narrowing concerns the principal tactics on which police rely to make arrests and control crime.

Preventive patrol, rapid response, and retrospective investigation almost completely replaced all other techniques. Most important, probably, the old links of foot patrol officers to their beats were severed. Their familiarity with their turf, their closeness to the neighborhoods and communities they patrolled, and the informal networks of friends, acquaintances, and informers—along with all the valuable information they represent—diminished or disappeared.

Something similar happened at the precinct level as departments went to great trouble to ensure that all communication with the public was centralized. Ordinary people and important figures and groups alike found their access and standing in precincts eliminated. Some departments discovered that residents persisted in calling "their" precinct houses even after centralized 911 systems were installed; they simply took the precinct phone numbers out of service.[26] Information about crime, criminals, or trouble brewing that did not come in properly—that is, centrally, as a call for police service—seldom came in at all.

Again the reformers achieved a useful objective: much greater accountability for the way police handled public requests for service. Every call that came into the department could be carefully logged. The record (or incident report) was updated in accordance with whatever action the police took, so the names of officers dispatched, types of additional resources allocated, and time the call was declared "dealt with" were all recorded. Supervisors could examine the written (or later computerized) record for any call, and the records were normally kept for several years. Any fudging now had to pass under the noses of the dispatcher and the supervisors and be recorded for posterity.[27]

These changes answered many of the criticisms that had spurred the reform movement and speak to the continuing interest that the police remain accountable, efficient, and under control. Worries that the police will get out of control are assuaged by the fact that they focus their energies on reactive approaches to serious crime. Higher standards and close administration have vastly reduced the corruption of police officers, and insulation from most aspects of city politics has put an end to electoral and partisan meddling. The achievements of the reform movement in reshaping policing have been enormous.

Regarding police departments almost exclusively as the front end of the criminal justice system continues to make a great deal of sense to police and public alike. That definition, in turn, continues to restrict the role the police can play in the life of cities. Their proper task is widely seen to be enforcing the criminal law against murderers, rapists, robbers, burglars, and auto thieves. It might be nice to have police help with other urban problems, but anything that takes away from these urgent tasks misuses their resources and leaves the cities vulnerable to increased criminal victimization. That, at least, is what the police often argue, and they tend to find a sympathetic audience.

THE LIMITATIONS OF PROFESSIONAL
LAW ENFORCEMENT

Confidence that the reform model is an adequate basis for a modern police agency is now beginning to be undermined by a host of unsettling insights into its limitations. We should say, in defense of the reformers, that they were only prescribing for the problems they faced, not those we face. They successfully identified the important directions for strategic change—for their time. The failings of reform-model policing that are appearing today are best taken as underscoring the need to look beyond that model, to adapt policing to new times and needs.

There are a number of good reasons for looking beyond the reform model, given the nature and extent of problems currently facing police departments. The starkest is the simple fact that the police seem to be failing in their primary mission of crime control. Crime rates remain at historic highs in the United States.[28] Clearance rates, which measure the fraction of reported crime solved (at least to police satisfaction), remain quite low: currently less than 30 percent of robberies (and only 56 percent of robberies are reported) and less than 15 percent of burglaries.[29] The police do not seem to be controlling crime.

There is unfairness, of course, in laying this charge solely on the doorstep of the police. A great many other factors influence levels of crime—including broad demographic, social, and economic trends—and many of these have been operating against the police over the last two decades.[30] But even the truth in the charge, and there is much, need not redound entirely to the discredit of the police. They are only the first step in the criminal justice system, and they can be no more effective than the rest of that system—prosecutors, courts, and prisons—allows them to be. That is to say, probably not very.

In an important sense, the U.S. criminal justice system is currently bankrupt. If the power of the police to control crime depends on arrests being followed by effective prosecutions and sentences, then it is clear that their efforts are being undermined. Although it is true that the United States now has more people in prison than at any time in its history, and more than any other country except the Soviet Union and South Africa, it is also true that the likelihood of a criminal offense being followed by a prison sentence is extremely low, less than 4 percent for robberies and burglaries.[31] Worse, there is evidence that until very recently the price of crime to offenders had been falling. Mark Kleiman has reported that the average robbery in 1958 resulted in a sentence of approximately 389 days. By 1986 that had fallen to 115 days. For burglary comparable figures are 61 days in 1958 and 21 days in 1986.[32] If the criminal code is a promise by society to punish criminal offenders, it is clear that that promise is being broken.

The police will say, with some justice, that that failure is not their fault, although it takes a leap of faith to accept that as a justification for business as usual. But there is worse news. Evidence is accumulating that the primary tactics of reform policing simply do not work particularly well to control crime or eliminate fear. Pursued with the best will and greatest expertise in the world, patrol, rapid response, and retrospective investigation do not do the job expected of them.

Kansas City's patrol experiment failed to find any difference in levels of crime when the intensity of patrol was widely varied.[33] Most crimes occur beyond the public view. The police see relatively little from the front seat of a patrolling car. Residents are not particularly sensitive to the number of times a patrol car passes. Quite aside from the research, the general inefficacy of random patrol is borne out by the experience of patrol officers themselves, many of whom go years—even whole careers—without happening on a felony. Random patrol is, more than anything else, random.

Rapid response also seems to have serious weaknesses as an anticrime tactic. Several examinations suggest that the speed of response to emergency calls has little impact on levels of crime and only a small impact on the likelihood that a crime will be solved.[34] As the pioneering Kansas City rapid response study showed, police often do not get a call until well after the crime has been committed. Witnesses often do not notice crimes in progress and often do not call when they do. Victims are too busy being victimized, and they call family and friends before they call the police. The police arrive in time to comfort the victim but not to catch the offender. These truths too are borne out by ordinary police experience. "Most of the time," says Wilshire's Captain Ernest Curtsinger, "irrespective of the call, you get there and the bad guy is gone and the real emergency situation is over. I would be willing to bet that in this division there aren't five calls in a month where if an officer had been there five minutes faster it would have had any impact on the outcome of the incident."[35]

More than anything else, the police are rediscovering that ordinary people and communities are the first line of defense in controlling crime and fear. The police cannot succeed without an effective partnership with the communities they serve. Without the eyes and ears of residents to extend the scope of police surveillance, the reach of police patrol is pathetically thin. Unless ordinary people are willing to call the police, rapid response is essentially useless. Unless ordinary people provide descriptions of offenders and accounts of events, detectives can neither solve crimes nor mount effective prosecutions. Citizens' vigilance and willingness to come forward are an integral part of police operations. If that piece of the machinery is not working well, the police, for all their sophistication and equipment, are rendered ineffective.

But the police cannot reasonably expect help from the public unless they give the public the help it wants, and this the police have not been doing. The majority of calls that come into police departments do not concern crime at all. Based on analyses of *dispatched* calls—which overrepresent crime calls since many noncrime calls are screened out before they reach dispatchers—about 50 percent to over 90 percent concern traffic, loud neighbors, lost pets, missing people, and an infinity of life's other pains and frictions.[36] All that ties them together is that the callers want help. Police officers, under the guidance of the reform model, arrive on the scene trained, equipped, and supported by their departments primarily to deal with crime. Where no serious crime has been committed, officers are under great pressure to get back in service so they can be dispatched to the next call. This approach wins few friends.

Even detectives, policing's elite, seem to have limited effectiveness. Evaluations have shown that retrospective investigations solve very few crimes indeed (although detectives will rarely admit this).[37] Only when the victims or witnesses are able to identify the offender are crimes usually solved. The others are essentially unsolvable because of the absence of useful clues. The mythology of detectives clearing cases through painstaking investigation has been largely debunked; neither legwork nor advanced forensic techniques are useful in solving the majority of cases (though both can be very useful indeed in proving cases in court).

These findings undermine confidence not only in the criminal justice system as a whole, but very specifically in the police. The reform model is very explicit in setting out what the police mean to do and how they mean to do it. It is increasingly clear that the prescribed means cannot achieve the prescribed ends: cannot now, and maybe never could.

There is one last sign of the limitations of the reform model: providing security is increasingly becoming a private rather than a public enterprise. This trend is easy to miss because private security takes so many different forms. Sometimes people work entirely alone: they decide to buy burglar alarms or iron grates for their windows.[38] Other times they join together in neighborhood watches or to patrol their neighborhoods.[39] Still other times community groups or large private institutions such as universities, hospitals, and industrial concerns establish their own security departments.[40] Sometimes private groups even hire public police officers to provide the security they need and cannot get by calling 911 or lobbying the police department.[41]

But in sum it is clear that private citizens are taking what they can get from the police and then adding further layers of private security.[42] In the last decade, total employment in private security has grown significantly. In 1980, 644,000 people were employed as private security guards. By 1990 that number had risen to 859,000. The comparable numbers for sworn police officers are 550,000 in 1980 and 643,000 today. The public market share has fallen from 46 to 42 percent.[43]

It would be wrong to see this movement toward private security as too much of a departure, for the reality is that there has never been any public monopoly on crime control. The police have always been fundamentally dependent on private citizens to help them fight crime, and citizens have always played their part not only by being willing to call the police but also by exercising more active self-defense. It is easy to forget that public police forces are only a century and a half old and that for all the time before their establishment much of the burden of self-defense and the apprehension of criminals fell on private agencies. The frank-pledge system, on which England relied for several centuries, made it the duty of every citizen to come to the aid of a fellow citizen if a crime had been committed.[44] That tradition survives today in laws that allow citizens to make arrests and to defend themselves against criminal victimization by arming themselves, keeping a dog, or purchasing a burglar alarm.[45] Private citizens have always been the first line of defense against crime, and their increased activism is to some degree positive and advantageous.

It is also potentially extremely dangerous. The most worrisome possibility is that private parties will be far less concerned than the police with constitutional niceties and far less disciplined in using force. Detroit residents burned down a crack house in 1988.[46] The same year in Baltimore a group of Black Muslims who had assumed responsibility for providing security to a public housing project were caught manhandling a suspected drug dealer.[47] In communities pressed beyond endurance by crime and drugs, such violence is understandable; it is also intolerable. One of the reasons Western civilization established a public system of justice was to preempt private vengeance and the escalating violence it seems to breed. The police exist not to visit vengeance on suspected offenders, but to make them stand still so that justice can be done. There is a world of difference between the two, symbolized on the one hand by Dirty Harry and on the other by the old westerns in which the sheriff stood in the door and held off the lynch mob. The failure of the police to control crime has made society increasingly understanding, even supportive, of vigilantism. Private security lends itself all too readily to abuse, even to mob justice. Neither can be allowed.

Private security is also invariably unevenly distributed. Rich people living in secure condominiums and well-off communities able to pay for private patrols will have a great deal more protection against criminal attack than poor people in public housing. Worse, the private security arrangements of the rich often allow them to enjoy more than their fair share of police protection. The increasingly common installation of home burglar alarms linked to local police stations, for example, gives homeowners with such alarms an access to police resources denied those without (as do private guards in department stores, silent alarms in banks and jewelry stores, and radio tags in automobiles). The police should be equally available to all people in trouble, not preferentially to those who can somehow purchase special standing.

The worst implication of the growth in private security, however, is that it may well undermine the very institution of the police. If people can simply buy protection for themselves, they have less reason to support a police that must serve everyone. If there is no reason to support the police, policing will atrophy, and the minimum level of security to which everyone is entitled will fall. As bad, the police will increasingly become an institution for poor people. We know from the history of public education and public housing how that status generally leads to even more rapid declines. From a parochial police perspective, the growth of private security is a mark of failure. It shows that the strategy that they are pursuing is not attracting the commitment of the nation's citizens. They are putting their money and time elsewhere. Policing, whether it knows it or not, may be facing a crisis.

If so, it is a crisis to which, as we argued in the last chapter, there are good reasons to hope for answers. But there will be far more to finding those answers than identifying useful new orientations and approaches, trying them out, and adopting the best. The reformers changed what police do and how they do it in many obvious ways. They did more than that, however. They also changed, in deep and subtle ways, what the police think of themselves and how police departments run themselves. The products of these changes—contemporary police culture and management—pose particularly steep challenges for police departments and executives interested in change and progress.

POLICE CULTURE

We have seen how the police came, during the later part of the reform period, to embrace an image of themselves as impartial, professional crime fighters. This image lies at the heart of the police value system; indeed, it is its foundation stone. This image is what police chiefs talk of at award dinners and budget time; it is what police officers talk of with their "civilian" friends. It is the face policing wishes to present to the public. It is real, or at least honest, as far as it goes; the police really do believe it.

It is not all the police believe, however. Behind it lie, usually secret and hidden, several other very powerful beliefs, often expressed in conversations between officers, embodied in departmental stories and legends, personified in police heroes.[48] But these beliefs bear little resemblance to what's laid down in the force instruction manual or prescribed through formal management structures and all too often have little to do with the chief executive's stated values (if there are any). Together, they are the building blocks of current police culture; they are the truths that officers feel in their bones, the touchstones that—unless changed—will continue to govern their behavior and attitudes. The strongest of them are as follows.

1. We are the only real crime fighters. Crime fighting is what the public wants from us. Other agencies, public or private, only play at it.
2. No one else understands the real nature of police work. That is, no one outside the police service—academics, politicians, and lawyers in particular—can comprehend what we have to do. The public is generally naive about police work.
3. Loyalty to colleagues counts above everything else. We have to stick together. Everyone else—including the public, politicians, and especially senior officers—seems to be out to make our job difficult.
4. It is impossible to win the war against crime without bending the rules. We are hopelessly shackled by unrealistic constraints foisted on us by civil liberties groups, thanks to the fecklessness of politicians.
5. Members of the public are basically unsupportive and unreasonably demanding. They all seem to think they know our job better than we do. They only want us when they need something done.
6. Patrol work is the pits. The detective branch and other specialties are relatively glorious, because they tackle serious crime. Patrol work is only for those who aren't smart enough to get out of it.

These are the beliefs that, for better or worse, now play a large part in fashioning police conduct. They reflect the values that are drummed into new recruits informally as soon as they have left the academy; they reflect the values that are perpetually reinforced among peers in locker rooms and cafeterias.

These beliefs are, in a very real sense, true. The general public really does have little idea of the nature of police work, and in expecting the police to control crime with their existing resources and tactics is making unreasonable demands. The police, having willingly adopted the role of professional crime fighter, finding themselves hampered—however justifiably—by restrictions on their investigative and interrogation techniques, and burdened by vast numbers of seemingly unimportant calls, often feel obliged to cheat to get results, and to justify that cheating by the importance of the crime-control mission they are charged with.

These beliefs rather accurately reflect the reality of reform policing as seen from "the sharp end"—the streets. Worse, they stand firmly in the way of recent attempts to update and upgrade police strategies, for they serve to cocoon the myths of the reform era's "professionalism." They preserve themselves by insulating the police from the impacts of societal change.

Belief 1—"We are the only real crime fighters"—prevents the police from sharing any part of the onerous burden of controlling crime, isolates them from other groups who share their interest in crime control, and pushes them into marginal and illegal acts to offset their inability to control crime by proper means. It devalues the part the community has to play in crime prevention and keeps the police from talking honestly about their inability to control crime. This belief is as well strongly endorsed by police unions, because it suggests that ever-rising crime rates should naturally lead to ever-increasing resources being devoted to the police.

Belief 2—"No one else understands the real nature of police work"—prevents any kind of open discussion with the community about the police role, limits the impact any academic research or writing can have on police officers, and discourages acceptance or adoption of any ideas (good or bad) that come from the private sector or other public agencies. It absolutely prohibits lateral entry into the service: no one is deemed capable of any important job in a police department unless he or she has already spent many years as a police officer.

Beliefs 3 and 4—loyalty to colleagues and the need to bend the rules—are probably the critical factors shielding and encouraging corruption in modern police agencies. The overriding obligation to show loyalty to colleagues prevents those officers with more sensitive consciences from reporting their less honorable colleagues, and acceptance of the need to bend the rules undermines the sanctity of the law. The credence broadly given to these beliefs has more influence on the level of corrupt practice than corruption probes, close supervision, or tight central control ever could. The need to bend the rules effectively opens the door to malpractice, and loyalty to colleagues prevents anyone from shutting it again.[49]

The subterranean existence of these two beliefs marks the limit of the reformers' civilizing influence. The reformers were not able to make the police believe that the sanctity of the law should override the goal of effective crime fighting. It is these beliefs, with smaller contributions from several others, that sometimes create the kind of police and police behavior that the public perennially fears: the police of forged evidence, falsified warrants, and street justice. These can be the beliefs of a police zealous, blinkered, and dangerously out of control.

Belief 5—"The public is basically unsupportive and unreasonable"—coupled with belief 2—No one understands us—creates a bunker mentality. Forays onto the streets are seen as exposure to a nasty, hostile world, exposure all the more unpleasant because it demeans the patrol officer, placing him or her at the beck and call of the very dregs of humanity (and the patrol officer soon discovers that a high proportion of calls do come from what he or she sees as "the dregs"). These beliefs combine into a pessimistic outlook on community life and a cynical view of human nature. They can ultimately lead to callousness, abuse of authority, and brutality, the means by which the disillusioned patrol officer levels the score.

Belief 6—"Patrol work is the pits"—portrays retrospective crime investigation, the work of detectives, as superior to crime prevention, which lies with patrol. The elevated status of detectives and specialists, who spend their time with victims, witnesses, and criminals, reduces the significance attached to officers' contact with the general public. This belief also denigrates all the noncrime functions patrol officers perform—traffic control, emergency medical treatment, and response to other service calls. All these come to be regarded as something other than "proper police work" (which, of course, is catching criminals); the service aspects of the patrol officer's job come to be seen as rather soft. "Community policing"—or anything that sounds remotely like it—is for "wets," or "grin-and-wave" or "rubber gun" squads.

Collectively these six beliefs preserve the myths that are central to the reform image of the police as a dedicated crime-fighting force. At worst they encourage and legitimize insensitive, unproductive, and even illegal behavior; at best they promote organizational insularity, introspection, and detachment. Replacing them with a more honorable, more realistic, and more productive set of beliefs must be one of the core tasks of any new policing. They are not immune to change, as we shall see later, but they are extremely strong, and their influence should not be underestimated.

Chief Frank Dyson was sandbagged by them when he tried to reform the Dallas Police Department in the early 1970s.[50] He advocated a people-oriented police force, sensitive and responsive, with a more rational relationship with the community based on mutual understanding. He called for renewed and innovative efforts in crime prevention and service delivery, deemphasizing the force's rigid law enforcement role with its accompanying militaristic organizational patterns. He proposed a problem-oriented approach with recourse to the criminal justice system as just one option. He talked of police officers being taught to accept and appreciate public scrutiny and review. His goals received broad political support; he was hailed as one of the most enlightened chiefs of the time.

He got nowhere. Within two years he, along with most of his senior advisers, had resigned. Internal opposition drove them out: his plans had been mercilessly sabotaged by his own officers, who were simply not ready or willing to accept the changes. The staying power of the reform culture turned out to be formidable.

MANAGEMENT STYLE

The reform model has also left a deep imprint on the management style of modern police departments. Through their efforts to curtail arbitrary or inappropriate uses of police authority and resources, the reformers placed the notions of tight supervision and control—the reduction of officers' discretion—at the core of police management philosophy.[51]

Police departments typically boast weighty instruction manuals, often running to several volumes and thousands of pages. These books are designed to prescribe the action to be taken in any foreseeable circumstance, from the crash of a military aircraft to the report of a rabid badger. They also carefully designate who is to make which decisions and whose approval must be obtained before certain courses of action are followed. They are huge partly because the range of police activity is huge and partly because each error in the department's past has been met with another rule.

Many officers regard the manuals as useful reference books, which they are. But many others see them primarily as instruments of control. Some senior officers explicitly regard them as disciplinary tools. According to one British police superintendent, responsible as head of research and planning in a provincial force for maintaining and updating its manual, "The whole object of having the force instruction book is that when something goes wrong, you need to be able to turn to it to find out whose head goes on the block."[52]

The comment reflects the dominant philosophy of police management. Tight control, with unambiguous rules backed up by fearsome disciplinary systems, remains the most common style. That style has its origins in the early days of city police forces, when officers were lazy, often drunk, and frequently brutal. For those officers, and those times, the reformers were quite right to demand tighter control.

The subsequent strength and persistence of this style has been furthered by the propensity of many police forces to hire ex-military personnel, whose familiarity with weapons, physical fitness, and exceptionally smart appearance in uniform has always endeared them to police recruiters. The middle- and upper-management ranks of police agencies have traditionally been, and still are, liberally laced with military people, and the military influence is very noticeable. "Appearance" and "bearing" rank high on the list of qualities to be commented on at staff appraisal time. Precison marching is still taught at police training centers, even though it is never needed in practical police work (the justification being that drill is a device to instill a sense of discipline and "pride in the uniform" in new recruits).

The reform movement further cemented this militaristic style of management. The reformers' answer to political interference and corruption was the establishment of rigid hierarchical lines of control leading to a commissioner who would be held accountable for the misconduct of his officers. As the list of police scandals grew ever longer, so newly appointed commissioners came to be judged more and more by whether they were able to clean up their departments.

Considerable weight came to be attached to what they managed to prevent their officers from doing, thus diminishing the attention paid to what the police department actually achieved.

It is still generally true that the chief looks bad if anything goes wrong anywhere in the department. The implications of this simple fact cascade all the way down the command chain. Precinct captains (and other department heads) know that the last thing they want to do is give the commissioner trouble. To keep the commissioner happy, they have to keep their commands from being the focus of any public criticism. They know that misconduct of any kind by any of their officers reflects poorly on them. They know that they will be judged at headquarters first on their ability to keep their commands free from problems and second on their ability to bring swift and effective punishment down on any recalcitrants. Tight control, backed up by strict discipline, becomes their aim.

Shift commanders all feel the same pressures. They know that the highest accolade they can get from their captain, in the day-to-day running of their squads, is "He or she really runs a tight ship." With that in mind, they seek to impress on patrol officers that they know all the tricks and are not likely to be fooled by even the most experienced officer. Being "streetwise," for a supervisor, is as much about anticipating and frustrating patrol officers' dishonorable inclinations as it is about fighting crime, solving problems, or understanding the curious ways members of the public behave.

Police supervisors are therefore expected, quite universally and quite unreasonably, to exercise absolute control over their patrol officers, according to the theory that close supervision is always effective, provided it is close enough. This theory is reflected in the attitude of a significant proportion of internal affairs investigators, who frequently repeat the maxim "For every patrol officer who needs disciplining, there is a supervisor who needs disciplining." The underlying assumption about any misconduct is that it must be routinely and directly attributable to a breakdown in supervision.

It is hardly surprising, then, to find that management style surpasses riots, fatal accidents, violent confrontations, and shootings as the major cause of stress for police officers. This finding, from a recent study commissioned by the Association of Chief Police Officers in Britain and conducted by the Home Office, wholly supports the comment of one participating constable that "there is more stress inside the nick [the police station] than outside on the streets."[53]

This dominant form of police management, like the dominant police values, represents a steep hurdle for any new policing. Nobody, from greenest recruit to most eminent chief, can expect a department to risk any new approach, however promising, when the entire structure is poised to attack at the first sign of error or failure. Creativity, innovation, and experimentation—individual and departmental—are all stifled. If policing is to change and progress, police management, like police culture, must also change.

Making such changes in strategy, culture, and management—or at least setting such changes in motion—can only, in contemporary policing, be the job of chiefs of police. The reform model's emphasis on centralization and the paramilitary style has put so much authority in chiefs' hands that no one else inside departments has the influence necessary, and the reform model has made policing so inward looking that no one outside departments has much influence at all. If policing is to progress, it must do so—at least initially—from within and from the top down. Chiefs must face the shortcomings of reform policing and craft at least the beginnings of a new way. They can no longer afford simply to keep things running smoothly. They must pioneer.

CHAPTER 3

■

Beyond the Modern Major General

Chiefs and Change

IN THIS CHAPTER we will meet seven chiefs who have responded thoughtfully and creatively, even boldly, to the trouble in which policing finds itself. While all of them believe that their core mission is to control crime and enforce the law, they have experimented with new and very different notions of missions and methods. Some, frustrated by the limitations of policing's traditional reactive response to crime, have made forays into crime prevention; others, aware that not only crime but also fear and disorder take their toll on individuals and communities, have made reducing fear and improving the quality of life key objectives; still others, knowing that they cannot do all these jobs alone, have forged close working partnerships with residents, communities, and local government. Some have encouraged their officers to look beyond incidents—crimes, disturbances, pleas for help—to the problems that caused the incidents and that the incidents in turn cause, and to try new ways, often far less dependent on arrest and the criminal justice system, to solve those problems.

These shifts in missions and methods have sparked corresponding changes in management and organization. These chiefs have reached outside their departments to community groups and other parts of local government for support and guidance. They want to be helpful and responsive, and they are willing to give up some of their departments' autonomy to achieve it. Inside their departments many of these chiefs have stepped away from policing's paramilitary trappings. They want creativity and flexibility from their officers and middle managers, and they are willing to trim their own authority to get it.

These are more than mere technical adjustments in the reform model. They point, as one of our chiefs will say, toward "a revolution in policing."[1] Although many of our chiefs were initially driven to change by some kind of crisis or manifest failure—a riot, the crack epidemic, pervasive public fear—many subsequently came to see their journey toward the new as immensely positive and hopeful. Many of them have come to believe, with Darrel Stephens, that the foundations of traditional policing are built on sand, and they are busy laying new footings. They—and we—believe that they are beginning to show that policing can do far more than most would now dare hope, not only to control crime but also to help with a wide variety of other social problems.

In abandoning the old and committing themselves and their departments to untried and uncertain paths, these chiefs are taking enormous risks. If they are wrong, the consequences for the cities and the public to whom and for whom they are responsible could be grave, the consequences for their own standing and careers dire. "I felt," one commented about setting in motion the wheels of change, "like I was stepping off a cliff."[2] In their boldness, and in the sustained artfulness and experimentation it will take to realize the most ambitious of their visions, the chiefs are breaking the mold of what it means to be a police chief. They are no longer what their predecessors largely were: modern major generals presiding over departments so established that they did not so much evolve as simply age. They are, instead, something new to the field, police *executives,* who believe that their departments' missions, operational methods, and administrative arrangements may all be adjusted to adapt to new demands and to exploit new opportunities. Their privilege, and their burden, is to point the way, not only for themselves and their departments, but for all the other police executives who so sorely need leave to search for better ways of policing.

DARYL GATES AND LOS ANGELES: COMMUNITY CRIME PREVENTION

Daryl Gates, of the Los Angeles Police Department, is in many ways the epitome of the reform police chief and his department a shining example of the best in reform policing. Gates is handsome, physically fit, of disciplined military bearing. He has had long and distinguished service in the department he now leads. He is an articulate and passionate champion of the reform model, of honest, professional crime control as the central mission of policing. He sees himself as standing for the virtues of moral discipline and integrity not only throughout his department but in the broader society. He is popular with his troops, for although he is a harsh taskmaster he unreservedly supports his officers when he feels their cause is just. In his bearing, in his philosophy, in his conviction, he reveals his steadfast commitment to keeping the Los Angeles Police Department at the forefront of reform policing in the United States.

Gates's department mirrors his values. It operates with a high degree of autonomy, discipline, and self-confidence. For four decades it has avoided major corruption scandals. It polices a vast terrain and varied population with half the officers per capita of some big city departments.[3] It boasts sophisticated technical specialties rivaling the expertise of much larger organizations. It is, perhaps, the only department in the United States that could have wrested from the Federal Bureau of Investigation the responsibility for ensuring the security of the 1984 Olympics.[4] Its personnel are in demand to lead other departments throughout the country. It is the apotheosis of reform policing.

For all its professionalism, or perhaps because it feels so secure in its professionalism that it can afford to bend the rules somewhat, the LAPD is home to several important experiments in something the reform model has never valued very highly: crime prevention.

The department's senior lead officers, or SLOs, whom we met as part of the Community Mobilization Project in chapter 1, were among the first American police officers explicitly charged with forging strong, active, pragmatic links with city residents. For almost twenty years the LAPD has worked to create, refine, and maintain the SLO's role, and the community ties associated with it, in the face of internal uncertainty and opposition, and of both internal and external demands for scarce resources.[5]

The SLO's job, despite its unique character, was generally aimed at fairly traditional police problems. In 1983, faced with what Gates regarded as a new scourge apparently immune to traditional police methods, the LAPD crafted a program called DARE—Drug Abuse Resistance Education—which takes officers off the streets and puts them in the schools to teach kids why and how to say no.[6] Together, the SLOs and DARE say a great deal about the appeal of community involvement and crime prevention to even the most proudly reform departments—and to some of the limits they face in such departments.

The LAPD's community policing program was born of fire, the fire that seared Los Angeles in the devastating Watts riot of 1965. Then chief William Parker, one of the stalwarts of the California cadre of police reformers, was first astonished that anything could go so badly wrong and then impotent to do anything about it. After a week thirty-one civilians were dead, much of Watts burned, and order restored only with the aid of 14,000 National Guardsmen.[7]

The LAPD's subsequent postmortem came to focus on its ties, or lack thereof, with the communities it policed, and particularly on its classically reform-model patrol arrangements. Parker had spent much of his long career in Los Angeles dismantling the city's old pattern of foot beats and moving his officers into radio cars. Although each patrol car was assigned to a particular area, the pattern of calls across the city largely determined where a car would operate, and cars were often dispatched well beyond their areas. In the wake of Watts, the LAPD realized for the first time that it had become hard for patrol officers to develop any special familiarity with their assigned area and that they tended to feel responsible first for their watch—for making sure nothing happened on their shift—rather than for the area itself. They had become focused on incidents rather than conditions. "When I joined the department," in the 1950s, says now chief of operations Robert Vernon, "there was nobody at the radio car level who was in charge of all three watches, nobody who had the responsibility of looking generally at the area."

That fact, in the opinion of Chief Ed Davis, who took over the department in 1969, had created a dangerous isolation from the currents of city life, and he determined to correct it. In 1970 he reestablished a beat system—officers still patrolled in cars, but they were formed into small teams given round-the-clock responsibility for a relatively small area within a precinct—and he created a new rank, the senior lead officer, to lead the teams. Senior lead officers patrolled and answered calls just as ordinary patrol officers did, but they were also expected to monitor conditions in their areas, organize neighborhood watch groups, and arrange meetings of local people to determine what they wanted and help them get it.

This idea was a genuine inspiration for its time; in most places it still would be. Although the practice is abating somewhat, even quite large municipal jurisdictions, in the interest of minimizing response time, often deploy their patrol cars anywhere the calls come in, with no regard whatsoever for continuity for either the officers or the public. Where jurisdictions are subdivided into patrol areas, boundaries often reflect administrative convenience rather than community realities; patrol areas frequently neatly bisect established neighborhoods. Arrangements for attending to, much less mobilizing, residents are almost unheard of. The LAPD had reason to be proud.

It also had reason to be surprised. As the new SLOs went about their business, they discovered—as would many other police officers who pursued similar paths—the unexpected and crucially important fact that the things that concerned the citizens were often not what the police thought they would be. They heard few complaints about serious crime, many more about drunks, rowdy teenagers, abandoned cars, vandalism, and the like. People craved police help, but they craved it on their own terms.

This discovery created a dilemma for the police. On the one

hand, if they were to show good faith in forming partnerships with the community, they had to take these concerns seriously. On the other hand, responding to these problems robbed time from patrol and investigative work, which made a poor fit with both the priorities and the self-image of professional crime-fighters. From the day-to-day standpoint of patrol officers, community work dragged them away from real police work into something different—and distinctly "soft." "They were saying, Wait, that's not our job," Vernon recalls. "We're arresters, we're citation writers, we're not coffee pourers and nice talkers to people." As one LAPD captain now recalls, "I was in the locker room working out, and I heard two guys who were senior leads. One was talking to the other about how he needed cookies for his meeting, and he was really concerned about 'Dammit, I can't find the cookies.' And the other one needed a movie projector. And I thought, 'Oh my God, what have we done with our finest?' "

As time went on, though, many officers began to see more utility in the new order. "Say on one block you're taking a third report of a stolen battery in a week," says Vernon. "Now this third victim is pretty hot, because he came out and got in his car and it wouldn't start. You say, 'You know what? You're the third guy on this block. How about hosting a meeting tomorrow night at your house, call in all your neighbors, and let's come up with a plan to get this guy.' I mean, you've got a crime victim here who's hot; he's ready to do anything. But you get the people mobilized and organize a watch all night, and the neighbors stake the street out, and they get the guy arrested. After a while we started doing a lot of meetings like that." Some officers, and some area captains, even started letting local priorities, as revealed in neighborhood meetings, affect department policy, for instance, shifting their attention from strict crime control to clearing neighborhood streets of abandoned cars.

The LAPD, however, never stopped trying to be both a classic reform department, devoted to patrol and rapid response to calls for service, and a community police department, responsive to local priorities and relying to a considerable degree on local resources. The balance was never very happily struck. The conflict was greatest for the SLOs, who were personally expected both to foster community involvement and to handle regular patrol duties. Their dilemma was basic: time spent attending to and organizing local residents was time not spent on the streets. The more meetings and special projects SLOs lined up, the less they were available to answer calls. In many of the department's areas, traditional policing values won out, and SLOs became little more than ordinary patrol officers, their community responsibilities effectively suspended. "The reason they can't do anything—it's not their fault—is because they're working patrol, working a radio car," says a more activist SLO. Especially after 1978, when California's Proposition 13 tax-abatement measure forced large personnel cutbacks, much of the department's commitment to its SLOs waned. In the words of one LAPD veteran, the SLOs "went into a drift."

The LAPD never lost its idea of community policing, however, and from time to time the balance tipped the other way and community policing won out. Thus, the Community Mobilization Project experiment in Wilshire came down unequivocally in favor of local organizing, order maintenance, and the precedence of cooperative projects between the public and the department over ordinary patrol and call response. The results, the officers and residents involved with the experiment believe, speak for themselves. In particular, Wilshire's SLOs have been entirely converted to the community-oriented philosophy. And in 1986 Daryl Gates called once again for elevating SLOs as the department's principal device for strengthening community mobilization.

Even before he made this call, however, he had undertaken another major crime-prevention program, one that not only took officers off the streets—thus potentially degrading response times—but also seemed, on its surface, perilously close to the kind of "social work" that the reform model rejected on principle and that police officers invariably eschew. That DARE, aimed at steering schoolchildren from drugs, so captured Gates's and the LAPD's imagination says a great deal about policing's openness to different kinds of crime prevention.

Some of what impelled the LAPD to craft DARE is all too painfully obvious. Traditional police work had simply failed against LA's drug trade. As a program brochure explains, the department

64

was arresting more narcotics suspects than ever before, three people in Los Angeles County were dying drug-related deaths every day (a 106-percent increase over five years), and drug use seemed to be reaching an ever-younger population.[8] This use was perhaps even more serious in LA than elsewhere, because the drug trade was so connected with the city's notorious youth gangs and because crack cocaine—"rock," as it is called in LA—surfaced much earlier there than most other places in the country.

Facing the failure of enforcement, the LAPD, in cooperation with the Los Angeles school system, turned to prevention. DARE officers teach classroom workshops on resisting the lure of drugs and peer pressure. Uniformed but unarmed officers use skits, exercises, and role playing to teach youngsters that real friends won't push them to drink and use drugs, that not everybody their age has or will dabble, that maturity means being assertive and independent, and that there are a variety of positive and nonconfrontational ways to fend off entreaties to alcohol and drug use. Eighty-one officers taught 230,000 students in 1989.[9]

It's not at all clear how well DARE works, and, given the program's long-term goal of preventing drug use in a very large and young population, its success won't be ascertainable even in principle for some time (though its failure might). DARE is, according to independent reviews, popular.[10] Its officers were almost universally well received by students, teachers, administrators, and parents. "Quite simply, the students love" the instructors, a 1986 National Institute of Justice report noted.[11]

The most important thing about DARE, in some ways, is simply that the LAPD, among the most reform of reform departments, decided to do it and has given it a solid institutional home. With its emphasis on incident-driven, after-the-fact law enforcement, the reform model never gave crime prevention a great deal of weight, and with its emphasis on patrol, rapid response, and investigation, it typically had no room at all for such exotica as partnerships with public education. DARE is proof positive that, at least in extremis, crime prevention is a plausible complement to traditional policing.

DARE's status as a jewel in Gates's crown is particularly noteworthy. Many departments have had programs aimed at crime prevention or reduction, which were popular with the public, that have nevertheless been either discarded or effectively shut off from the departmental mainstream. "Crime-prevention" bureaus, like "community-relations" bureaus, are notorious departmental backwaters, home—or commonly assumed to be by the rest of the force—to officers without the skills, courage, or backbone for real police work. Officers who visit schools for "Officer Friendly" or similar community-relations programs are routinely derided by their colleagues on the street, though, as with the DARE officers, kids love to see them. Chiefs, more sensitive than street officers to the value of positive community relations, often support such programs, but not the way Gates embraced DARE.

What is special about DARE is the way it speaks to both the reform model's explicit values—crime fighting—and important elements of its hidden culture. Police culture holds that nobody understands the real world, the world of the street, like the police do. When the police saw society threatened by civil unrest in the 1960s, a threat they feared much of society was missing or underestimating, they coined the phrase *the thin blue line* to denote the contribution they felt they made to stemming the tide.[12] DARE is the thin blue line operating at a moral level. Gates saw Los Angeles—and "the United States, Western Europe and much of the Third World," as a DARE brochure says—threatened by drugs, and he felt that the cause of that threat was the failure of family and other social institutions to teach the young proper values.[13] His sense of his department— that it was a model of probity and good conduct, and thus fit to give moral instruction—made him unusually ready to step in and, in co-operation with the schools, try to fill the gap.

We take no position here on the question of the LAPD's special standing as a moral force, and we do not know—though we hope— that DARE will do the job it was designed for. But we do see DARE as a welcome example showing that even the most consciously reform police departments, when faced with problems not amenable to solution through law enforcement, will turn to other, more preventive problem-solving methods, if those methods are in accord with their values and culture. And as policing takes on more and more jobs less suitable to law enforcement, as we believe it should, and changes its culture to support those jobs, as we believe it must, creative and unusual preventive strategies and tactics will become more and more common.

NEIL BEHAN AND BALTIMORE COUNTY: A FIGHT AGAINST FEAR

Neil Behan, chief of the Baltimore County Police Department, is cut from a different cloth than Daryl Gates. Where Gates is pristine, forceful, and distant, Behan is professorial, introspective, and engaging. They share an overall commitment to the moral code of police professionalism—to the honesty and integrity of the force—but Behan is far less sure than Gates that the reform model holds all the operational answers. In particular, Behan has come to challenge both the reform model's reactive approach and its insistence that all serious police work is anticrime work. Is it important for the police to take issues other than crime seriously? Behan, who got a chance to pursue some of his own ideas when he took over the Baltimore County department in 1977 after a career in New York City, thought so, even if he wasn't sure how. Is there a way—an honest, constitutional way—to do police work without having to wait for the crime to be committed and the damage done? He thought so, even if he didn't have a complete plan in mind.

Behan was moved to action after two particularly frightening murders traumatized Baltimore County in 1981.[14] The killings underscored, as far as he was concerned, fear's status as a problem distinct from crime. Neither murder was the sort that was likely to be repeated, and police caught the suspects almost immediately, but county residents' concerns were not assuaged. If the police could do things to reduce fear directly, Behan concluded, those things were likely to be different than what they already did to fight crime. Just what those fear-reducing activities might be, he will frankly admit, he had very little idea, except that he wanted officers working far more closely with residents. He was content to set the goal and support his officers while they figured out how to get there.

Behan created three units, each consisting of fifteen volunteer officers led by a lieutenant and reporting to one of the department's three area patrol commanders. He assigned them to motorcycles—after his staff convinced him horses would be unworkable—to signal greater accessibility to the community and make them recognizable within and outside the department as a new kind of patrol officer. And he ordered his area commanders not to use them for regular patrol functions and activities. The three COPE (Citizen-Oriented Police Enforcement) teams hit the streets in July 1982.

They knew they weren't supposed to fight fear simply by fighting crime, but they didn't really know what to do instead: no other department in the country had tried to do what they were doing. They went through a phase in which they simply saturated troubled neighborhoods, walking, slowly riding their high-profile motorcycles, and talking with residents, on the principle that seeing lots of cops would make people feel safer. Sometimes that worked, but sometimes it backfired when residents assumed there must be something really frightful going on to command the presence of so many officers. They went through a crime-prevention phase, encouraging residents to lock their doors and secure their property. That kept them busier, but it didn't seem to quell fear. By the end of the first year, the program seemed to some participants to have stalled out.

Behan and the project team brought in Herman Goldstein for advice. Goldstein ran seminars introducing his problem-solving notion: that police should look at patterns and causes of incidents and use creative means to attack the conditions that promote crime and other problems. COPE officers loved the idea. During the spring and summer of 1983, the program's strategy was retooled. Fear problems were to be exhaustively researched using surveys and other information-gathering techniques. COPE teams would "brainstorm" to find new and creative solutions. Officers assigned to each project would write a detailed "action-plan" diagnosing the problems and describing proposed solutions. Public and private agencies were encouraged to help. COPE officers were to use any legal means they could think of—including, on Goldstein's recommendation, traditional police tactics—to solve the county's fear problems.

COPE units soon scored significant successes. One was called into Garden Village, a large public housing project with a long history of antagonism toward the police. Officers surveyed the community, analyzed crime statistics, and photographed the dismal deterioration of the project. Armed with these data, they arrested several local serious offenders and persuaded the Baltimore Gas and Electric Company to repair streetlights, the County Highway Department to pave the alleyways, and the Department of Recreation and Parks to construct a new park. Fear, measured by household surveys, decreased dramatically in the community, and police popularity soared to the point that officers in the project on a drug raid were greeted with applause rather than the usual taunts and complaints of harassment.

Another COPE unit was mobilized by a community of elderly terrorized by the brutal beating of a sixty-nine-year-old woman. The woman could identify her assailant but was so afraid she moved away instead. A neighborhood meeting sponsored by the COPE officers disclosed that the offense was one of a series of burglaries committed by neighboring teenagers who had invaded the area through a hole in a fence. Further, they discovered that while the burglaries had been reported to the local precinct, local officers were unaware of how afraid residents had become.

As in Garden Village, the COPE officers first responded to the environmental problems, fixing the fence and installing lights in areas where the teenagers had once lurked. In addition, they went to extraordinary lengths to persuade the victim to testify, including a promise to provide vans to transport neighborhood supporters to the trial. As it turned out, the burglar was not convicted. But COPE's efforts produced a different and perhaps more valuable result: fear decreased, the victim moved back, reported crime plummeted, and enthusiasm for the police increased.

COPE continued to string up success stories, and after a few years some precinct commanders began to train their regular patrol officers in the program's problem-solving approach. Behan caught in COPE a glimpse of the future of policing. "All the pieces of the puzzle are there," he says. "The use of a wide range of alternative responses. The engagement of the community. A bigger and more flexible role for individual officers, the deemphasis of military structure, and a more thoughtful analysis of the problems police are expected to handle. If you fit all these pieces together, you have the beginning of a new vision of what police work could become. If COPE is adopted, it will mean a revolution in policing."

DARREL STEPHENS AND NEWPORT NEWS: PROBLEM SOLVING

Darrel Stephens, chief of police in Newport News from 1983 to 1986 and now head of the Police Executive Research Forum, thinks approaches like COPE can be adopted not just by the odd team of officers but by whole departments and aimed at not just new but traditional police problems. Stephens is by nature unassuming and soft-spoken, a thinker and learner. In his days as a patrol officer, his principal frustrations were the lack of time to think about the problems he encountered and the limitations of the remedies he had available. To him, as to Neil Behan, Herman Goldstein's problem-solving vision made a great deal of sense. It made a virtue of discretion, which policing had tried to deny and discourage. It promised to tap the talent and creativity of police officers and to eliminate some of their frustrations and anxieties. With that, some of the cynicism might also go.

Stephens was determined that this new approach be departmentwide. When Newport News began its problem-solving experiment in 1984, he had already laid the groundwork for transforming his very traditional department into something markedly different.[15] He promulgated a "philosophy of service" that required police managers to develop neighborhood watch groups and communicate with them through newsletters and personal correspondence, and that emphasized the resolution of neighborhood problems rather than arrests, crime statistics, or calls for service. This was directly contrary to the old management style, which emphasized distance from the community. Stephens published a set of organizational values that put the protection of individual constitutional rights at the top of the list. The apprehension of criminals, often treated as the most important objective, was included somewhat grudgingly as one among many ways of preventing crime. Stephens introduced many forms of participative management and encouraged open communication throughout the department.

On this base he meant to build what he called problem-oriented policing. "We felt that there was a need to develop a more structured approach to analyzing and addressing crime and service problems," he says. "We also felt that it was important to test that approach in a way that involved the entire police department, not just a special unit set off to the side, not just confining the thinking process to a planning or crime analysis unit."[16]

Stephens thinks he largely succeeded. The story of New Briarfield from chapter 1 is one notable example, but more important than any single success is the fact that during his three years in the department Stephens changed it to the point that there are *many* such stories, peopled by different officers focused on disparate problems: citywide crime problems such as domestic violence and gas station robberies, neighborhood crime problems such as business district and residential burglaries, neighborhood disorder problems such as illegal drinking and hooliganism. In every case officers partially freed from the reactive discipline of answering emergency calls were able to frame, analyze, and respond to—often very creatively—long-standing difficulties. One officer working on a downtown prostitution problem got to know his enemy so well that he frequently broke up imminent liaisons by introducing the male-transvestite hookers by name to their astonished, and horrified, johns. "We reoriented the thinking process of the whole department to say that we can best use our time to focus on the problems of the community," Stephens says. It is something he finds very heartening.

So he should. Neil Behan, fighting fear in Baltimore, showed that ordinary police officers can change both mission and tactics to their own satisfaction and the public's benefit. Darrel Stephens, fighting crime in Newport News, showed, or at least took a huge step toward showing, that a whole department can do the same.

JOHN AVERY AND NEW SOUTH WALES: COMMUNITY RESPONSIVENESS OVER TECHNICAL SPECIALIZATION

John Avery, commissioner of police in New South Wales, Australia, has fierce eyes and a determined jaw. His presence is imposing, but his nature, and his managerial style, is deliberate. There is something of the scholar in his background and outlook. He has for many years shaped the educational policy of his department, and he has written a first-rate book on policing, called *The Police: Force or Service?* which argues for responsive policing tailored to community needs.[17] He is exceedingly devoted to his colleagues and his department, and he has high ambitions for both. It has been his fate, however, in his six years as commissioner, to have his devotion tried and his vision tested. He has been forced both to preside over the disgrace and to craft the rehabilitation of his department. In the process he has moved it from the path of specialized, professional crime control to one offering far more broadly defined and responsive help to the people it serves.

It was a very big job. The New South Wales Police Department employs some 16,000 people.[18] It is responsible not only for Sydney, a sprawling city of several million souls, but also for a rural area twice the size of Texas with less than half the population. It consisted, when Avery assumed command, of three essentially different arms, almost three separate departments: an ordinary metropolitan patrol force, a rural constabulary, and an investigative agency based in Sydney but available to the whole state as needed. And it had fallen prey to a common failing among reform departments, of valuing and rewarding only the most specialized and elite elements of its crime-fighting force.

In New South Wales detectives were the heroes, the heart and soul of the department. They had a prized reputation for conducting tough, sophisticated investigations, tinged—not unpleasantly, many thought—with a slight odor of brutality and aggressive zeal. They often earned more and had more overtime available than patrol officers, and they had far more discretion in their work, more access to training, altogether more status, and more media attention. The investigative force was also the only place where initiative and performance counted for much. In the rest of the department, advancement mostly occurred along a treadmill in which vacancies were created by retirements and automatically filled by the next person in line. (For many years the most closely examined document in the department was the quarterly report that listed every employee by name in order of seniority; the commissioner was number one and the most recently hired constable 12,764.) Not surprisingly, ambitious, motivated, and resourceful officers wanted to be detectives.

The rest of the department lost accordingly. Those who saw value and promise in service functions as well as crime fighting, who championed the patrol force and the rural constabulary, got short shrift. In this the New South Wales Police Department exaggerated the tendency of most departments to put street officers at the bottom of the status heap and specialist units, especially detectives, at the top. It is a rare department that does not reward patrol officers by giving them a wholly different kind of job; it is not an uncommon department that views patrol officers as those who are too new, or too stupid, to get off the street. Reform policing does not overly value patrol work.

Eventually, in their enthusiasm and independence, the New South Wales investigators went too far. They were caught using illegal methods like wiretaps to gather evidence, even manufacturing evidence outright. Worse, they were caught in close, corrupt relations with organized crime figures. A royal commission established to review the organization and operation of the department recommended a thorough housecleaning.[19] To carry it out, it reached down six or seven rungs of the seniority ladder and named John Avery commissioner. The move was unprecedented and shattering: Avery still vividly recalls the shock and hostility with which his colleagues greeted his appointment. Several of his disappointed superiors explicitly vowed to undermine him; only one promised to help. And as a sign of things to come, the commission called for, and the legislature established, a three-member police board, with Avery holding one seat. The board had various oversight powers; most important, it could require the department to submit an annual strategic plan for its review and could fill all departmental positions above the rank of captain.

Avery's first priority, consistent with both his mandate and his character, was cleaning up the aftermath of the corruption scandal. He spent two years doing little else. Many senior officials and prominent detectives were prosecuted, retired, or allowed to resign. It was hard, bruising work for a man who felt his loyalties to his colleagues and his department deeply. On a more positive note, Avery managed to strengthen the academy's programs and raise educational standards throughout the department. But he still felt far from his goal of reshaping the force into a fundamentally more valuable service.

With the help and support of the police board, Avery began to shift his department toward something he called "community policing," by which he meant thoughtful, service-oriented policing aimed at enhancing the quality of life throughout the department's varied domain. They used a number of tools to begin the change. They published a set of official values meant to guide planning and operations; in contrast to the implicit values of the last thirty years, the new statement explicitly emphasized service and integrity over crime fighting and law enforcement. They required the department to submit an annual "strategic plan" setting out its basic goals for the next year, and Avery made it clear that he wanted his people thinking about ways in which they could make a new, positive contribution. The police board backed him up by making its primary criteria for promotion integrity and the development of fresh approaches.

While his people were mulling these changes over, Avery took the department apart and put it back together again. Its old structure, based on the reform ideal of centralized, functional commands, was dissolved in favor of decentralized, geographically based commands. The most obvious, and painful, part of the change was dismantling the central detective branch, most of whose personnel were farmed out to the new field commands. Community-relations, juvenile, and traffic divisions were also broken up, but moving the detectives was far more dramatic. They had been the soul of the department and many continued to be most hostile to Avery's reforms. Now, in a

Beyond the Modern Major General

direct attack on their standing, they found themselves working for officers who had made their careers in patrol (or, worse, traffic). They did not go gently, but they went.

Avery did not reorganize simply to weaken the detectives' hold on his department. He wanted, also and perhaps foremost, to strengthen the police's ability to live up to his service ideal. His primary insight was that shifting authority to geographic commands would change the nature of commanders' responsibility. Instead of being accountable for how a particular specialty—investigations, traffic control, crime prevention, narcotics—was performed, commanders focused on general conditions in their areas. They were responsible for their communities, their turf. With the specialists reporting to them, they had at their disposal all the powers of the department. It was their job to see that they were put to good use. Nobody had had that job in the old department.

Geographic command likewise transformed what it meant to lead. In specialized units it was natural for ranking officers to think of themselves as qualified to lead by virtue of superior skills. The chief of detectives was, presumably, the best detective around; his job was to oversee his subordinates' work. In geographic commands, senior officers could not easily claim to be the best at all the functions they were newly responsible for. They were unlikely to be, simultaneously, ace detectives, skilled traffic engineers, and sensitive youth counselors. Their job became to focus the energies of diverse experts on the joint task of producing security, order, and safety in their areas. They became, most significantly, managers rather than supervisors. The change helped give them time to think, freed them from the habits of mind of particular specialties, and let them focus on team building and innovation.

Finally, geographic command created the potential for new kinds of relationships with the community. In the old department, as in most reform departments, only two kinds of officials—the commissioner and street officers—routinely had contact with the public. Everybody else was largely insulated. They looked up to receive instructions and down to give them; they rarely had to look outside. If the community wanted to say something, or have something done, it was hard to make contact at any receptive level. The commissioner was too lofty, and patrol officers too powerless. But with geographic command, new parts of the department were put in contact with the world. Captains were natural contacts for local problems and served as pipelines, when necessary, to other reaches of the department. Different-sized groups, with different-sized issues, could find someone to talk to.

In New South Wales, as in every department, the question inevitably arose, What should the department do as special demands emerged, from the public and elsewhere? They always do: at one time it will be street drug dealing, at another domestic assault, at still another parking enforcement. The usual response from police chiefs is to ignore the demand, hoping it will fade; issue an order for the ranks to attend to it, knowing that the order itself will shortly fade; or create a special unit to act on it. Special units have great appeal for chiefs. They are tangible evidence of commitment (useful for press releases); they will do something; they may even do something useful, since they typically attract people who are resourceful, ambitious, and interested in the problem; and they are easy to monitor and supervise.

Avery recognized, however, that special units have distinct liabilities as well. They draw assets away from the rest of the department and thus create hostility. They tend to reduce other units' attention to the problem; domestic violence becomes the province not of the patrol force but of the domestic violence unit. They tend to monopolize any expertise they develop. And they ran counter to Avery's determination to push responsibility and accountability out to his new commands. What was the point of working so hard on geographic organization if the most important work ended up being done elsewhere?

Avery's answer was to replace the idea of special units with the idea of special programs. If a problem was important enough to justify a unit, he reasoned, it was important enough that all parts of the department should try to solve it. The managers of his programs now operate analogously to his geographic commanders: they don't tackle the problem themselves, or manage those who do; instead, they focus the department's attention on coming to terms with it. They convene task forces, develop a plan of attack, monitor performance, persuade, exhort, and cajole. They become expert in the techniques and status of the program by staying in touch with what the operational arms of the department are doing. Learning takes place and expertise develops throughout the department, and stays there.

John Avery has set himself an ambitious program, with much yet to be tried and proven. But even now it is clear that he has a distinct vision of what policing could be, and of the structure and tools his department needs to realize that vision. He has taught a major department that policing need not be insular to be effective, or tough to be valuable. He has created a model of how his department can marshal its strengths rather than divide them, and how it can turn those strengths to the service of the people and communities of New South Wales.

KEVIN TUCKER AND PHILADELPHIA: EMBRACING ACCOUNTABILITY

Nothing ranked higher on the reform agenda than prying police departments from the clutches of outside political influence. Reformers had seen too much police involvement in rigged elections and machine politics, and too many police departments battered when administrations changed, to countenance anything less than absolute insulation. It was a point they largely won. Even in those cities—meaning probably most cities—where the break was less than absolute, the ideology of reform policing required that relations between police and other authorities have at the very least the appearance of distance. Chiefs bristled at overt efforts to influence their departments. Autonomy, if it was not a reality, never ceased to be an aspiration.

Autonomy, however, has been an extremely mixed blessing. The days of serious police meddling in municipal politics are over, but at the cost of departments that are isolated, unresponsive, suspicious, and far less effective than they might be. Autonomy inhibits the police from being close and attentive to the communities they serve and deprives them of resources—information, influence, and the various capacities of municipal government—they badly need. It is one of the reform model's most unfortunate legacies.

Kevin Tucker, appointed police commissioner in Philadelphia in January 1986, sought another way.[20] The summer before Tucker's appointment, Philadelphia police had bombed and laid siege to the downtown stronghold of MOVE, a militant black separatist group, killing most of the people inside and burning an entire city block. His mandate was to restore public confidence and police morale and to make any changes necessary to reform the department: to prevent any idiocies like the bombing and to avoid embarrassments like the high-level corruption scandal that rocked the department shortly thereafter. It was not, he found, a mandate that he could or wanted to carry out in isolation from the rest of the city. Making the Philadelphia Police Department work meant insisting both that the department open itself to outside influence and that the city as a whole assume some responsibility for what its police did. In finding ways to make those things happen, Tucker ventured an experiment in what might be called postreform political relations: constructing ties to city government and other centers of municipal power that were political without being partisan and potent without being hidden, improper, or self-serving. Tucker's work is a demonstration that the police need not, and should not, shrink from the larger political life of the cities they serve.

Tucker, a plainspoken former high official of the United States Secret Service, brought two crucial assets to his new job: a reputation for honesty and integrity, and a talent for management. Both were critical—to Mayor Wilson Goode, who was fighting for his political life in the wake of the bomb debacle, and to Philadelphia's business community, which had backed Goode over former mayor and commissioner of police Frank Rizzo. But Tucker did not have the kind of background or clout that commanded instant respect from either his new department or his new political overseers. Guarding presidents and tracking down forgers was not the sort of thing that impressed Philadelphia's tough street cops, nor was managing an enforcement agency at the federal level—with its lavish resources and neat separation from political interference—much like running a police department in a fiscally strapped city with a powerful and contentious city council.

Tucker assumed from the beginning that his main job was to professionalize the department—which had been acting anything but professionally of late—through the usual internal changes and reforms. He knew perfectly well that his legitimacy was shaky, so he made obtaining a clear mandate his first order of business. To get it, he established the Philadelphia Police Study Task Force, with members recruited from four key groups: civic-minded members of the city's business community, black community leaders from Philadelphia's neighborhoods, heads of important city public and nonprofit organizations, and nationally recognized experts in policing. Tucker charged the group with developing a "detailed management blueprint" for the department.

The task force set out with a classically reform focus, looking at the mechanics of fighting internal corruption, improving training, optimizing shift schedules, and the like. Tucker soon came to believe, however, that unless the community demanded it, he would have little leverage to implement a reform agenda, and unless the community was willing to invest in the police, he would lack the means to build the capabilities he needed and to sugarcoat the distasteful medicine of reform. The realization that the city as a whole, not just the chief, had to provide the impetus for change shifted the task force's direction. Instead of writing its report for the police department, it addressed itself to the broader community. It wrote its report not only as a management blueprint, with hundreds of specific recommendations, but also as a call for a new partnership between the community and the police—the reconstitution of an effective, mutually challenging relationship, with an emphasis on community policing, enhanced service and accountability, decentralization, and improved management.

The publication of the task force report accomplished what Tucker had intended. Its themes created a great deal of excitement in the press, the business community, and, to a lesser degree, Philadelphia's ethnic neighborhoods. It won general applause and gave Tucker the popular support he needed.

Tucker's, and the department's, course had been set. To keep to it, however, required sustained, grueling political and organizational work. Having learned the importance of external prodding and support, Tucker sought to continue the influence of the task force by creating an outside Implementation Committee (later rechristened the Police Commissioner's Council) to oversee his response to the task force recommendations. The committee was chaired by an influential local businessman named William Eagleson, who had been an active member of the task force. It included the other Philadelphians who had served on the task force and some new recruits from the city. The national experts were thanked for their efforts and excused. The Implementation Committee published a nine-month progress report, testified often before the city council, operated behind the scenes to ensure that the mayor and city council supported the reforms, and provided a supportive audience to those in the department who were working hard to implement reforms.

Tucker's allies needed that kind of help. They faced, in the upper levels of the department, a well-connected and powerful old guard—with ready access to press and politicians and a great deal of internal influence—whose glowering presence dampened enthusiasm for reform. They faced confusion about what Tucker wanted, about just what this new community policing was and how they were supposed to get there. Most important, perhaps, they faced uncertainty over Tucker's tenure. The new commissioner had a less than cozy relationship with the city council and showed a dangerous penchant for threatening to resign when his will was thwarted. His departmental supporters worried, with reason, that one day the city would call his bluff.

In that environment every bit of guidance and support counted. Tucker did what he could, but other parties in the city, with the chief's blessing, offered vital help shouldering the responsibility for progress. As a report by the Police Commissioner's Council noted, "To realize the possibilities of a new relationship between Philadelphians and their police force, it is necessary that a broad and powerful constituency for change develop. Otherwise, the staying hand of tradition and inertia will continue to guide the department's future."[21] The council saw itself as the core of that constituency: a loyal, but watchful and critical, harbinger of progress. It kept public watch on Tucker's programs, lined up civic and business support for particular initiatives, honored officers noteworthy for new-style community policing, and chided the city when it failed to take what the council deemed proper steps: for example, when it refused to make a high school diploma a requirement for joining the department. It made itself, in effect, the conscience of the "new partnership" between Philadelphia and its police that the original task force had called for. Making liberal use of both praise and goad, the council refused to let either party take its eyes off the mark.

Where the previous generation's chiefs would have chafed at such interference, Tucker embraced the council's role. His problem was not the gross political meddling of the earlier era but a kind of malaise, shared by city and department, that needed simultaneous solution. He knew that he could not do it alone, but perhaps he and others could do it together.

The main hurdle to success, he came to believe, was the department's middle management. The bottom of the department, patrol officers and detectives, he believed would be willing to change if he could convince them of the new approach's merits. The top of the department he could work on himself. That left, however, a large number of midlevel officials who, by the way they dealt with new ideas and rewarded and disciplined the officers under them, could spell success or failure for his reforms.

His answer was to invest in management training for many of these middle managers, something the department had never before done. He contracted with the Police Executive Research Forum to run special classes aimed at conveying the ideas behind, and management techniques appropriate to, a decentralized, community-oriented style of policing. And he arranged with Philadelphia businesses to include police managers in their own in-house management workshops. He could, he hoped, use that education not only to smooth the way for his ideas but also to create a cadre of managers who, over the balance of their careers, would develop their own as experience and circumstances required.

Tucker did quit, eventually. In most cities, without his active commitment and guidance, his reforms would very likely have died a quiet death. In Philadelphia the constituency for change remained intact. The new chief, Willie Williams, who came from inside the department, found that he had both outside pressures and inside partners to help him. With luck, as Tucker's agenda takes hold and becomes the department's normal way of doing business, the focus of outside groups will shift from the problems of immediate change to the long-term issues of maintaining an open and effective relationship between police and city. The Philadelphia police, if they go the distance, will set a new example: a department that is neither a political tool, as in the old days, nor politically alienated, as in more recent ones, but a cooperative and conscientious partner in municipal life.

SIR KENNETH NEWMAN AND LONDON: PUTTING IT ALL TOGETHER

Sir Kenneth Newman, commissioner of the London Metropolitan Police (better known as the Met, or as Scotland Yard) from 1982 to 1987, looks little like a police commissioner, even less like someone who had led the Royal Ulster Constabulary in Northern Ireland against IRA and Protestant terrorism. He is small and scholarly, and peers out at the world like an owl from behind thick glasses and, more often than not, a dense wreath of pipe smoke. He invariably speaks not just in complete sentences but in entire paragraphs. He is a bold thinker and strategist who brought to the London Met a complete new model of policing. Where his fellow chiefs have taken aim at this part or that of reform policing, Newman has tossed the whole paradigm aside and replaced it with a new one: something he calls "neighborhood policing." Neighborhood policing represents wholesale change—in the department's goals, its tactics, its relations with London's communities, its values and management. The concept makes of many of the ideas that have informed other provocative but less ambitious police innovations—in Los Angeles, Baltimore, and similar places—an integrated and comprehensive whole. It is one of contemporary policing's boldest experiments.[22]

This transformation, like many of policing's major departures, was born of crisis. Newman was appointed commissioner in the aftermath of the worst antipolice riots London had ever seen. Until that time Scotland Yard had taken considerable pride in—and enjoyed an enviable international reputation for—a blend of policing that ran from imperturbable bobbies, who patrolled unarmed and spoke politely to even the most degraded citizens, to sophisticated experts in terrorism and hostage negotiation. The riots, however, took a nick out of the Met's self-confidence, just as the Watts riots fifteen years earlier had prompted soul-searching in the Los Angeles Police Department.

London's Watts was Brixton, one of the city's poorest, highest-unemployment, and most racially and ethnically mixed neighborhoods. Brixton had the highest incidence of street crime in England, double the robbery rate of the next worst area in London, and ostentatiously public drug use and dealing. Relations between the Met and the Brixton community were notably poor. Particularly despised was the Special Patrol Group, or SPG, one of the Met's answers to situations like Brixton where normal policing methods seemed inadequate. The SPG, which operated out of a central headquarters, could be deployed temporarily, as necessary, to work with divisional officers on special projects. Typically, the unit flooded an area with officers for several days to combat drugs or street crime; some of the SPG would be in uniform, some in plain clothes, and they would make vastly more than the usual number of stops—official acts short of arrest that permit searches and interrogation—to try to make crime at least temporarily impracticable.

Units like the SPG, and the tactics they employed, were rather considerably at odds with the popular image of London's bobbies steadfastly walking their time-honored beats. The Met had in fact turned from its traditional walking beats to motorized patrol and such specialized squads—hallmarks of police professionalization on the American model—only in the late 1960s and 1970s, in an attempt to make the most of a force that was then considerably understrength. For the first time London's police force became primarily response—radio call—oriented. A relatively small second tier of "home beat"

83

officers continued to walk the same beat each day, making a special effort to keep in touch with the community by visiting schools, helping organize sports matches, making themselves available to residents, and the like.

The reactive side of the force had the upper hand, though, at least until April 1981 when Brixton launched a fateful SPG-style sweep dubbed Swamp '81 (the SPG itself was not involved). Over the next ten days police stopped 1,000 people and arrested 150. On Friday, April 10, Brixton erupted. Officers found a young black man wandering on the streets, stabbed and dazed, and were attacked by bystanders who thought the police had assaulted the man during an arrest. Rioting broke out, died down, recommenced on Saturday, and continued sporadically until Monday night. Police from all over London were brought in to retake control of the streets. The conflict was a mixture of antipolice violence, with bricks and Molotov cocktails (their first appearance in England) for weapons, and considerable arson, vandalism, and looting (there were no firearms and ultimately no deaths; "Gun contol works," *The Economist* wrote afterward).[23] The eruption was not racial; whites attacked the police with enthusiasm, and *The Economist* reported that young blacks protected elderly white women living off Railton Road, where the violence was worst (and where scorch marks left by piles of burning tires are still visible).[24] When it was over, 279 police and 45 civilians had been injured, twenty-eight buildings burned, and a large number of local businesses permanently closed. Less serious "copycat" riots were sparked elsewhere in London and in a number of England's other inner cities.

England was shocked. Much of the blame came to rest on the Met itself. Although Swamp '81 led to 150 arrests, *The Economist* wrote, "They had stopped 1000 people; that meant 850 people stopped without justification. The mixture was ready to explode."[25] Brixton Division was pilloried in the press for rejecting or ignoring neighborhood opinion and for isolating its own home beat officers, who had not even been notified of Swamp '81. The leader of the Lambeth borough council called the Met "an army of occupation within the borough"; a prominent black Brixton barrister called the SPG "stormtroopers."[26]

It was into this mess that Newman stepped when he took over the Met in the fall of 1982. London's police, he soon decided, needed a fundamental and departmentwide reorientation. For the first time since Sir Robert Peel had established the force in 1829 as the prototype for all modern policing, the Met was about to have a thorough shaking up. Newman meant to mobilize the public and open the department up to community direction, desquad the force and shift priority to patrol operations, and move large areas of responsibility from headquarters to the field. Most, if not all, of this had been thought about and done elsewhere; nowhere had it all been done simultaneously and on such a large scale. It felt, he says, "like I was stepping off a cliff."

He began with the idea that the Met was taking on an impossible job, and raising impossible expectations, by accepting sole responsibility for fighting crime. "The majority of crime facing the Metropolitan Police is of a frustratingly fleeting and transient nature," he wrote in an early report to the Home Secretary. "However effective the police are able to be within their existing resources against the millions of opportunities provided by parked vehicles and available premises, their achievements will appear insignificant alongside the bulk of opportunist crime."[27] There appeared to be no particular prospect for a substantial increase in the Met's establishment, but Newman said later, even had there been, "I suppose it would have [taken] something on the order of 10,000 men, at least, [to make a significant difference], and I'm not sure that even then you could guarantee you'd make any impact, because the great majority of crime is so random and opportunistic."

Newman was convinced, however, that the Met could do something; it simply could not do it alone. "We had to set about, somehow, mobilizing the great latent resource that resides in the public itself," he says. "Not just exhorting the public to cooperate, but actually providing a coherent framework within which they can cooperate."

The "coherent framework" Newman desired for cooperation between police and public took the form of a putative bargain he drew up between the public and the police, a bargain he called (with a bow to Locke and other social contract theorists) the "notional contract." In return, the commissioner wrote, "for the police service striving to protect the rights, freedom and property of the individual in accordance with the law of the land, the individual contributes toward this endeavor by actively cooperating with the police in the discharge of their duty."[28]

In practice, this meant that Londoners should, with police support, set up neighborhood watch schemes to alert police to crimes in progress, mark their property, undertake "target hardening" to make residences and businesses more resistant to burglary, and notify police of known criminals. For their part, police should be far more sensitive and responsive to community wants and needs than they had been. In the wake of the Brixton troubles, Parliament had decreed that the Met set up neighborhood "consultative committees" to promote community involvement in police planning and operations. Newman seized on the idea and directed his divisional (precinct) superintendents to draw up annual plans in cooperation with the committees (which tended to be made up of local politicians, businesspeople, and neighborhood activists) and to meet with them regularly to discuss police activities and anything else that might come up.

The idea was to move police and public perceptions and priorities closer together, but it did not come easily. Newman recounts escorting his newly appointed chief superintendent for the Brixton area to a neighborhood meeting. The hall was jammed with angry citizens. The podium was besieged by microphones and flooded by the lights of television cameras. Newman stood up first, briefly introduced his chief superintendent, and sat down to join the audience and see what his newly appointed commander would do. The commander sweated and stumbled his way through this first exposure. By the fifth such meeting, however, he was an accomplished performer: articulate, graceful, responsive without being slavish. Press coverage and neighborhood support both improved immediately.

Newman went one step further to get London's advice: he took a poll. "If you're going to serve in a way that is congruent with public wishes, one can borrow from the private sector and engage in a bit of market research," he says. "We took on professional help from national polling organizations and actually asked the public what they wanted. Part of the survey set out to ascertain what troubled the public most. The survey showed that they were most worried about burglary and street robbery. We [also] wanted to establish a baseline for the evaluation of our subsequent activities. So one part of the baseline was the public's present perception of the quality of police service."

If divisions were to respond to their neighborhoods' wishes, they needed latitude and autonomy, and Newman published an order in the department insisting on "the recognition of the Division as the fundamental unit of policing," with (according to another paper) "maximum practical control over the resources necessary to coordinate policing within its boundaries, and provide a comprehensive service responsive to community needs." The commissioner and his superintendents alike knew, however, that latitude and autonomy they did not have. "We say to chief superintendents on divisions, this is your bit of London, police it," says a member of a planning team Newman established. "Then he finds out that a great number of the resources needed to police it are actually outside his control. The flying squad and the central CID (criminal investigations department) looking at drugs and various other things are floating over it without any input from him, or any ability on his part to control. He gets all the letters on his desk complaining about parking, one of the things that really drives residents up the wall. But he hasn't got control over deploying the traffic wardens; that's done from a central branch that deals with traffic. It's dictated to him, all the posts that he's got to fill within his structure for all the particular reasons, and he ends up with a few of the rawest recruits who he can move around on the ground to deal with problems. By that time he really hasn't got much to play with."

The commissioner's shorthand for fixing the problem was "de-squadding the force." "In the past, there had been a tendency to create a squad for everything," Newman says. "For every problem that arose, abstract some personnel from a line or patrol function to focus on this new task. Over the years this process had led to a total imbalance of the force between headquarters and divisions. The obvious thing to do was to de-squad the force." In a major shake-up, the traffic department was reduced by 200 officers, 10 percent of other headquarters squads returned to basic line commands, some 1,200 headquarters posts shifted to the field, and a level of territorial command eliminated entirely. The changes not only made more resources available to the field but also, quite deliberately, enhanced the status of divisional superintendents.

Newman also embraced and expanded an experiment in neighborhood policing that had begun on a very limited scale under the previous commissioner. The cornerstone of neighborhood policing Met style is—as in other departments we've described—geographic responsibility: patrol officers are assigned to more or less manageable beats and are responsible for reaching out to residents, organizing neighborhood watches and other crime-prevention schemes, and in general responding to local needs. David McDonald, who was an inspector in Hackney Division when the scheme was introduced there, welcomed neighborhood policing as a return to the Met's roots. "There is nothing new in neighborhood policing," he says. "When I joined twenty years ago you had a beat you walked for eight hours; you never had a radio and you lived on your wits. You had to speak to the community because you relied on them totally, and you were seen very much as part of that community. And then suddenly we were put in vehicles, and we became detached from the community we were trying to police. The gap widened and widened, until suddenly someone said, enough's enough. Let's put the brakes on and stop this. It took a very brave man to say that, and if nothing else neighborhood policing has given us the opportunity to stop and reassess the way we've been going."

McDonald credits neighborhood policing with turning around one of Hackney's worst housing estates. In the division's view, the estate had to be a high-crime or at least high-fear-of-crime area, even though reported crime was quite low. Few calls for assistance came from the estate, so Hackney police spent little time there, but when neighborhood policing was instituted, constables began increasingly to patrol it and cultivate contacts with its residents.

What they found was as bad as they'd always suspected. "It was all bubbling down there," McDonald says. Once the division's constables had been there for a bit, reported crime rose sharply, but some time later on it started to go back down again. "They got in at the ground floor and were able to nip it in the bud," McDonald says. "By being there, by having a high profile on the streets, getting in with the clubs, getting the confidence not only of the black population but of the little old ladies, the whites who had lived there all their lives and now were frightened to go out on the streets. I felt that that contributed, certainly, toward preventing [what could have been] serious riots down on that estate."

Ian Russel, then a Hackney Division inspector as well, thought that the new system also did a great deal toward improving constables' opinions of the area's populace. "It used to be, before we started with neighborhood policing, constables thought everybody in Hackney was against them," Russel recalls. But practicing neighborhood policing, "they started getting stopped in the street by people who wanted to talk to them. It was amazing; they couldn't believe it! They got very protective of their little patches. These guys, in this shitty area, had a totally different attitude, in a matter of months, toward the people they were policing."

In London, then, neighborhood policing, and the departmental reforms set up to support it, scored some notable successes. It was not all smooth and positive. The Met's neighborhood policing divisions suffered from overwork and lack of resources, so much so that some of them—including Hackney—eventually went back to a far more response-oriented style. Divisions throughout the Met still complain that Scotland Yard has not given them the promised authority over local operations. And at Scotland Yard itself Newman's reforms were painful, drawn out, and—particularly with specialist squads—often unpopular. The jury is therefore still out on the success of the commissioner's endeavors (Newman himself retired in 1987, leaving the job to his successor to complete). But Newman proved that there could be a model for a different way to run a large, multifaceted, and powerful police department, a model dedicated at every level to sensitive, responsive, service-oriented, problem-solving policing.

LEE BROWN AND HOUSTON: NEIGHBORHOOD
POLICING AND THE TRIUMPH
OF DEMOCRATIC VALUES

Lee Brown, chief of the Houston Police Department from 1982 to early 1990, gives, if anything, more reason for hope than does Kenneth Newman. Newman, though a maverick, was one of British policing's stalwarts, and London and the Met never seriously questioned his legitimacy or his motives. Not so with Houston and Lee Brown. Brown is black; the department and the city's powerful were white. He was an outsider in a department that valued its own. He came under the unfamiliar banner of neighborhood policing into a department that had long prided itself on taking names and kicking ass. Despite all this he reformed the Houston Police Department perhaps more thoroughly and fundamentally than Newman did the Met. That he did it, and how he did it, suggests that not even the most entrenched police departments need be immune to growth.[29]

Before Brown's arrival, Houston's was a police force that the reform movement had all but passed by. It prided itself on a peculiar brand of tough, shadowy, no-quarter policing. Tim James, who rose to become the department's general counsel, says of his early days as a tactical squad officer in 1968, "Our mission was very simply to stop crime in the high-crime areas. In units of four and five we would go into the bad-ass clubs and check the patrons for papers, guns, drugs, with very little regard for the subtleties, the niceties, the constitutional nuances. If there was a liquor license, that was probable cause enough for us. We went in looking for violators. We made hundreds of felony arrests." Things were often worse than that, if department lore is to be believed. Old-timers on the force today still boast, according to newer officers, that in the good old days a burglar caught in a house was likely to die there. The department's public behavior was sometimes little better. "I remember," James says of Houston's relatively minor riots in 1968, "that we had all seen pictures of the looting on television. We were all mobilized one night, and I remember standing out in the parking lot among the cruisers. Herman Short [then police chief] came out and climbed up on top of one of the cruisers with a bullhorn. He said, 'There will be no looting in Houston. Looters will be shot on sight. Get on your loud-speakers and tell them to stay inside their homes and they'll be safe.' It sent chills up and down my spine. We left the parking lot in a convoy of cruisers, driving slowly, lights flashing."

Matters improved little over the next decade. Chief Pappy Bond deregulated the police force, allowing officers to wear what they wanted and arm themselves as they wished. Cowboy boots and pearl-handled automatics became much in evidence. When more officers were needed, a national campaign was mounted to attract candidates who wanted to come to "where the action was." The result was appalling. "In the first part of 1977," says Mary Sinderson, an assistant U.S. attorney for the Southern District of Texas, "the Houston Police Department was killing people left and right. It was just about a bloodbath, something like thirteen people in a three-month period. In the middle of that, the Joe Campos Torres case came along." In the words of Harry Caldwell, who would soon be put in charge of the department, five police officers took Torres "drunk from a bar, whipped his ass, and threw him in Buffalo Bayou." Torres, his hands handcuffed behind his back, drowned. An officer testified at the subsequent trial that another officer had said, "I always wanted to see a wetback swim."

Bond resigned in the ensuing scandal. He was replaced by Cald-well, who had headed the department's Community Relations De-partment. Caldwell thought his task was to "establish accountability." He failed. Houston's officers wanted no part of his strict, by-the-book policing, and Caldwell was more or less driven from office. He was replaced by B. K. Johnson, one of the department's own. Hous-ton's minorities soon came to regard Johnson as anathema. He once tested an open microphone at a public meeting by reciting a portion of "Little Black Sambo." In response to requests from the Hispanic community for better policing in their neighborhoods to deal with a rash of homicides, Johnson promised to send fleets of patrol cars. "Don't be upset when you see them," he said. "We're not trying to harass you. We really don't have time for that." An organizer of Houston's large gay community was shot and killed by a police of-ficer.

By the fall of 1981 the city's minority communities were up in arms. Kathy Whitmire, running on a platform of reform and good management, and supported by a "rainbow alliance" of newly arrived professionals and Houston's varied minority populations, was elected mayor. In one of her first and most visible acts, she appointed Lee Brown chief of police. He was the first black, and the first outsider, to head the Houston Police Department.

Brown had as illustrious a background as any figure of his generation in American policing. He began his career in San Jose, starting as a patrolman and leaving eight years later as an assistant to the chief. After teaching criminal justice and public administration at Portland State and Howard universities, he took over as sheriff and director of public safety in Multnomah County, Oregon, then turned down an invitation to be deputy administrator of the federal Law Enforcement Assistance Administration to take over as director of public safety in Atlanta, Georgia, just in time to manage the investigation of that city's horrific series of child murders. He had big plans for Houston, many of them superficially like those of the other chiefs we have introduced here. Brown is a firm believer in community policing, and he meant to do much as they had in decentralizing his new department's authority, enhancing its responsiveness, breaking the power of detectives and other special squads, and building the problem-solving discretion of patrols.

He had a different approach to making those changes than did many of his fellow chiefs, however. He was convinced, probably more than any of them, that community policing is not simply a matter of good ideas and programs built on them but requires—if it is to work, and to last—a complete transformation of policing and police departments. Community policing would not take root, he had come to believe, in "organizations whose administrative systems and managerial styles were designed for more traditional models of policing."[30] His job, he thought, was to change the Houston department's *style:* how it thought, how it worked, what it believed, what it valued. More important than any particular plan or program was the involvement of all parts of the department, and of city government and neighborhoods, and the consequent development of a style of policing that enlisted and benefited from the contributions of police, community, and the relationships between them.

Over the ensuing years Brown instituted variations of many of
the changes and programs we have already seen. He did so in a
remarkable spirit, however. Like Neil Behan, but on a grand scale,
he knew where he wanted to go, but he did not presume that he
knew how to get there. He saw his programs—new beat plans and
neighborhood responsibilities for officers, fear-reduction experiments, community planning boards, reshaping of departmental discipline and incentives, and much more—as opportunities for his
department to learn, to find its own way. He trusted that it could,
and that the journey would lead to a department that suits Houston,
its people, and its conditions. "Brown opened up the windows and
the doors of this department to let the sunshine and fresh air in,"
says Assistant Chief Tom Koby. "Brown posed the question, Don't
you think there might be a better way?"[31] The department, consequently, is a ferment of innovation, the Link Valley success described
in chapter 1 being only one of the most dramatic examples. What
works is adopted, what doesn't is taken as an informative detour.
Where—and if—it will all end nobody, including Brown, knows.
But he seems to have succeeded in orienting his entire department
toward creativity and progress, and blunting to an extraordinary degree conventional policing's fear of and resistance to change.

Something particularly distinctive, and creditable, about
Brown's work in Houston is the emphasis he put on democratic
values and the creativity with which he wove those values into the
daily workings and management of the department. One of his first
official acts was the promulgation of an explicit, formal set of departmental values. They were markedly different from the ones that
had prevailed, unspoken, before his arrival. His values emphasize
"crime prevention" as well as "vigorous law enforcement." They
stress "the involvement of the community in all aspects of policing
which directly impact the quality of community life." Finally, and
most important, they stress the crucial importance of democratic
values and fairness in the execution of the police function. These
values were meant to cut deeply into the department's culture and
even to reconstitute the implicit deal that had existed between the
city's establishment and its police.

Brown thought a new deal could be struck with the citizens of

Houston. Instead of a department that was indulged so that it would do the dirty work of protecting society, Brown would settle for no less than a department trusted, and supported, to do right. Instead of a department that had systematically cut itself off from parts of the local community by dealing only with the traditional power structure and going outside the city for personnel, Brown planned a department tied to the city's residents and neighborhoods by staff drawn from its diverse population. Instead of a department that did what and how it pleased, Brown imagined a department that focused its resources on the problems that communities thought were important.

Brown also meant his value statement to guide the department's daily operations. He was convinced that while rules and procedures are helpful in directing departmental operations, they cannot deal adequately with the varied circumstances that officers confront in ordinary operations. Nor can they guarantee proper conduct, because so much of officers' work occurs beyond effective supervision. If a manager wishes to ensure an appropriate response to varied circumstances from employees who work largely independently, the only possible control mechanism seems to be to inculcate proper habits of mind among the employees. Thus, Brown thought that ingraining his values was not only a key instrument of reform and change but also the one effective way of controlling officers' conduct.

Brown, like the other six executives described in this chapter, brought his department a long way. Like Sir Kenneth Newman, he departed before it was fully settled into its new style, leaving for perhaps the biggest and hardest job in American policing, chief of the New York City Police Department. But he succeeded in establishing the idea that just and proper conduct is always and under all circumstances expected of Houston's officers. That Brown, starting from where he did, could make the credo of democratic values and accountability stick in Houston—of all places—and marry it to a program of ambitious experiments in neighborhood and problem-solving policing and fear reduction is a sign of considerable promise for policing everywhere.

CHAPTER 4

■

Toward a New Policing
The Issues

Emerging from the programs, experiments, and wholesale reconstructions we have just seen is a new conception of how police departments must change to meet the challenges of the contemporary world. This conception is by no means fully developed. Despite compelling notions such as "problem-solving policing" and "community policing," there is as yet no mature successor to the reform model.[1] The best executives and the best departments are groping toward a new vision of policing.[2]

Much of this groping involves efforts to cope with the contradictions, and to escape from some of the constraints, of the reform model. Having committed themselves to controlling crime, the police are seeking more effective means: through crime prevention, problem solving, and community involvement. Having made themselves accessible to the public through 911 systems, the police must learn to handle the torrent of varied demands the phone lines bring from anxious, frightened, or angry citizens. Having insulated themselves from the community to avoid inappropriate politicization, the police are looking for ways to make themselves knowledgeable about and responsive to community wants and needs. Having adopted rigid paramilitary hierarchies to exert control over officers, the police must look for ways to encourage the creativity and flexibility strict supervision stifles, and ensure the good conduct it cannot in fact guarantee.

Some of the innovations essayed by our seven chiefs, and the ones that are perhaps at first glance most exciting, go directly to policing's substantive mission and principal methods. Fear reduction and order maintenance represent important additions to the police's mission. Community crime prevention and problem solving represent important shifts from random patrol as a primary method. These are clear, dramatic, and promising developments, and, insofar as any recent changes in policing have commanded widespread attention, it is understandable that these have.

Some of the most important innovations, however, are institutional and managerial. They have to do with reordering the relationships between police departments and the communities they police, and between police executives and the officers they must direct, control, and inspire. Sir Kenneth Newman's desire that London's communities help the Met plan and evaluate its activities—even if they overruled the department's own proclivities—and Neil Behan's efforts to empower patrol officers to design COPE, and to struggle, falter, and even fail in the process, may seem tame compared with the immediacy and vigor of a New Briarfield or a Garden Village. In fact, they are not, for a very important reason: in a world where the exact answer to the question of how cities might best be policed remains unclear—where community policing as practiced in London and problem solving as practiced in Newport News may or may not work in the long run or in other cities—what becomes important is the design of a method for finding that answer.

In policing, that means finding ways to reconnect the police to their communities so that the police can learn what their problems are and ways to use the initiative and knowledge dormant within police departments to devise the proper responses. One of the ways policing has gone astray in the past is by investing too much in trying to find particular answers to particular substantive problems—burglary or homicide or drugs—and neglecting the larger questions of how departments should be constituted and how they should relate to the public they serve. As policing sheds the reform model and its reliance on a few methods, it will inevitably enter a time of experiment, of trial and error. Some things will work; some, inevitably, won't. Having the right idea about how to work with the public, and how to organize and use the police, will probably be more important than debating the effectiveness and merit of particular programs.

With this in mind, we explore here the issues that the chiefs of chapter 3 raise about the future of policing. There are, on examination, relatively few key strategic questions. Some concern the basic mission of the police and their principal operational methods: for example, the potential for shifting from a reactive to a preventive approach to crime, how the police should regard citizens' wishes for help with matters other than crime, and how the police might successfully manage their overwhelming volume of calls for service. Others concern the proper structure of relationships between the department and the community: for example, how the police might make themselves accountable to and how they might order their relationships to encourage assistance and cooperation from the community. Still others are managerial, focusing on the internal relationships between executives, midlevel managers, and officers: for example, whether departments should be organized around functional specializations or geographic areas, and to what extent departments' operations should be decentralized.

We sketch these issues and their import below. Different chiefs, different departments, different cities will view them differently and formulate different responses to the problems they pose. How they do so—and how their responses fare in the streets, in squad rooms, in city halls, and in neighborhoods—will determine the direction policing takes in the future. It may even lead to a new consensus about what policing can and should be, a new strategic vision to extend the reform vision that has so long guided policing.

CRIME CONTROL: REACTIVE OR PREVENTIVE?

The New Briarfields of the policing world—ordinary crime problems tackled with forethought and tenacity, with an eye to long-term results—are rare indeed. The current strategy of policing is based largely on reacting to crimes as, or more usually after, they occur. That is the inevitable result of relying on motorized patrol, rapid response to calls for service, and retrospective investigation of crimes as the principal tactics of policing. A crucially important question facing modern police executives is whether they have reached the limits of these tactics and what alternatives might now be considered. Of particular importance is the question of whether police organizations can break out of their reactive approach to crime and find more effective proactive and preventive alternatives.

Before rejecting the reactive approach as inherently weaker and less satisfying than more active preventive efforts, it is worth recalling the most significant advantage of reactive tactics: that they limit police intervention in public life to those few occasions when it is fully justified. If the police wait until a crime has been committed and reported, there is always a predicate for their intervention. A crime has occurred. A citizen has requested assistance. The scope of police interests is well defined. Thus, reactive tactics prevent the police from shuffling through the drawers of social life; they are kept at the surface until there is a strong reason for them to intervene. So strong is the association of reactive tactics with propriety, in the minds of police and public alike, that the very idea of another mode of operations often smacks of the police state, bringing to mind the secret intelligence files of big-city departments in the 1960s or police infiltration of civil rights and radical groups.

The reactive strategy also has some preventive effects. Police patrols and retrospective investigations threaten offenders and potential offenders, and certainly deter some crimes. For all that, the reactive strategy suffers from important and obvious limitations. Unless police are on the scene, or witnesses call them to it, a crime is a tree falling in the forest. Invisible crimes like embezzlement and the illegal disposal of toxic wastes almost never come readily to police attention; consensual crimes like prostitution and drug dealing rarely do; likewise, crimes whose victims are afraid to call or be seen to deal with the police. Obviously, there is much of importance that eludes the reactive strategy.[3]

These limitations, together with the commonsense feeling that it would be better to prevent a crime from happening than allow it to occur and then solve it, have always frustrated the police. They have historically taken two paths to try to do better. One has emerged from extensions of the basic logic of patrol, investigation, and apprehension. They have tried "directed patrol" techniques: some targeted on places where offenses are likely to occur, some targeted on people who are particularly likely to commit offenses.[4] They have also adapted undercover techniques to deal with ordinary street crimes such as robbery and burglary. Anticrime squads send officers into the streets posing as attractive mugging victims.[5] Sting operations set the police up as fences to snare burglars.[6] And the police have experimented with focusing investigative efforts on offenders who seem to be among the most active and dangerous, to increase the likelihood that they will be arrested and incapacitated.[7] Some of these have worked, at least to some degree, although they have never been entirely free from the taint of entrapment and harassment. They have not, at least to date, made large differences in either the level of urban crime or the quality of urban life.

Other, more recent proactive methods, however, focus not on offenders but on what might be thought of as crime-causing circumstances. The idea is that crimes can be caused or facilitated by situations that create frustrations or opportunities: domestic disturbances that escalate into homicides; bars in which drunken fights among strangers are particularly likely; insecure, robbery-prone late-night convenience stores and gas stations. All these situations spawn crime and could be altered by the police: not only by putting a police officer on the scene but also by enlisting others who have a stake in controlling the crimes or some capacity to help.[8]

These methods of crime control are often described as problem-solving approaches. Their logic lies in the notion that crime analysis need not be limited to the when and the where or even the who of crime; it can also probe what sorts of proximate social activities and conditions are leading to the offenses, and what could be done about them. In principle such approaches might actually prevent crime, not through the usual mechanisms of deterrence and incapacitation, and not by getting at the root causes of crime, but simply by removing some relatively superficial conditions in a community or in social transactions that are causing crimes to occur. COPE officers, for instance, on one occasion dissolved a racial conflict by prevailing on the county to move two bus stops that brought violence-prone groups of black and white youth together (the stops were later peacefully restored after COPE and community attention to the underlying problems). The promise of such efforts has been shown, at least in isolation, in places like Newport News, Houston, and Philadelphia. Whether they can make a large, lasting impact on urban conditions is the next major question.

The police have also sought to increase their capacity to prevent crime by mobilizing citizens to assist them.[9] The most limited form of such efforts had been simply to encourage citizens to call the police more promptly and reliably when they witness a crime.[10] Other efforts have encouraged property marking or installing locks and other security devices to guard against burglary.[11] Still others encourage citizens to patrol their own neighborhoods, provide escort services to vulnerable victims, or improve street lighting and the environmental conditions that lead to crime.[12] The most ambitious efforts yet seen are full-blown partnerships between the police and community groups in which, as in Link Valley, each party assumes responsibility for part of a complex, cooperative undertaking that neither could have carried out alone.[13] As with problem-solving efforts, these community mobilization projects have produced local successes. And, as with problem solving, whether the efforts can be widened and sustained enough to have an appreciable impact on overall levels of crime and the quality of life is the next question.

Regardless, however, of the early returns on either problem solving or community crime prevention, it would be a mistake to forget that they must be compared not with some successful ideal but with the very real reform tactics of patrol, rapid response, and investigation, whose limitations are becoming obvious. Although there may be opportunities for improving those tactics at the margin—through directed patrol, improved forensic techniques, or the like—they seem limited enough to make problem solving, community crime control, and similar approaches worth considerable investment and exploration.

CRIME FIGHTING VERSUS FEAR REDUCTION, ORDER MAINTENANCE, AND EMERGENCY SERVICE

The COPEs of the policing world—police work aimed at targets, like fear, that are not necessarily directly related to crime—are even rarer than the New Briarfields. For the last forty years crime control has been the raison d'être of police organizations. It has been the goal that has rallied public support and inspired police officers, that has established the terms in which the police were held accountable. It has been the objective toward which virtually all actions of the police department were directed and the touchstone against which all proposed changes in policies and procedures were judged. Such at least was the theory, for both public and police consumption.

On the street the reality has always been quite different. Most police officers, most of the time, were not engaged in crime fighting.[14] True, there were detectives who tried to solve crimes by interviewing victims, witnesses, and offenders. And true, patrol officers were sometimes dispatched to respond to crimes in progress and spent much of the rest of their time staying ready to respond to such calls. But the calls to which the police generally responded did not involve serious crimes.

Instead, the police spent a great deal of their time dealing with varied disputes and emergencies. Domestic disturbances have, in police circles, long stood as the symbol of such demands because they were both disputes and social emergencies (and they often, in time, produced serious crimes).[15] But there were many other kinds of disputes and emergencies that escalated to involve police. Landlords and tenants argued about whether the tenant owed the landlord rent or whether the landlord owed the tenant more heat. Neighborhood groups quarrelled about whether a neighborhood street would be used for dancing to celebrate Rosh Hashanah or for the final game of a neighborhood stickball tournament. A depressed man would threaten to jump from the roof of a six-story building. A fourteen-year-old girl, recently arrived from a rural area, would be discovered wandering the streets at 3:00 A.M. with no money and

101

no place to go. Such events became police problems because the police were conveniently available, with access to necessary services such as transportation, medical care, and sometimes shelter; and because solving them often required the use of authority and law.

Such activities were almost always viewed as peripheral to the dominant police mission, annoying distractions that degraded police capabilities to deal with serious crime and wasted the special talents and training of professional police officers. They were resented and their claims on police services minimized. No special training to mediate disputes or handle social or medical emergencies was provided.[16] No special recognition was given those who performed such tasks well. No accounting for the quantity and quality of such services was offered as a justification for increased police budgets. The work was done, but it was done in the breach.

Policing is now rethinking this basic stance toward "nuisance" calls. Instead of denying that these matters are police problems or fobbing them off on other city agencies, police executives are beginning to think about how to include such claims within their conceptions of their overall mission and how to prepare their organizations to deal with these issues more effectively.

Different chiefs are doing so for different reasons. For some, this shift is nothing more than a bow to the inevitable. They don't like this part of their mission, or see any particular value in it, but they acknowledge that these functions are invariably demanded of police departments, and they are prepared to adapt to what they cannot change.

Others feel inclined to do these jobs because they see links between dispute resolution, crisis intervention, and effective crime control. Sometimes the link is quite direct. Disputes, left unattended, often lead to assaults, sometimes to robberies and burglaries, sometimes even to homicides. Social crises like lost children and the alcoholic homeless often invite crimes. Responses to these situations can be seen, at least in part, as crime prevention.

Other times, the link to improved crime control is less direct. By doing these other jobs well, these chiefs hope, the police create a presence in and a relationship with the community that increases the effectiveness of the alliance between the community and the police against serious crime. Citizens learn that they can trust the police to respond usefully to their concerns, and as a result the community is more willing to call the police with information about crimes that have been or are about to be committed. In the end the community has more self-confidence about resisting crime.

Still other police executives find these jobs important and intrinsically valuable; they need not be justified in terms of their contributions to the crime-control function but can stand alone as important police contributions to their communities. These executives note that the police play a significant role in guarding the health of their communities by preventing injuries. They note that the police contribute to social welfare by intervening in cases of domestic violence. And they note that the police enhance the quality of justice in their communities not only by preparing cases for criminal prosecution but also by justly mediating a variety of minor disputes that will never reach the courts. Police departments, these chiefs believe, should do these things simply because they can do them well. They offer immediate accessibility, general resourcefulness and skill, and, when it is appropriate, the power to invoke the authority of the state. In short, in the words of Robert Peel, the police are the only organization that assumes the general duties of citizens as its full-time, paid occupation.

Whether police departments are better aimed at a narrow mission of crime fighting or at a broader one of contributing to the quality of community life is one of the perennial questions facing police executives. In the past many have fought to narrow their mission to what they judged the most appropriate and valuable use of their agencies, namely, the protection of citizens and their property from criminals. That effort has not, however, succeeded in taking the police from important activities such as traffic enforcement in which their general law enforcement capabilities serve social purposes such as injury prevention; nor has it ruled out initiatives by police executives in realms such as drug abuse education; nor has it prevented individual citizens from asking the police to fill a variety of other functions. These persistent anomalies are forcing a reconsideration of the police mission. With that reconsideration is coming a new appreciation of the contribution that dispute resolution, order maintenance, and emergency service can make not only to crime control but also to the general quality of life in a community.

MANAGING RAPID RESPONSE: ESCAPING THE TYRANNY OF 911

In Boston, in 1985, a young nurse was assaulted in the hallway of her apartment.[17] The attack lasted a considerable time and created a great deal of noise. A neighbor called the police, but somehow the calls were lost, and officers arrived long after the woman had been raped and killed. In the furor that ensued, it was charged that the disaster was no accident. Several months previously, in the heat of a tough campaign, Mayor Kevin White had committed the Boston Police Department to the politically popular course of putting more officers on neighborhood foot patrol. The number of radio officers was inevitably reduced citywide. The nurse's murder seemed to many an awful result of an ill-advised, politically motivated shift in department policy. To others it seemed no less awful, but not inevitable either: a failure of procedure and performance rather than the sure consequence of a promising change in Boston's policing.

It is in such tragic circumstances that cities and police departments must often come to grips with the problems inherent in reform policing's commitment to providing prompt patrol response to emergency calls for service. The equation is simple. The more officers a department reserves to answer 911 calls, the swifter and more sure the emergency response, but the fewer people and less time left for doing *anything* else, such as foot patrol, neighborhood organizing, crime prevention, and the like. Outside police departments the issue generally arises only when something goes badly wrong, and the popular pressure is almost always in favor of minimizing response times. Inside departments, by contrast, the issue is constant, and nowhere more than in innovative departments trying somehow to move beyond the strictures of reform policing. There the desire is to figure out some way to contain the demands of rapid response. Los Angeles's senior lead officers, Baltimore's COPE teams, Newport News's problem-solving officers: all do their good work in the scant time left over from chasing radio calls. Nobody would think to deny the central importance of delivering immediate aid in life-threatening situations, but thoughtful police executives are beginning to doubt the wisdom of policing's marriage to 911. As one participant at Harvard's Executive Session on Policing remarked, "We have created a monster."[18]

So eminent has the place of response time become that in many cases good response time has become *the* test of a patrol force, and often of a department. Because response times are easily quantifiable, under some degree of executive control, and widely believed to be connected to successful crime control, they have come to be used by mayors, city managers, and newspapers to judge the competence of police managers. They are used by departments to analyze personnel needs and to justify increased budget requests.

This was, perhaps, fine as long as departments could easily handle their call load—which they could for a time in the early days of 911—but most departments can no longer do that. Over the last decade the volume of calls has increased dramatically while police resources have remained constant or declined.[19] The patrol forces of many departments are hostage, day in and day out, to the unending tolling of the 911 bell. Rapid response has generated so much pressure in police departments that many police executives feel they have little room to maneuver.

Even *that* might be fine if rapid response delivered on its crime-control promise, but, as we have already argued, it probably doesn't. Most 911 calls don't concern crimes. The ones that do don't usually reach the police in time to allow immediate apprehension of the criminals. Worse, perhaps, rapid response—and the emphasis on individual calls for service it imposes—distracts the police from understanding and responding to the conditions and trends that underlie the calls. If merchants are experiencing a plague of shoplifting, or a neighborhood an epidemic of drug dealing, *it is not the patrol officers' job to notice the pattern and do something about it;* it is their job to take individual complaints from individual people. The most remarkable testament to this fundamental failing is the recent discovery that an extraordinarily large proportion of emergency calls in many cities come from a few, sometimes a very few, addresses.[20] The most remarkable aspect of this finding is that it was a finding at all, that police departments could have failed to learn it in the course of their routine business. Individual patrol officers knew where their hot spots were, perhaps even the whole patrol force knew, but their departments, locked into rapid response, were often incapable of registering that knowledge and acting on it.

Rapid response has also become, in a perverse way, a threat to good relations between the police and the people they serve. Anyone with a phone or a dime can claim several hundred dollars' worth of public resources in the form of a dispatched police officer, and people make 911 calls often, for a wide variety of purposes, and in the full expectation that they will get service. The police, however, are over-worked and have a narrow, and generally narrowing, definition of what they are willing to do. The stage is set for encounters in which citizens end up angry and dissatisfied and the police end up feeling badly used.

Police departments have tried a number of ways to take the edge off the rapid response problem, most aimed at enhancing efficiency and increasing resources. Vehicle locator systems and computer-aided dispatching have improved dispatchers' abilities to assign calls to the closest patrol cars.[21] Departments that have a ghost of a chance of succeeding fight the political battles for more patrol strength (de-partments rarely try to shift other resources into patrol; a rank or unit that provides a refuge from street work is very difficult to elim-inate).[22] These moves can help, but generally not very much for very long.

A more fundamental attack on the problem, using a variety of measures described generally as "differentiated response," has tried to take advantage of the growing realization that relatively few 911 calls merit full-blown emergency treatment.[23] They rely on more careful analysis of calls to distinguish the ones that merit a rapid response; management of citizen expectations about how soon a response will be made; and suggestions that citizens use mail or other forms of communication for situations that are not particularly ur-gent. Darrel Stephens relied heavily on these techniques to create enough room in the Newport News Police Department to experi-ment with problem-solving techniques.

The most radical approaches, however, essentially break the mold of police thinking about rapid response. One tack is to face what appear to be the facts and fight the political and administrative battles necessary to dethrone response time as the main measure of police efficiency and effectiveness. This is sometimes done as part of an effort to introduce differentiated response; it is what Wilshire's Community Mobilization Project officers hoped to do when they demonstrated the efficacy of a style of policing that devalued rapid response. This is, needless to say, risky. Support for rapid response, in police and other circles, remains very high, and it is extremely difficult to make the case for anything else.

Another tack is to shift to a kind of policing that could actually solve some of the problems now drowning departments in calls for service. Cities that have introduced foot patrol and community policing have, promisingly, actually experienced reductions in calls for service.[24] In part, police officers simply hear from citizens face-to-face what the problems are without the necessity of a phone call, a dispatch, and a radio run. But it may also be that community-based, problem-solving police responses are more effective in reducing future calls for service than is the current style of policing.

What is difficult—and admittedly dangerous—about this approach is that it will surely take some time for a police department to make such a shift in style. In the transition period it is quite possible that response times will suffer. That might be taken both inside and outside the department as a good and sufficient reason to stay with the traditional style of policing. It is also possible that the new styles of policing will be effective in reducing calls for service, but by less than is required to supply the personnel the new styles need. Thus, rapid response may still suffer, and the question of how valuable it is to have very low response times will need to be addressed again.

None of these possibilities, from the vantage of a chief's office, seems particularly inviting, but there is no escaping it: police executives must somehow come to terms with the pressure to keep response times low. The police have established rapid response as an important operational objective and have spared no effort to hone their performance. They must now decide how they are going to manage the unintended consequences of their success. The bravest are exploring ways to get off this treadmill rather than remain hostage to an enterprise that seems to have reached the limits of its effectiveness.

PROFESSIONAL INDEPENDENCE VERSUS POLITICAL ACCOUNTABILITY AND COMMUNITY RESPONSIVENESS

One of the central objectives and most important accomplishments of the reform era was the depoliticization of police departments. The reformers envisioned a police department founded not on the basis of community support for the enterprise but instead on that of law and professional expertise. They thought it particularly important that the bonds of mutual dependence linking precincts to local political power be broken. Otherwise the police would be suborned by the locally powerful, and the goal of fair and impartial enforcement of the law would be frustrated.

In the modern era the legacy of this past has been a view—shared by mayors, police executives, police union officials, editorial writers, and ordinary citizens—that the police department should be free from political interference.[25] (That different parties defined what counted as interference quite differently does not detract from the nearly universal acceptance of the premise.) In extreme cases this view has caused the police to imagine that as long as they follow the dictates of the law, and follow the best standards of their profession, they should be neither answerable nor responsive to political or community figures. They have resented and resisted efforts by elected politicians to hold them accountable, either directly or through special review boards.

In the beginning, this independent stand seemed extremely valuable to both police executives and the departments they led. It seemed to give them a great deal of discretion and autonomy in charting their direction, to allow for orderly efforts to develop the organization along rational lines, and to protect them from the vagaries of politics. In reality, as some in the police have come to understand, the claim of professional independence has not helped the police all that much, for they are, and must be, fundamentally accountable to the community and its political leaders.[26] Whether they have behaved according to the law or in professionally competent ways is a matter ultimately to be decided by the community— not by themselves or their professional peers. This fact becomes painfully apparent in moments of crisis or scandal—when the police have been revealed to be incompetent or badly motivated—and they and their executives look for support from the community. It is perhaps no accident that so many of the executives discussed in chapter 3 took office following a public scandal involving their department.

Today, some police executives are seeking to establish their legitimacy and manage their accountability by going in exactly the opposite direction. Instead of insulating themselves from the politics of their communities, they embrace accountability and seek much closer working relationships with political overseers and community representatives. They try to establish a compact with the community that will define their terms of accountability. In negotiating that compact they are responsive to what the community wants as well as to what they think is important to supply. They agree to meet the community's demands in ways that the community finds tolerable as well as in ways that they prefer to offer the service. In exchange for their responsiveness and performance in dealing with community needs, the police expect continuing political support.

There is a clear risk in moving in this direction. To many, both in policing and outside it, any steps toward enhancing police responsiveness to communities or political overseers risks opening police departments once again to inappropriate political influences.[27] Neither politicians nor police have a sufficiently unblemished record to ignore the hazard in bringing together what was once, for very good reason, pulled asunder. The danger today, however, is probably not electioneering or simple corruption; these abuses may blemish any new style of policing from time to time, as they occasionally still do reform policing, but they will never again be considered the norm or fail to be fought when they surface. The danger in a less isolated modern policing is more subtle: that groups who win the police's ear will try to use that influence, with questionable propriety, to their own advantage. It is a problem that will surely arise, probably often, and—given the racial, ethnic, economic, and other tensions that pervade cities and their communities—the prospect of the police opening themselves to it is enough to give real pause.

As Kevin Tucker, our examplar of a chief who crafted a new political relationship with the typical powers—duly elected and otherwise—of a big city, discovered, these are not easy questions. He faced them, albeit in a rather low-key way, in an early quarrel that pitted him against the Philadelphia City Council over whether the police would continue to be stationed in schools throughout the city.[28] A previous commissioner, in response to worries about rising levels of violence in schools, had yielded to council demands that he station officers in the schools. When Tucker became commissioner these officers were badly needed to help respond to the crushing burden of calls for service. To Tucker's mind, while the officers were no doubt contributing to security in the schools, they could be more effectively and more widely used if they were folded into the general patrol force. Moreover, he thought it was the school board's responsibility to provide for security in the schools. The city council disagreed. So did the superintendent of schools. A crisis loomed.

As in all such crises, two things were at stake. One was the substantive question of whether the police officers were more valuable to the city sitting in the schools or responding to radio calls. The other was the procedural question of who got to decide such issues. For reform police chiefs the procedural question was extremely important. They simply had to establish their independence from political bodies such as the city council, particularly on matters of deployment, or they would soon have their forces nibbled to death by politicians' special claims. Consequently, Tucker was initially inclined to view the furor over the schools in terms of a challenge to his authority and to resist the pressure with all his might. His stand drew support from some, but not all, quarters of the city.

Police chiefs know, however, that as a matter of prudence and principle they must be to some degree responsive to duly elected representatives of the people. After all, these officials appoint chiefs and can remove them. They also represent, along with the courts, a higher authority to which police chiefs are, like it or not, bound to be subservient. The chiefs' standing with political authority is based only on what they can muster from their own claims to expertise or impartiality in responding to all the needs of the city. If no political force or court backs their claims to represent citywide interests in a fight with political authority, they will simply disappear from office.

Moreover, in Philadelphia it was not in fact obvious where the officers would be most valuable. There was a plausible argument that they would be put to better use dealing with citywide threats to life and property than guaranteeing the safety of those particular children attending public schools. There was also a plausible argument that security in the schools was a key citywide priority and represented an important effort not only to ensure that students could go to school safely but also to teach them that society would not tolerate, and they should not indulge in, violence. Deciding which was paramount was not a matter for police expertise; it was a political question that Tucker could not in all honesty claim the right to decide.

In the end Tucker and the council reached a compromise that put foot-patrol officers in the schools for a good part of their shift but left them free to take emergency calls when necessary. The shape of that solution doesn't particularly matter; what does is that it emerged from a negotiation in which the merits of the issue were reasonably effectively debated. Tucker was forced in the process to engage the question of what values he was really protecting by guarding the police against political interference. The comfortable symbolism of police commissioners refusing to kowtow to political officials was clearly inappropriate. Tucker wasn't an insular chief to begin with, and the situation made clear that chiefs have to be at least somewhat responsive and accountable to elected officials on crucial substantive questions about how the police might best be used. It was still true that if politicians made such judgments with parochial interests in mind or simply did not understand that having details in schools degraded the capacity of the police to perform other functions, then merely responding to their wishes would also be wrong. But striking some enlightened balance between autonomy and slavishness no longer seemed like an option; it seemed like a necessity.

Thus, chiefs like Kevin Tucker (and John Avery and Sir Kenneth Newman) are beginning to give up reform policing's conviction that an independent, professional police executive has to be wholly insulated from political judgments—from politicians, neighborhood groups, or others—about what the police should be doing. They are beginning to think instead that their job is to define a set of values they must defend while trying to be responsive to community concerns: for example, to uphold citywide interests against local interests, to ensure that the poor and disadvantaged do not lose out to the rich and powerful in struggles for police services, to use their expertise to give their best judgment about where the crucial problems of the city lie and how the police might best deal with them, and to make sure that their officers live up to the challenge of economizing on the use of their force and authority.

To do all this honestly and well, chiefs must have some degree of independence and autonomy. That is the hard-won prize of the reform era. But autonomy alone is both too much and too little. Finding the right balance between independence on the one hand and accountability and responsiveness on the other is a key moral and political challenge for today's chiefs. They can no longer hide simply by shouting "interference" whenever an outsider has an idea about what the police should do. They must be prepared to join, in earnest, the debate about what values should guide policing.

OPERATIONAL AUTONOMY VERSUS RELIANCE ON THE COMMUNITY

Their recent history has encouraged the police to think of themselves as not only politically independent but operationally autonomous. To a degree the police were set apart from the community and other organizations not as a matter of policy but by the nature of their work. They worked round the clock and were uniquely trained and authorized to use force. They confronted human tragedy in ways that few other organizations did. These factors helped in the creation of a very strong, very inward-looking police culture.

The police also championed the cause of independence as a

matter of organizational ideology. To the extent that they thought themselves operationally linked to other governmental organizations, they tended to see themselves as the entry point for the criminal justice system: the first step in the long process of producing justice for those accused of crimes.

An important part of their drive for professionalism was to try to create within their departments all the skills and resources they needed to deal with the problems for which they felt responsible. They also focused, quite naturally, on developing their own technology and equipment. Operational autonomy and professional competence meant being expert in dealing with crime and monopolizing that expertise. Success lay in being able to control crime effectively without having to depend on others.

To the extent that this drive increased the police's ability to deal with criminal offenses, it was exceedingly valuable. But this thrust of the reform strategy is also beginning to show its limitations. The police are finding out that they need assistance from the community to deal effectively with crime. They are discovering that they need better collaboration with other agencies of city government to deal effectively with the disputes, disorder, and other problems that constitute or lie behind a great deal of their work, and that—effectively addressed—hold the potential for creating a better working partnership with communities in dealing with crime. They are beginning to look less at what prosecutors and judges could do to help them and more at what the city as a whole could do.

It is these observations that have persuaded chiefs like Sir Kenneth Newman and Lee Brown to essay the greatest departures from the path laid out by reform policing. They have deliberately sought to open their organizations to effective collaboration with citizens at every level: from the chief's office through the precinct captains to the patrol officers. They have reorganized to put the full resources of their forces at the disposal of low levels of the organization. They have sought help from citizens in controlling crime and disorder. They have rallied support from other government agencies to deal with the problems that the community and the police together view as most important.

These comprehensive reforms are the radical result of cold,

frank appraisal. Their architects want a closer, more productive relationship with the cities they serve. They want help from residents and city government, and they are willing to change their ways to get it. To the extent that mobilizing cities and fighting crime and fear effectively require altering their organizations, administration, and the roles of their people—as well as their own roles—these chiefs are ready to make these alterations. The promise of Wilshire and New Briarfield and Link Valley is too great—and the vision of cities whose sorest problems are routinely addressed with all the means at police, municipal, and private disposal too attractive—not to take the steps necessary to forge such powerful new partnerships. How to form those partnerships, and how to manage them so they remain productive, legitimate, and just, is one of the core challenges facing a new policing.

SPECIALIZED VERSUS GEOGRAPHIC ORGANIZATION

One of Sir Kenneth Newman's most important, and canniest, moves was to "desquad" the London Metropolitan Force, shifting people from Scotland Yard's many specialized bureaus—drugs, homicide, traffic, juvenile, and the like—into its precincts (divisions, in Met parlance). He did so in part to free patrol officers for the community surveys, crime analysis, and crime prevention of his new neighborhood policing. More subtly, but no less—perhaps more—importantly, he did so to shift a critical mass of the Met's power and authority out of headquarters, where it had been growing ever more concentrated since 1829, and into its geographic divisions. Ed Davis tried to do the same in the 1970s in Los Angeles, and John Avery is trying to do so now in New South Wales. The weight of two generations of policing, and the dominant wishes and desires of contemporary police culture, lies against them, but they have strong arguments for bucking the tide.

Specialized squads, starting with headquarters vice units in the early reform days and going on from there, have been among the most prominent, and most valued, elements of reform policing. They have embodied what is most advanced, most professional, about the field, and they have commanded commensurate status. There was a period, for example, when police professionalism simply required the development of an investigative bureau with access to a crime lab. Later, professionalism required the creation of SWAT teams ready to handle hostage situations. More recently, police professionalism has been tied to improved capacities for discovering patterns in serial murders and developing new methods and teams for profiling such killers. To a considerable degree policing's attempts to come to grips with the problems society presented it with can be traced in the creation and evolution of such units. Only patrol looks much the same now as it did fifty years ago. The same, but smaller. More than a quarter of the personnel in most departments now work in special squads, almost all people who otherwise would be available for patrol work.[29]

There are clear advantages to doing things this way. Important police problems often require skills and approaches ordinary police officers don't have. Investigations are different from patrolling, so it makes sense to have a detective bureau. Rape investigations are different from burglary investigations; a special unit can help ensure that rape victims are treated well. Community-relations skills were seen as different from law-enforcement skills; therefore a separate "grin-and-wave" squad was needed to show up in schools, attend community meetings, and march in parades. When policing has to develop new abilities, specialized units concentrate the job in a small number of people with the appropriate responsibility and aptitude. If often works well.

Creating a special unit is also a clear, public, and decisive act, which has great appeal to police executives confronting new problems. If people thought domestic violence, or racial strife, was particularly urgent, forming a new team with an imposing title was always a popular move. Long before it could be expected to produce results (or, just as important, fail to do so), chiefs could get credit for quick and determined action. (The London Met even has a saying: "When in doubt, form a squad and rush about.")[30]

There are also problems, less clear but increasingly important to chiefs like Newman and Avery, with doing things this way. Most obviously and inescapably, special squads drain strength and resources from patrol operations. This wasn't so bad when departments' call loads were relatively low, but these days it matters a lot. (One often hears wry comments from patrol officers—usually, not coincidentally, those in the most thoroughly reform forces—that it would be nice if the department created a special unit to do patrol work.) Special squads also drain talent. As in New South Wales, though generally to a lesser degree, special squads become the places where officers with ambition and imagination can gain recognition. Patrol loses initiative, flexibility, and overall status.

Specialized squads can even, in a perverse way, ultimately reduce a department's power to deal with the problems they were created to handle. In the short run, of course, there is a burst of energy as the department's leading lights are brought together and allowed to focus exclusively on the new job. Less noticeably, however, the rest of the force often quietly gives up whatever part it had previously played. If it is an investigative problem, the patrol force lets the detectives do the work. If it is a drug problem, it lets the narcotics squad do the work. In some cases this is not bad—nobody expects, or probably wants, every officer to be an expert sniper or conversant in the latest nuances of forensic genetics—but if much of the department stops attending to major aspects of the ordinary police function, a great deal is lost. Only the specialized squads, which as the bloom of newness fades often become both overworked and inflexible, remain.

The most basic problem of the functionally specialized squads, however, and the element that has most spurred organizational reforms in places like London and New South Wales, is that they work against the effective organization of the police along geographic boundaries and thus their ability to serve and support neighborhoods and communities. Modern police departments often *appear* geographically organized—they divide their cities into precincts, districts, and so on, each with its distinctive character—and for the patrol force that is indeed the reality. But patrol is no longer the heart of most departments; its people, even its senior people, hold relatively little sway. Patrol commanders can do little, sometimes nothing, for the residents of their areas except adjust patrol operations. If communities need special emphasis on investigations, or juveniles, or drugs, they have to find some way to persuade the head of a central squad to give it to them, which is rarely easy. Modern departments have made it very hard for the public to mobilize the police to work on their problems. One obvious answer to this difficulty—assigning members of the special units to geographic commands and thereby creating functionally complete police departments throughout the city—has been strongly resisted by the squads, who have taken it as an encroachment on their stature and expertise.

Since the beginning of reform policing, the squads seem to have gotten the better of the argument. This has been especially true for detectives, who not only had particularly elite status but also were so closely identified with fighting crime and locking up bad guys that they could resist almost any threat to dislodge them. It has been true for most other specialists as well. More recently, here and there, the squads have been losing the argument. The appeal of establishing close and cooperative relations with neighborhoods and community institutions is so strong that some chiefs are choosing to break up headquarters units and reassign their people and responsibilities to field commands.

This is a big step for a department. The role of supervisors, especially precinct commanders, changes; they become responsible for developing and deploying a broader set of capabilities and for achieving results across a wider front. Because they can no longer be expert in all the functional areas for which they are responsible, their job becomes the challenging task of ensuring that people with different capabilities work together well to accomplish a number of different goals. The role of officers changes; they are expected to have more varied skills than when they were just patrol officers and there was a world of specialists to back them up. That is a good thing if one thinks one is dealing with talented professionals; it is bad if one thinks patrol officers are little more than drones. We think, as we shall argue at length in chapter 8, that patrol officers can be remarkably able and creative, and we therefore think that it is quite a good thing.

Reducing a department's reliance on special squads also, for all its apparent advantages, poses a problem for chiefs, who need to find ways to retain their cumulative expertise. Chiefs also need to be able to account for their departments' performance in the specialized areas the squads handled. John Avery is trying to do this through special programs that draw in many geographic commands. He thinks the arrangement strikes an effective balance among the goals of developing specialized expertise, keeping the organization focused on and accountable for especially important programs, and ensuring that the full weight of the force acts on high-priority problems.

There may be other ways; the movement, if that is what it turns out to be, toward reempowering field commands is in its infancy, and there is much yet to be learned. The question, however, has surely been joined. Good police departments can no longer simply assume that decentralizing patrol and centralizing most everything else is the wisest or most effective course. The promise of serving community needs and enlisting community support is too high to fall victim to tradition and standard operating procedures. How the police can best organize to realize that promise has become, and will remain, a key issue.

CENTRALIZED VERSUS DECENTRALIZED AUTHORITY

When Kevin Tucker became commissioner of police in Philadelphia, he began to hold regular meetings with his command staff to discuss organizational problems and proposed solutions. He was startled to find that his staff sat silently unless directly questioned and then answered only in the most general or obvious terms. They would not get more specific until he offered clues about his own views. Then they would offer responses closely aligned with what Tucker had said. When challenged to give a different answer, the staff became first uncomfortable, then angry. They felt, it became clear, that they were being set up by their new chief.

From Tucker's perspective, his principal commanders were waiting for him to do all the work of identifying the problems, inventing solutions, and giving the appropriate orders. It felt to him like they were acting as though he was the only one in the organization who was allowed to think, while everyone else was simply supposed to carry out orders. Not that the orders would necessarily be carried out; he knew well enough that his subordinates would undermine many. But the appearance was of extraordinary deference to his authority.

A similar pattern applied throughout the department. At each level the lower rank waited for the higher to indicate what it wanted done, then grudgingly carried out the order. For its part, the higher rank wanted to appear to be in complete operational control. Supervisors prided themselves on knowing exactly what was going on with their troops on the streets. They wanted to know the daily status of patrol activity. They were truly in their element when they appeared suddenly to oversee a police operation, stood by until someone made a mistake, and then assumed control. Lower-level officers were expected to keep their superiors minutely informed and to seek advice whenever they were at all uncertain about what to do.

These patterns, typical of modern police departments, are the hallmarks of a highly centralized organization. Wisdom, authority, and legitimacy are at the top of the organization; operations are at the bottom. The principal management problem is to ensure that the people at the bottom react to situations exactly as the chief would wish. The principal means relied on to produce this result are the development of detailed policies and procedures (most contemporary police departments boast amazingly enormous rule books), the creation of a dense structure of supervision so that much of the organization's conduct can be directly controlled, and stern disciplinary action in response to violations. The ideal manager in such a department has superior knowledge of and experience in policing, knows and strictly enforces the rules, and is a model for subordinates.

Many things conspire to make this style the dominant mode of administration in police departments. The paramilitary aspects—embodied in ranks, uniforms, and a unified chain of command—suggest a highly centralized organization. Officers themselves may feel comfortable in a world of rules because it fills a need for order and certainty in a disorderly, uncertain business, and because if they go by the book they cannot be blamed for failure or misbehavior. The public demands highly centralized authority because it wants someone prominent to blame if something goes wrong. That usually means chiefs, who in self-protection naturally try to make sure that everyone, from deputy chiefs to crossing guards, is doing exactly what is expected of them.

For all the considerable merits of tried and codified operating procedures, high standards, and strict accountability, getting them via a centralized, paramilitary style has important liabilities for police departments. The emphasis on procedure and discipline blunts the initiative and adaptability of officers in the field. The system encourages officers to think in terms of avoiding blame rather than doing a good job, it teaches them to check with their superiors before taking any unusual action, and it places heavy emphasis on treating all cases as though they were similar even when there are circumstances that make them seem different to the officers on the scene. As a result, the department does less work, and less particularly adapted work, than it would if the officers were given freer reign.

The centralized style is also inconsistent with the concept of police as professionals. Most professional organizations—hospitals, law offices, universities—have few explicit rules governing their staffs' discretion, and few layers of supervision. Everyone understands that professionals face complex, unpredictable situations that require a certain amount of intelligent improvisation rather than the application of cookbook rules. Moreover, operational control in professional organizations is achieved by the long periods of training and apprenticeship that those who join a profession must endure, and by the confidence that, in addition to technical skills, values appropriate to the profession were inculcated during that training. Thus, the benefits of initiative can be obtained without losing control.

Police officers, for all their field's talk about professionalism, are treated not like professionals but like factory workers. The duties and methods of their jobs are presumed to have been well worked out. Someone else has already done the thinking; only their faithful adherence to procedure and their willingness to show up for work are required. Their superiors, for the most part, merely supervise and discipline.

To the extent that this conception undercuts officers' considerable abilities to contribute and offends their sense of professional pride, something important is lost to police departments. Even worse is the long-denied but increasingly inescapable fact that it relies on a fictitious, and entirely inappropriate, picture of the operational realities of police work. Police work is not rote; it is varied, unpredictable, and full—for better or worse—of surprises that cannot be covered by precise rules. The rules can operate as guidelines, and as a basis for judging officers' performance, but they cannot dictate the correct response to every situation. There is no escaping the fundamental nature of the street. The street is, and always will be, largely unsupervised. Most of policing's important decisions—to stay or not, to arrest or not, to shoot or not—are made on the spur, and often in the heat, of the moment.[31]

The fact that the rules do not cover every situation but are nonetheless used for disciplinary purposes tends to make officers cynical about them. They are seen as punitive rather than helpful; they seem to protect bosses, not street officers, from exposure and blame. This all seems particularly galling because supervisors, wanting results as well as proper conduct, often wink at rule violations by officers until it becomes in their interest not to do so, at which point the hammer comes down.

The wide gulf between the reality of police work, which depends on individual initiative and adaptiveness, and the false ideology of control means that police and their supervisors live in a murky world of subtle lies and deceptions. The forms of control and discipline are honored, with a mutual if unspoken understanding that the reality is quite different. Nonetheless, the forms are powerful enough to claim victims if the reality is discovered to depart too much from the form. Whether one becomes such a casualty seems to be arbitrarily rather than reasonably determined. Falling victim to disciplinary action is like being the only one standing in an exposed field to be struck by lightning: it could have happened to anyone, but it happened to you. Indeed, recent studies have discovered that the principal cause of stress among police officers is not street work but their feelings of vulnerability to arbitrary punishment by their own commanders![32]

In response to the limitations and the shortcomings of the centralized administrative style, some police executives are trying to make a virtue of necessity by decentralizing responsibility. In some cases this means putting the principal operational commanders, rather than chiefs alone, out in the public eye. That is what Sir Kenneth Newman did when he took one of his commanders to a community meeting and introduced him to the attendant mob as the person with whom they would have to work.

At other times it means thinning out the ranks of supervisors and encouraging officers to make decisions themselves, as recommended by the Philadelphia Study Task Force.[33] Such actions also require the department to set up mechanisms for effective after-the-fact evaluations of officer conduct—with increased weight given to the public's reactions and complaints—as an alternative to before-the-fact supervisory control. Performance and results come to count for more than simple adherence to procedure.

Still other times, it means reducing the number of specific rules and increasing the role of well-articulated general values: as guides to behavior and as the basis for establishing officer culpability in specific instances. Commissioners Avery, Tucker, Newman, and Brown have all emphasized the development of broad value statements as operational guides for their departments. The West Midlands Police Department decided to give up its bulky manual in favor of a simple credo outlining its values.[34] Evaluating and disciplining officers ceases to be a matter of checking the book to see whose head should roll and becomes one of comparing conduct with the department's basic outlook and priorities.

Such changes are very difficult. It is extremely uncomfortable for police executives to sit on top of organizations composed of hundreds or thousands of people carrying guns and the authority of the state and rely on their officers' professional training and values to keep misbehavior in check. They are much more inclined to reach for detailed control over what the officers do by hiring staffs to write rules, supervisors to ensure that the officers abide by the rules, and then more staffs and supervisors to ensure that the supervisors supervise appropriately. The cruel facts—that this elaborate superstructure cannot effectively reach street operations, that chiefs are ultimately reliant on officers' training and values anyway, and that the supervisory structure paradoxically tends to insulate officers from accountability for their conduct by creating an atmosphere of winks and nods—are all easily ignored in the effort to control the organization's operations and protect against charges of managerial negligence or incompetence.

Yet some, paying more attention to the operating realities of policing, are seeking to enhance professionalism and accountability by stripping away these levels of supervision so that officers can and must confront their tasks and responsibilities to citizens directly. Creating healthy values, and articulating and imposing them in such a way that policing gains flexibility and creativity without increased space for misconduct, is their crucial challenge.

These issues define the rack on which modern police executives, and their departments, are being twisted. The old conventions and traditions anchor the police firmly in one position: focused on crime control to the exclusion of all other contributions they might make to the quality of life in cities; committed to patrol, rapid response to calls for service, retrospective investigations, and arrests as their principal operational methods; determined to maintain their professional independence against political interference; confident that they alone can control crime if only the other parts of the system would do their minimal part; heavily invested in the technical specialties now enshrined in centralized offices; and accustomed to the discipline (and reassurances) of tightly centralized organizations.

Operational realities, new challenges, and fresh ideas about management are pushing them in quite a different direction: toward a broader engagement with the community's fears and problems; a wider set of operational methods that use thought, mediation, and mobilization of the public and other agencies rather than the power of the law; public accountability rather than professional independence; shared responsibility for and coproduction of crime control; geographic decentralization rather than functional specialization; and management emphasizing creativity and values rather than paramilitary discipline.

The new torque on policing is painful to those accustomed to past traditions. But it is equally painful to remain anchored to the past. We are convinced that the pressures can be relieved by stepping boldly into the future—toward the new opportunities and challenges. Exactly how far, and along which dimensions, remains unclear. Indeed, we do not think there is a general answer to this question. Each executive, each department, each community will have to reach its own conclusions. This difficult process is inescapable for three reasons.

First, many departments still have important work to do in meeting the standards and challenges of the reform model of policing. The fact that this model dominates police thought and practices does not mean that it is uniformly adhered to throughout the country. The reform model's commitment to professional standards of education, conduct, technical competence, and especially commitment to constitutional values has yet to be met by many departments. They must finish the work of meeting those standards; or, instead of advancing toward a new era of policing, they might well sink back into the problems of the political era.

Second, certain linkages and interconnections prevent executives, departments, and communities from freely choosing a position on each of these issues. For example, if one shifts from reacting to crime to prevention of crime, one inevitably ends up shifting to problem-solving or community mobilization methods; and one cannot shift to these without to some degree decentralizing the organization and reducing reliance on patrol and rapid response. Similarly, if one shifts to a geographically decentralized organization, it is almost impossible to remain focused exclusively on crime issues, because community groups will nominate other issues for the police to handle. In short, moves in one direction will make moves in another direction necessary and inevitable. Or, put differently, a move in one direction will be impossible unless other changes are made. The choices about these strategic issues come bundled together, not neatly separated.

Third, what is valuable and feasible to do with a police department will depend a great deal on local conditions. Communities face different substantive problems. They also have different political cultures, with differing openness to change and innovation. The departments themselves will have different histories that affect the feasibility of particular changes. Philadelphia after the bombing of

MOVE was different from Baltimore County facing widespread fear, which was different in turn from Los Angeles in the grip of gangs and drugs. Our seven chiefs stand out in part for refusing to fit their departments to the Procrustean bed of the reform model, and instead inventing particular responses—community policing, COPE, DARE—to their particular problems. The future of policing will see far more of this sort of diversity, and properly and productively so.

But while it is foolish to prescribe a model of policing to be followed in all places and at all times, we are still entirely certain that policing must change. We are also reasonably clear about the directions change must take, and the several instruments that police executives and communities must grasp to begin the process. It is to these matters that we turn in the second part of this book.

PART II

■

Reconstituting the Police

CHAPTER 5

■

Managing for Change:

The Police and Values

O N THE STRENGTH of the early experiments in a new style of policing, we are convinced that the field must move toward more open, more cooperative departments—toward accountability and partnerships—and toward less reactive, more creative strategies and tactics—toward thoughtful, entrepreneurial approaches. Community policing, with its emphasis on openness and partnerships (as practiced in embryonic form in Los Angeles, New South Wales, London, and Houston), has broadened police awareness and extended police capabilities. The police have been willing to accept community help in both setting priorities and carrying out operations. Problem-solving policing, with its emphasis on thoughtful police work (as practiced in Newport News and Baltimore County) has challenged police to pay renewed attention to the causes and patterns of crime. It has also added to their arsenal new techniques of analysis, dispute resolution, and crime prevention, and an increased willingness to engage in productive cooperative relationships with other municipal agencies.

Wilshire's Community Mobilization Project is a testament to the power of melding these two ideas. Senior lead officers endorsed both the precepts behind community policing—that the community should be served as it wishes and should lend any help it can—and those behind problem solving—that thought and creative solutions should be brought to bear on important police problems. By trimming trees and vanquishing drunks, they won the support of area residents. With that support, they beat back the drug dealers. With new ideas and a little help from their friends, they did what scarcely anybody expects of the police anymore: they turned around a failing neighborhood.

Unfortunately, a neighborhood is not a city, and a precinct is not a big-city department. Wilshire is, so far, a story, a promise, not an answer to all the questions policing faces. It is by no means clear that the ideas we have seen to date are sufficient. We cannot yet point to unambiguous evidence that these approaches, applied on a departmentwide scale, can produce sustained results—in particular, that they can successfully address serious crime. In these respects and many others, the verdicts on community policing and problem-solving policing are still pending. Time and trial will, we trust, tell.

But the point is not whether community policing, problem-solving policing, or any of the other tentative steps policing is taking have yet shown broad superiority to the reform model. Even overwhelming evidence for their success would not—or should not—mean the end of the pursuit of better policing; it would only make the next step somewhat clearer. The point is that policing is beginning its struggle to emerge from the limitations imposed by the reform model. The significance and the appeal of ideas like community partnerships and mobilization, problem solving, fear reduction, decentralization for responsiveness, and the like are not so much that they work well—although they may—but that they show that policing is not, as it has so long thought, bound to a narrow set of ends and means. Just what policing can be nobody now knows, any more than the turn-of-the-century reformers could have envisioned today's 911 systems and SWAT teams. What we know now is only that policing can be more than it is, and that the direction of change must be toward a broader base of support and guidance, less rigid and more professional management, and smarter, less mechanical, and more proactive methods.

Nothing will be as important to this movement than that the police adopt new and very different values. We have argued that if the police are to escape the impossible position in which they now find themselves, if they are to move beyond the limits of the reform model, they need a new belief about their role in society. We have also argued that such a fundamental change cannot occur without the leadership and support of a new breed of police chief. Their primary job will not be to redeploy their people, institute problem solving, organize neighborhood meetings, or carry out any of the other technical tasks of a new policing. Important though those things will be, the main task facing these chiefs will be to change the expectations that citizens and communities have of police departments, and that the police have of themselves. In short, it will be to change the fundamental culture of policing.

Police departments are typically rigid bureaucracies, fiercely defensive of the status quo. Their considerable institutional momentum stands as a major barrier to change or development. Police officers who believe and behave as the reform model has led them to do will at first not be comfortable with the new conceptions, may not even be capable of pursuing them. Police chiefs who suddenly commit their organizations to a new strategy will throw them into confusion and resistance. To move successfully from the reform model to a new style of policing, chiefs must change the basic nature of their departments. Only then will their reforms take root.

A new attention to values is important to policing for two distinct, if closely related, reasons. First, attention to values can help executives change the culture and behavior of their organizations. By articulating the values that are to guide the organization's conduct, an executive can garner outside support, establish the terms by which the organization will be held accountable, and challenge and guide employees. The specification and promulgation of values is a key managerial tool in changing an organization's culture.

Second, the values that currently inhere in policing, both those explicitly articulated and those implicitly held, are in many ways pathological. They prevent the police from discovering their full potential to contribute to the communities they serve and sometimes lead them to scandal and disgrace. They must be replaced with higher values that reveal the opportunities and obligations of policing and keep the police in the public's high esteem. This is, as we shall see, a lofty—but attainable—goal.

ESTABLISHING TERMS OF ACCOUNTABILITY

It is significant that many of the chiefs we met in chapter 3 took office following a scandal or dramatic failure to perform: John Avery became commissioner in New South Wales following the discovery that detectives had been manufacturing evidence; Kevin Tucker became commissioner in Philadelphia shortly after the notorious MOVE incident and just as a corruption scandal was breaking; Sir Kenneth Newman became head of the London Met following the Brixton riots; Lee Brown became chief in Houston after a police killing and an election that had discredited many of the department's old policies. Such scandals are the public sector's equivalent of bankruptcy. Citizens, who have been asked to give up their money—and to some degree their freedom—to allow the police to operate, have become disenchanted with the police and have withdrawn their credit. The chiefs are removed, and new teams are invited in to see whether they can't do better.

Such events are managerially significant because they give the incoming executives a broader scope to make changes than would be available if the scandal had not erupted or the bankruptcy not been revealed. Old commitments to particular people, units, and ways of doing things come unglued. People who were confident and powerful become uncertain and unable to command the same degree of loyalty. Resources frozen into particular uses suddenly become available for reallocation. The attention of the organization comes to be focused on the new executive, who has been chosen to lead it out of ignominy. Crisis empowers leaders. The values they articulate have strength because they light the path forward.

Scandal and disaster also give executives a chance to redefine their external relations. All those who supported the old regime will be slightly discredited and cautious. The critics who toppled the old regime will be looking for someone to champion their values. The majority of the public, who are generally passive and uninterested, will be paying unusual attention to the department, its new leader, and the directions it plans to take. In the ferment there is an opportunity to strike a different deal with the public on the basis of a fresh agreement on the fundamental values the department should pursue.

Sir Kenneth Newman, Lee Brown, and, to a somewhat lesser degree, John Avery, all used value statements to exploit these opportunities. Darryl Gates in Los Angeles used his departmental policies to serve a similar function in less tumultuous circumstances. It is Kevin Tucker's story, however, that is most instructive.[1]

When Tucker was appointed commissioner in Philadelphia, it was clear that he needed to do something to restore the public credibility and improve the performance of a by then notorious department. As part of that process, Tucker decided to commission a survey on what Philadelphia thought of its police. The results were a surprise. Tucker was leading a department that had just burned down an entire city block in a bungled effort to control a radical political organization and that was suffering a corruption scandal reaching high into the ranks. But the good citizens of Philadelphia rated it fairly high—70 percent as good or excellent overall. Only 5 percent said it was doing a poor job.[2]

Even more surprising was the public's response to questions about police misconduct. Did citizens think the police were rude? Fifty percent said yes. Did they think the police took bribes? Forty-nine percent said yes. Did the police use unnecessary force? Sixty-six percent said yes.[3] Yet the department still rated high in their regard.

Tucker's interpretation of these results was devastating. It seemed that the citizens of Philadelphia were quite content with a police department that was falling far short of embodying the values of the reform model, much less any newer style of policing. The deal between the citizens and the police appeared to be that if the police did a good job of fighting crime and responding to calls for service, they could be indulged a little in other ways. As one Philadelphia police officer explained, for the police force to be willing to do the job of "shoveling shit," they had to be allowed to sleep on the job, be rude, harass defendants, and extort bribes.[4]

We suspect that this deal—trading at least the appearance of crime-fighting effectiveness for the indulgence of a certain amount of misconduct—is often implicitly made between the police and their communities. It is a crummy deal. It is so crummy that it can never be discussed openly. It is the stuff of locker-rooms and sly jokes rather than official policy. But the deal—the understanding—is always there in the background. It is what allows the police to cut corners in crime-control efforts, as often for self-expression as for effectiveness. It often feels like the right deal to make—a recognition, however unhappy, of the values that must guide policing. But it is ill founded and unstable. If revealed, it will be denied. It cannot be used to protect police who are found to be behaving consistently with the implicit deal but inconsistently with the far more pious explicit deal. In the backlash individuals will be scapegoated, careers will be sacrificed, department morale will collapse. And, above all else, it is beneath a civilized people to win security by authorizing thuggery and malfeasance.

To prevent all this from happening again in Philadelphia, Tucker sought a new compact between the police and the city's residents. This deal emphasized a working partnership between the community and the police, but it also committed the police to live up to the values that Tucker believed a professional department should adhere to. Tucker's value statement began by quoting Plato to the effect that "good government is wise, brave, temperate, and just"; it referred to officers as "citizens who earn their police badges voluntarily" and established an absolute injunction against private gain and the violation of the Constitution or other law. It called on officers to "appreciate and care for the needs of the people they serve" and "exercise common sense in a manner that conveys common decency." It admitted that police work is demanding and disappointing but emphasized that it "provides officers the opportunity to contribute in an immeasurable way to the common good."[5]

Tucker knew that these could become the department's real values only if the community continued to demand them. To ensure that it would, he not only published his report and his value statement as the basic charter for the future of Philadelphia's police, he also created a citizens' oversight commission to monitor progress in reaching the report's goals and to keep the heat on for compliance with the statement's new values. In this he was following the lead of John Avery, who had his police board, and Sir Kenneth Newman, who defined his "notional contract," and was taking an important first step in transforming the culture of policing in his department.

NEW VALUES FOR A NEW POLICING

Undoubtedly the greatest strength of the police reform movement was its effort to redefine the values of policing. For the crass values of protecting one's political or economic friends, or the dangerous value of fighting crime by any effective means, it intended to substitute powerful constitutional and legal values such as equal enforcement of the law and respect for the civil liberties of defendants. Unfortunately, the reform movement has been only partially successful in inculcating these values in police departments. It has succeeded in establishing the virtue of equal enforcement of the law and in creating conditions under which police can enforce the law without fear or favor. It has succeeded in banishing police methods that are illegal, brutal, or particularly intrusive, at least to the extent that such methods are employed only surreptitiously or when the police or the public is particularly provoked. But it has failed to make the police see themselves as what they are, what they must be: important guardians of the civil liberties of ordinary citizens.

Many—particularly hard-bitten police officers and those who have been the unfortunate object of their attentions—will be reluctant to see the police as key protectors of vital freedoms. Yet that is one of the fundamental reasons the police exist. The alternative to the police is private vengeance. Society long ago rejected that solution—at least partly on the ground that it would risk injustice to those accused of crimes. The police are society's agents in producing an ideal of justice in which suspects' rights are protected. They are trained in the law and the use of force precisely so that they may use both more accurately, more precisely, and with more

135

respect for civil liberties than would ordinary citizens or private security guards.

This idea—that the police are some of the most important protectors rather than the most determined attackers of civil liberties—does not seem strange to those police executives who have tried to strike a new, more promising deal with their communities. In particular it does not seem surprising to the black chiefs who have achieved prominence in the United States. They know full well that the law can be and has been a protector of minority interests as well as an instrument of oppression.[6] They know that the police have, for example, protected free speech and the integration of public housing projects and schools (even though, as individuals, officers often disagreed with the speakers and the desegregation laws). And they are determined to protect the constitutional values that have provided what little protection they could muster from a society whose racism lies at best only a little beneath the surface.

Fortunately, their influence seems to be spreading. Harvard's Executive Session on Policing polled chiefs who participated in its sessions about the values they had established to guide their organizations. Their responses fell into a pattern—not only in terms of what values were represented but also in the order in which they appeared.[7] The list was something like this:

1. Police should fully embrace democratic and constitutional values.
2. Police should define their role in the community broadly to achieve their greatest value.
3. Police should seek close relationships with the communities they serve to ensure responsiveness.
4. Police should conduct themselves in an exemplary manner in their private and public lives.
5. Police departments should provide a decent working environment.
6. Police should emphasize crime prevention and the maintenance of order as well as crime control and law enforcement.
7. Police should use public resources economically and fairly.
8. Police should conduct themselves with professional integrity.

This list reveals the remarkable extent to which democratic values and the protection of civil liberties have emerged as two of policing's most prominent concerns. In this respect, the new style of policing seems finally to be delivering on some of the most important promises of the reform style.

It may be that the reform movement was only partially successful in inculcating these key legal values because the reformers never saw police officers as people who could be trusted with such important matters. Restraint, respect, decency, and so on were upper-class values. They were the sorts of things best left to judges and lawyers, not the blue-collar people who became police officers. From the reformers' perspective, the problem was usually how the people with the proper values could control the police, not how they could elevate the rank and file to a position of similar virtue.

If that perspective was once appropriate, it no longer seems so. The reform movement has succeeded in drawing into policing people who are well educated and who believe, or are well prepared to believe, in democratic values. They accept, or can be taught to accept, their obligations to enforce the law fairly and impartially and to protect civil liberties. We have paid far too high a price for continuing to assume that we could not expect, and demand, that police officers understand and do their duty.

GOVERNING DISCRETION

The same assumption has guided the ways police attempt to keep discipline in the ranks, and it has driven the price even higher. We have already seen how the reform movement's suspicions of ordinary police officers, and its commitment to controlling their conduct, left a deep imprint on the administrative systems and management style of police organizations. Elaborate mechanisms of rules, close supervision, and staff inspection created the appearance of effective control over police officers' conduct and protected senior officers from charges of managerial negligence. They were clear evidence of zeal for rooting out misconduct and foresight in organizing and directing the force. Whether they actually succeeded is far more dubious.

137

There can be few other jobs that provide opportunity for so much discretion.[8] In fact, one of the notable peculiarities of the police service is that it provides the greatest discretion to those at the lowest rather than the highest rank. Despite the supposedly all-pervasive supervision by radio, patrol officers spend the largest part of their day out of sight and out of the immediate reach of their supervisors. At the same time they carry with them the invested authority of the state and some formidable weaponry. Patrol officers have an irreducible degree of discretion, and with that discretion phenomenal power to do good or evil.[9]

Many police officers will deny the extent of their discretion. They describe themselves instead as "impartial enforcers of the law." As we have seen, police work is not at all limited to law enforcement, but even in that relatively small part of normal police work that is, this description is a sham. No patrol officer enforces all of the law all of the time; all are highly selective.[10] Few will normally pass up the chance to make a career-enhancing felony bust, but here are a dozen common reasons—omitting practices that are blatantly corrupt—why particular laws may not be enforced at particular times:

1. Because the officer doesn't feel like it
2. Because the officer feels that a word of advice would be more appropriate
3. Because the offender is a police officer (or someone else who is deemed to deserve special exemption)
4. Because there is such widespread abuse that the officer is unable or unwilling to find grounds to discriminate (for instance, where parking restrictions are widely ignored)
5. Because the officer has some other priority to attend to
6. Because the law in question is unpopular or about to be reviewed or repealed
7. Because the law is a civil law, which police regard as outside their purview
8. Because there is an overriding obligation to preserve the peace (for example, when a minor arrest might spark a brawl or even a riot)

9. Because the police lack the necessary resources (as for investigation of serious computer fraud)
10. Because the crime is victimless or the victim is a large institution deemed capable of taking care of itself (for instance, in some mortgage or insurance frauds)
11. Because there is a government department (or even private enterprise) better equipped to enforce a particular law
12. Because the police are unable to enforce the law without making the situation worse (for example, in riot and in many racial situations)

At first sight it appears that only the first five of these reasons fall within the officer's individual discretion. But closer examination shows that all the others depend, directly or indirectly, on the way the police department has come to view its role, and hence allocate its resources. The scope of police action is not fixed by law, as some claim (of the twelve considerations given, only 7 and 11 are likely to be determined to any great extent by the law); it depends, mostly, on the way the police department sees itself—which is fundamentally a manifestation of the predominant organizational values.

Organizational values, then, play a large part in determining an officer's actions in law enforcement: and law enforcement is reputed to be the least ambiguous of police roles. If values play such a great role here, how much more crucial are they in guiding an officer's approach to noncrime emergency calls, domestic disturbances, road accidents, political demonstrations, and industrial disputes, where the role of police is much more ambiguous? What about the manner in which officers speak to members of the public and the relationships they may or may not forge with the community?[11] These will depend almost entirely on officers' beliefs about their role and their job.

Besides being of dubious effectiveness, management through rules and close supervision is very costly.[12] The direct cost is paying all those people to develop the rules, supervise the officers, and investigate those who supervise the officers. But the indirect costs may be even greater. Management by rules and supervision gives little room for creativity or initiative, because it is designed to give little room for anything at all. It is based on the premise that giving

139

officers latitude spells trouble. These regimes provide scant opportunity for learning and development because—as a way of thinking—they focus on adherence to prescribed practices rather than on examination of problems or formulation of new strategies. They encourage officers to devote themselves to avoidance of mistakes, and the surest way to avoid mistakes is to keep out of the way. "Keep your nose clean and you'll do OK" is the advice new recruits receive from more experienced colleagues.[13] They quickly learn that situations requiring the exercise of judgment (generally situations in which the role of police is most ambiguous and which therefore demand difficult decisions) are, for their career prospects, the most dangerous. They will soon be taught that the organization can remember mistakes for years; mistakes, however good the intention, can result in dreaded notes on their personal files, which will come back to haunt them when they apply for a promotion or posting. A brief comment such as "this officer lacks judgment," scribbled by some senior officer in the margin of an appraisal report, has retarded many a promising police career long after the senior officer has moved away and the unfortunate patrol officer has learned better.

Finally, the disciplinary management style turns out to be phenomenally destructive of human resources. It creates a punishing environment that, as we have already noted, seems even more onerous than the street. According to the English officers who participated in a study of the sources of police stress, the aspects of poor management that have the strongest adverse effect on the performance and health of all officers were

Unjust criticism or scapegoating
Lack of counseling skills
Unrealistic expectations
Contemptuous attitudes toward constables [patrol officers]
Lack of concern for the individual
Lack of communication
Excessive autocracy and lack of consultation[14]

Given that controlling the conduct of officers through rules, supervision, and discipline is likely ineffective and expensive, is there an alternative? The public interest in controlling the officers' conduct cannot be denied. The question is what better form that control might take.

One alternative would be a shift to a style of management that is more characteristic of fully developed professional organizations, such as hospitals, architectural firms, or law offices. In these organizations the assumption is that those who do the work—the doctors, nurses, architects, and lawyers—are principals of the enterprise, not mere employees. They can be counted on not only to have appropriate skills, but to reflect appropriate values in the decisions they make and the work they do. The structures of such organizations are relatively flat, with wide spans of control to reflect the sense that workers can generally be counted on to do the right thing and that they are ultimately accountable for their own behavior. Workers in these organizations cannot fob the responsibility for mistakes onto wrong instructions by supervisors.

In such enterprises employees are expected to take the initiative in defining and acting on problems. They consult with their peers and superiors for advice, but they are not required to submit their every new plan for review before taking action. Control is maintained by periodic reviews of results and performance. These reviews are objective and based on facts, but they consider principally the extent to which employees lived up to the enterprise's ultimate values, not whether they stuck to established procedures or avoided all error. In short, employees gain status and discretion at the price of after-the-fact accountability for results.

Police organizations have sought professional status and discretion largely through noting the uniqueness and urgency of the work they do and the technical skills they possess. But they have missed the importance of embracing a set of values—values that properly reflect the public's most idealistic aspirations for their conduct—as a key instrument of professional advancement. They have been reluctant to accept after-the-fact accountability for their actions, preferring the safety of compliance with rules. And they have failed to build organizations based on principles of professionalism rather than mechanical control. If they are to progress, the police must be persuaded to embrace new values, accept a

141

different kind of accountability, and devise organizational forms consistent with the culture of a new professionalism.[15]

OVERCOMING RESISTANCE TO CHANGE

So persuading the police will be far more difficult than in most, perhaps virtually any, other fields and organizations, for the police form, to a most unusual degree, a closed society, little exposed and less amenable to outside influence.[16] Two principal factors accentuate the closed nature of police communities and support the strongly self-reinforcing character of their value systems. The first is the difficulty most patrol officers face in having anything like normal contacts outside police circles; the second is the fact that, because of the dangers inherent in police work, the outside world is perceived as, if not actively hostile, certainly uninformed and unhelpful.

A broad and normal social life is denied police officers for a number of reasons. The first and perhaps most obvious factor is the harsh reality of shift work. Police departments vary in their shift patterns, but the division of the day into three eight-hour shifts is fairly standard for patrol officers. In most cases the night shift begins at 10:00 or 11:00 P.M., occasionally at midnight. Going on duty at such times, together with preparation and traveling time, rules out socializing in the evening. For those on the afternoon shift, finishing late in the evening rules out social engagements except late-night drinking sessions with police colleagues, which frequently carry on into the early hours. Even the early-morning shift (usually starting at 6:00 A.M.) presents problems for the previous evening; officers either go to bed very early or face extreme fatigue.

Patrol officers who work shifts are therefore effectively barred from socializing for at least 60 percent of their evenings. Because the rest of the world tends to do its visiting during the evenings, the net result is the complete decimation of an officer's normal social life. The situation is further exacerbated by the unpredictability of shift changes, the likelihood of being retained on duty (for instance, to deal with prisoners), and the average officer's insatiable appetite for overtime (on either public or private duty).

All these problems are shared by nonpolice shift workers in security, nursing, and the provision of other emergency services as well as a host of manual and technical jobs in manufacturing, energy services, transportation, and the like. Even their closest friends outside the workplace cannot keep track of their shift patterns and so tend to assume that these shift workers are unavailable. But policing may be the only profession that demands shift work and also requires a close sense of community involvement and awareness. Hence unsocial hours are an especially serious problem for the police.

There are many, mostly specialist, posts in police departments that carry normal office hours and allow a much more normal social life. People who hold such posts are often despised by their shift-working colleagues and are referred to in terms of derision, such as *nine-to-fiver*. This term says, "This person is now incapable of understanding the problems facing us front-line troops; from the safety of an office, he or she spends the day making retrospective judgments about what we did in the heat of the moment." The term *nine-to-fiver* is, in fact, extremely rude. It carries with it a suggestion of betrayal. It is a sure indication that police officers in posts involving regular (and short) office hours begin to move out of the mainstream of police culture. In the eyes of many patrol officers, the vast majority of nine-to-fivers have switched sides.

The second factor that drives police officers closer together and further from the public is the nature of their job. To begin with, there is the element of danger.* The statistics for injuries and fatalities tell us that policing is a relatively safe occupation compared with fire fighting, shipbuilding, or forestry.[17] But it is not so much the accident level as the perceived degree and frequency of threat that affects behavior and attitudes. Most industrial accidents are totally unexpected. By contrast, police are forever anticipating violence. Police work *feels* dangerous. Calls to domestic disturbances or "intruders on premises" always raise the adrenaline level and heighten officers' awareness of their dependence on their colleagues, even

---

*The incidence of fatal injuries and injuries involving days lost from work for police is reported as 2.37 events per 100 workers for 1987. The national (U.S.) rate for all industries was 1.86. But policing was safer than fire department work (5.36); ship and boat building (4.20); or forestry (4.10).

when the call turns out to have been overstated (as is usually the case) and can be resolved without either violence or assistance.

Continual exposure to the unknown and the unpredictable, coupled with high levels of perceived danger, provides fertile ground for the seeds of what some have called a bunker mentality. A high proportion of officers' interactions with the public are either antagonistic or potentially so (assuming their job is essentially reactive), and the police gradually become more and more conscious of the violent, brutal, and destructive elements in society and less and less conscious of the decent, law-abiding majority. Collegiate loyalty gets stronger, feelings of obligation to the general public weaker.

Police work is also unusual and frequently exciting. Officers routinely see aspects of human behavior that other folk may not see even once in a lifetime. They are forced to confront the morbid, the bizarre, the obscene, the ridiculous, the pathetic, and the distressing.[18] They have to deal with each, both practically and emotionally, on a daily basis. They follow disaster, heartbreak, and turmoil wherever they strike. Measured in terms of life experience, there are few jobs like it. Officers mature extremely rapidly, and in a way that either equips them to face up to the whole spectrum of human experience or protects them from its impact. Very few friends outside the police service will be able to share their experiences. In many cases the duty of confidentiality prevents officers from even talking about aspects of their jobs with outsiders. Collegiate relationships become even closer, and outside friendships come to seem somehow inadequate. For patrol officers, even other—meaning higher—levels of the department, specialists, and nine-to-fivers no longer on street duty seem alien. The insulation of the lower levels of a police department becomes very considerable indeed.

WORKING TOWARD CHANGE

These barriers can be breached, but not with the ordinary tools of police management and supervision. For an initial clue about how, we can turn to Tom Peters and Robert Waterman's study of ways the leaders of notably successful private-sector companies diffused new sets of values through their organizations. Peters and Waterman started with the assumption that this takes exceptional personal charisma, which would put the task beyond most of us. Thankfully they concluded that it was less a question of charisma and more one of personal commitment to the new values and persistence in communicating them to staff.

The "gurus" of successful companies seem to have had a knack for framing their critical values in appealing and memorable ways. Hence Peters and Waterman's description of their value systems as "simple—even beautiful."[19] What, therefore, are the simple and compelling values that will distinguish the new style of police departments? Here are a few suggestions, all of which are alien to the vast majority of existing police cultures:

1. *The Constitution always comes first.*
2. *Close to the people.*
3. *Beat work matters most.*
4. *Behind every incident lies a problem.*
5. *Prevention is better than a cure.*
6. *If it might work, try it.*
7. *Integrity has no price.*
8. *Police are model citizens.*
9. *Respect every individual.*

But it is not enough for values to be articulated in an elegant way. Peters and Waterman discovered that successful leaders had one particular quality in common: they were renowned for the amount of time they spent talking with their junior staff. Thomas J. Watson, Jr., of IBM and William Hewlett of Hewlett-Packard, for instance, are both described as "legendary for walking the plant floors."[20] They knew that values cannot be communicated effectively second- or thirdhand. To make a difference, workers have to hear it from the boss.

There is a particularly valuable lesson here for police executives.

Police rank structures are themselves a principal obstacle to effective communication of new values. A typical British police force (of say 3,000 officers) has nine ranks; the larger metropolitan forces have even more. In American forces the number of ranks can vary from nine to thirteen. (This is in contrast to the worldwide Catholic church, which does a fairly good job of disseminating values to 850 million members with just five layers.)

The typical working day for an officer of almost any rank provides personal contact with the rank immediately above and the one immediately below. Perhaps 80 percent or more of time spent with officers of other ranks is within this close band. The majority of the remaining 20 percent of an officer's time is spent with the next closest ranks, leaving an extremely small portion spent with significantly differing ranks. Worse, the few occasions when officers get to speak to those who are, comparatively, very senior tend to be extremely formal and stilted.

Consider for a moment where else we find structures of many thin layers. Weather forecasters are constantly reminding us that many thin layers of clothing provide much better insulation against extreme cold than a few thick layers. Television advertisements for the latest and best in diapers tell us that their secret lies in extra layers. Wherever many thin layers are a plus, their advantage appears to be the ability to insulate against the transmission of heat, cold, wet, electricity, or some other potentially unpleasant element.

Police departments are no different. Their rank structures provide an extremely effective barrier to communication between a chief executive and operational officers. The fact of many thin layers, with interpersonal contact confined to narrow bands, enables each rank to be comfortable in its predominant value set while the top and bottom of the organization need share no common values at all. The deputy chief will agree with 90 percent of what the chief thinks. The assistant chief will agree with 90 percent of what the deputy thinks, all the way down the line to the officer on the beat, who might share 90 percent of the values of his or her sergeant. Thus the workplace is made comfortable because there is not much diversity in attitude among those with whom each officer has regular contact. What few differences exist between adjacent ranks are played down for the sake of peaceful coexistence. Yet the accumulation of all those small changes in outlook, down the length of such tall rank structures, can make up a complete change in outlook. The chief executive can believe that the whole force is busy with the ideas that last month he or she asked a deputy to ask captains to implement, while in fact the sergeant is telling his or her officers that the latest missive from those cookies at headquarters "who have forgotten what this job is all about" shouldn't actually affect them at all. Not one of the departments we visited in the course of writing this book failed to reveal both chiefs more or less confident of the progress and popularity of their reforms and quantities of officers adamantly and colorfully opposed.

The rank structure, then, has to be bypassed in times of change if there is to be any hope of the operational ranks coming to understand what their chief officers are trying to get them to think about. It means that the chief must talk to the officers, and must do so at length. The fact that, as officers well know, the chief is short of time adds a great deal of weight to any personal communication he or she chooses to make.

There is good reason why patrol officers as well as middle managers should be principal targets for the communication of new values: policing's unusual distribution of discretion. A patrol officer is more in the business of dispensing justice or injustice than is a sergeant, and patrol officers make decisions that affect the community with much greater regularity than do lieutenants. We have noted that values are most fully revealed when discretion is exercised; hence the patrol officer has a far greater potential impact on the successful implementation of a new ethos than do supervisors. Patrol officers also have far greater scope and opportunity for acting in a manner that publicly refutes the assertion that anything has changed in the department.

The legacy of militaristic management also poses problems as chiefs work toward change. They have to grapple with the fact that patrol officers are deeply resentful of virtually anything new that comes out of headquarters. Patrol officers feel that nothing from headquarters ever made their job easier, and rarely failed to make it more difficult. As one English patrol inspector recently wrote in a Christmas card to one of the authors: "It seems that hardly a day passes without some new set of rules, some new policy, or some new idea. I sometimes wonder if we will survive." This is the typical perception from the receiving (operational) end of the traditional process of centralized control: It all comes from headquarters; it is all imposed; it is all thought up by somebody else—probably somebody with a carpeted office who has time to sit and think these things up. We are too busy already; too busy doing "real police work" to pay serious attention to any more of their fanciful schemes. We already have more rules and procedures than we can possibly remember. There is no time for trying new schemes out—it takes all day just to avoid making any mistakes.

Above all, patrol officers are not accustomed to being listened to. They feel that no senior officer has ever really wanted to hear their problems and concerns. They are accustomed to telling senior officers, on the few occasions when they meet them, what they think those officers want to hear. (They do this, incidentally, out of loyalty to their immediate supervisors, who would be embarrassed by any frank exchange.) They have borne the burden of juggling the demands of headquarters (which they see as politically motivated) with the practical realities of patrol work. This is a very real phenomenon. The Police Executive Research Forum (PERF), in its evaluation of Darrel Stephens's problem-solving experiment in Newport News, counted it a major victory that patrol officers assigned certain "problems" by their superiors were actually willing to volunteer that they were not problems at all and therefore not worthy of effort.[21] To PERF—and anybody else familiar with police departments—it seemed just as likely that the officers would simply mutter vilely to themselves and go through the useless motions of carrying out their assignments. (Nor is this problem restricted to the lowest ranks; some captains, lieutenants, and sergeants will say that they have actually had to hide good work from headquarters simply because it did not fit with the demands the hierarchy was making at the time.)

If patrol officers are told that headquarters wants to hear their ideas and feelings, their first reaction will be incredulity. If they hear it themselves, from the boss, they may begin to wonder what is happening. But they will remain highly skeptical for a long time and will be most reluctant to play their part until they are certain that they will suffer no repercussions from the captain for what they said to someone from downtown. A captain from the Philadelphia Police Department captured the problem nicely. "The trouble with ideas about greater discretion and innovation and participative management," he said, "is that, when they come down through the hierarchy, they get to look just like yet another new system being rammed down your throat."[22]

Some police executives have taken the trouble to draw up a printed document describing the values they want the department to adopt. Several have circulated it to every officer as a means of ensuring that the message does not get filtered or distorted as it goes down through the ranks. As a device for making new values known, that is a very good start, but only a start. Distribution of such a document is no guarantee that the values it embodies will become part of the organizational fabric. Those who receive it will probably read it (if it's short enough),[23] but they will not believe that their working environment has changed until they experience it in practice. They will have to see dissent and failures tolerated before they believe that it's safe to make suggestions and try new things. They will have to see that the old performance measures are genuinely dead and buried before they will change what they do every day. And they will need to witness the demise or containment of a few of the department's bombastic autocrats before they will believe that the management style is being transformed.

The police chief's biggest job in moving toward a new policing, then, is to frame values for a higher police culture and to ensure that every aspect of the department's operation is suffused with the new culture. That includes management style, performance measures, staff appraisal systems, promotion systems, the training academy, and (perhaps most important) disciplinary procedures. It also includes the arrangements police organizations employ to make themselves open and accountable to the public they serve. We turn to these arrangements next.

CHAPTER 6

■

Openness
and Accountability

$\mathbf{P}$OLICE DEPARTMENTS, and the executives who lead them, are entrusted with important public resources.[1] The most obvious are tax dollars, taken from citizens by force of law. Less obvious is authority: to bring the power of the state to bear on those suspected of wrongdoing and, when needful, to use force to impose the law. Private citizens surrender authority, no less than money, to the police. It comes not from their pocketbook but from their precious stock of liberty.

In any democracy, both tax dollars and public authority are in short supply. They are supplied to public enterprises only with great reluctance, and their use is closely monitored by citizens and their representatives. Citizens expect and demand that public monies granted to the police will be used efficiently and fairly. They demand the same of authority.

The very reasonableness of these demands behooves the police to consider carefully their obligations to remain, or to become, properly accountable and to embrace—rather than, as so often at present, eschew—relationships with the public that promote understanding and facilitate guidance. Only genuine openness and accountability will produce rather than obstruct progress toward more effective and responsive policing.

THE CURRENT FOUNDATIONS OF LEGITIMACY

Having quite deliberately isolated themselves from most of their old sources of public and political support, which the reform movement deemed improper and corrupt beyond rehabilitation, the police currently seek to shore up their legitimacy on three basic pillars. The first is the enduring popularity of crime control. Provided crime remains an urgent concern and that the police continue to be viewed as the best hope for crime fighting, they will enjoy considerable support. The second is their claim of professional impartiality and competence. It is thus that they seek to assure concerned citizens that money and authority will be used efficiently, properly, and fairly (the fact that the police can today plausibly make this claim is the proudest achievement of the reform strategy). The third is their commitment to serve and protect individual citizens, especially through a patrol force dedicated to rapid response. This is the most tangible and direct promise the police make: you call and we'll come. Other commitments are relatively abstract and build less concrete support; getting to citizens when they call is visible, immediate, and immensely popular.

But these pillars are showing their cracks. The first is crumbling altogether. It is becoming increasingly obvious that the police are not winning the war against crime. Public support for police efforts is no longer automatically granted. Even if the end still attracts support, traditional police means do so less and less. Indeed, as we saw in chapter 2, citizens who can are increasingly turning to private security rather than the police to protect themselves.

The second pillar is undermined by occasional but persistent instances of police incompetence, unfairness, or outright abuse. The episodes the public seems to care about most do not generally involve the misuse of public funds and only somewhat more frequently the failure to deal with a particular crime problem. Instead, the most

151

common and devastating criticisms focus on alleged police failures to enforce the law equitably, or to use force economically and fairly. Through the police-action-sparked riots that have plagued Miami, through the stop-and-search scandals that have recently rocked a host of American cities, through innumerable lesser and more local taints and abuses, the police remain vulnerable to the consequences of their actual and perceived misdeeds.[2]

Indeed, only these kinds of complaints have succeeded in breaching the barriers of police independence. When the police suffer corruption and failure, they are more or less trusted to put their own house back in order. When they shoot speeders and abuse black youths, often they are not. Special commissions of outsiders—that is, nonpolice—are established to make investigations.[3] Civilian boards are authorized to review complaints of police misconduct.[4] Even without—or sometimes regardless of or despite—these special arrangements, individual citizens who believe they have been injured by police misconduct may, and increasingly do, seek redress through civil suits against police officers, police departments, even entire city governments.[5]

The result is that the police are far more accountable to the public for the fairness and economy with which they use force and authority than for the use they make of public dollars. This oversight tends to come in response to specific complaints about the misconduct of individual officers or, less often, departmental sanctioning of patterns of such misconduct. This intense focus on incidents of police abuse is entirely natural, given the reluctance of a free people to countenance violent abridgments of their liberty and given that the stakes are often very high when the police go over the line.

Concern about police abuse is fed, however, by the unfortunate fact that the police have often failed to represent themselves as—or indeed to be—eager to respect and protect the public's rights and liberties. They often rail against the laws and policies that demand their good behavior and forecast dire consequences if new restrictions are imposed on gathering evidence or obtaining confessions. (To be fair, some of the most vehement opposition to Miranda rights, the exclusionary rule, and the like has come not from them but from the political right claiming to speak for them: but the police rarely demur.)[6] As long as they fail to respect lawfulness, restraint, and fairness at least as much as the rest of society does, the public will be justified in suspecting both police motives and police conduct in using force. And the ambiguity and pressure of police work guarantee plenty of episodes to fuel concern. When a suspect is shot in an alley, sometimes no amount of investigation will reveal whether the killing was correct, honestly mistaken, reckless, or evilly calculated. Where there are substantial doubts about the police's outlook and motives, the worst will always seem—and unfortunately be—a possibility.

Commissions, civilian review boards, and other such bodies have not generally been greatly able either to improve police conduct or enhance police legitimacy.[7] Partly this is because the police have stubbornly resisted even these limited intrusions into their autonomy. But it is also because reviewers' focus on individual instances of misconduct, rather than on the police's overall behavior and performance, is greatly problematic. From the public's perspective, the publicity given to occasional awful incidents merely confirms suspicions that the police are dangerous. From the police's perspective, the sole concern with abuse undermines the fairness of oversight, because the great preponderance of their work—fair, proper, and restrained under the most difficult circumstances—goes unremarked. Relations between the boards and the police are as a consequence generally neither easy nor productive.

The third pillar on which policing now stands—the promise of instant service to citizens—is, as we have seen, being undermined by the conflict between the reform model's commitment to crime control and the public's desire for a much broader kind of help. The result is often encounters in which both citizens and the police are frustrated and disappointed. The appeal of rapid response is so great that it is rarely subjected to any public criticism, but it no longer seems able to deliver on the promise it once represented.

A NEW APPROACH TO LEGITIMACY

Police need a new kind of governing relationship with their public, not just because the old one is faltering but because it does not let them do the good they might. They have to find a framework of accountability that helps them to discriminate between improper political interference and well-motivated democratic influences, that helps them to expose the former, while accepting and utilizing the latter in pursuit of better policing.

We are not going to dwell on or prescribe particular institutional arrangements. What really counts in establishing effective cooperation between the police and the public is what the police think of their public and what the public thinks of its police. Neither picture is at the moment terribly encouraging. In many cases police and public have little love for one another, nor much mutual understanding, nor much respect. In some cases they hold each other in contempt. They certainly pay little attention to each other's hopes and desires. The police too often regard public priorities as ill informed and irrelevant, and the public too often dwells endlessly on isolated instances of corruption and brutality, in large part for want of any broader conception of what the police are about.

The simple fact is that police and public seem to know very little about one another. The opportunity to do some serious learning about each other is invariably painful: but often extremely healthy and enlightening.

THE BENEFITS OF A NEW OPENNESS

Between January and March 1982 BBC Television screened a series, called "Police," of groundbreaking documentaries about Commissioner Peter Imbert's Thames Valley Police Force. Television cameras recorded at length ordinary police officers doing ordinary police work. The privilege of being a fly on policing's wall was hard won; as filmmaker Roger Graef recalls, he approached four English forces unsuccessfully before Imbert acceded. "None of them were prepared to allow us unrestricted access," Graef says. "They all asked for conditions that were unacceptable to us. Peter Imbert was the first to agree, without restrictions. He told me he thought this was the kind of thing a modern police force ought to be doing—but that he was sure it was a decision he would ultimately regret."[8]

The show was a huge success, running a close second to "Dallas" for the three months it was on the air. "People were just fascinated to see what police work was really like. They just had no idea," Graef says. One episode, however, provoked a public outcry. It showed the treatment given to a working-class woman who went to her local police station to make an allegation of rape. In particular it showed her being interviewed by Detective Constable Brian Kirk, who was seen by many as unbelievably insensitive. He was testing the genuineness of the allegation, and doing so involved some harsh cross-examination. The common—though untested—police assumption that roughly 60 percent of rape allegations are false presumably justified, in the detective's view, the approach he took. In the eyes of Thames Valley Police, it was a disastrous episode. According to the producer, "It made the most almighty stink. That episode was previewed on the main nine o'clock news that evening—and extracts of the interview were shown by CBS and Stockholm News. . . . It led to questions in the House [of Commons]. I remember after the preview Peter Imbert saying he wished he had a veto over it. But he knew he didn't—and he didn't try. That's to his great credit—he had a lot of influence with the BBC. He did not try to stop it."[9]

Despite Thames Valley's embarrassment, however, the exposure it suffered was immensely productive. England completely revamped the way its police handle rape complaints. They no longer interview complainants of sexual assault in police stations; instead they use hospitals, clinics, or specially prepared "rape centres" to provide less intimidating surroundings. The manner of interview has certainly changed, and medical examination is mandated. Five years later, it is generally agreed that the British police treat rape complainants with much improved sensitivity and respect.

There is a lesson here for policing in general. Openness and accountability are two of the most important means public institutions use to ensure that their values and objectives accord with society's wishes. Under the reform model, the police have rejected openness in favor of ideological isolation from outside influence, and they have, as we shall see, viewed their accountability in narrow, legalistic terms. The strictures of shift work and the isolating tendency of the job tend to wall them off even further from the influence and interests of ordinary people. The result has been police departments, even the profession as a whole, insulated from the thinking of the public they are supposed to serve. Public examination of the police's inner workings is viewed with suspicion; change sparked by such examination is often seen as a sign of weakness. Instead of adapting gradually and fluidly to the legitimate and ever-changing needs of the people and cities around them, the police focus inward on their own needs, values, and traditions. When change comes, it tends, as in Thames Valley, to come through crisis.

In the meantime the police and the public continue to hold many contrary beliefs about policing's methods and objectives. Witness the difference in attitudes toward foot patrol. Almost without exception the public clamors for more foot patrols and in some cities has offered to pay more taxes to get them; the public greatly appreciates the reassurance of a familiar, friendly police officer who has time to listen.[10] Yet the majority of police departments continue to view foot patrol as their last priority, even as a punishment detail. If by some fluke a shift supervisor has filled all the cars and still has spare capacity, an officer may actually be assigned to a foot beat.[11] That officer will probably be a very junior one, or a senior one who somehow has got into the supervisor's bad graces.

Other examples of the divergence of outlook between police and public abound. The public would regard it as bizarre that police officers should ever be given a quota of traffic violations to write or keep running scores of officers' arrests when all it wants is free-flowing traffic (not prosecutions) and safe streets (not arrests). And the public is often disgusted when it learns of racist, corrupt, or violent behavior by police officers, while in many departments the police themselves are still willing to ostracize any of their number who reveal or testify against such behavior.

This distance between police and public must be reduced. The way forward for policing clearly lies in increased openness, responsiveness, and accountability, not through episodic crisis and embarrassment but as a regular habit. Two promising avenues lie open: reconstructing the police's attitudes toward and mechanisms for dealing with community and political influence to overcome institutional insulation; and recasting the roles of several important parts of typical police departments to organize for responsiveness. The first is the most basic and the most important.

OVERCOMING INSTITUTIONAL INSULATION

The development of policing through the reform era has provided police managers with some good defenses against attempts by outsiders to influence police practice. Commissioners were appointed with citywide responsibilities, and precinct captains were made accountable to headquarters rather than to the ward politicians they had previously served. Amalgamations welded small-town police departments into larger, professionally independent forces. The response, by now traditional, of police executives to political interference in the running of their organizations became something like this: "These are operational matters and as such are for determination by professional police officers. We alone are capable of making the correct judgment on the basis of our professional experience."

Some critics quite rightly ask how, under this powerful notion of professionalism, the police can be properly controlled. When politicians insist on questioning the adequacy of mechanisms for governing the police, police chiefs frequently respond, "We are accountable to the law, and our actions, if necessary, can be tested in the courts."[12] The response is accurate, so far as it goes; the police are held accountable to the law through civil liability. But there are at least two problems with this kind of defense, one minor and one major.

The minor one relates to using the law as the final arbiter of police actions: its scope is much too narrow. Of course police actions should be within the law, and transgressions of the law should be punished; further, it is obviously police executives' responsibility to prevent such transgressions. However, very few police decisions come anywhere near the limits of legality. "Accountability to the law" accomplishes little other than controlling obvious abuses of police power. It places restrictions only at one edge of the domain of possible police action, while being incapable of redirecting the mainstream of policy and practice. Most notably, accountability to the law fails to address any of the important questions concerning allocation of the department's resources, questions the community at large finds vitally important.

But the major problem with the traditional police response to political pressure is that it fails to distinguish between genuine concerns and political opportunism. "Professional autonomy" has tended to be used as a ground for rejecting any outside influence, however well or badly motivated. The availability of this blanket rejection has absolved police chiefs of responsibility for determining which voices should be given credence and which should not. They simply reject all voices and continue to trust their organization's internal agenda. All of this adds to the public perception of the police as a closed institution, set on its own preordained course and impervious to society's broader concerns.

The consequences of such insularity can be severe. The Reverend Hind, a clergyman in the Brixton area of London, spoke to *The Times* of London shortly after the riots of April 1981 about the Special Patrol Group in Brixton and their extensive use of "stop-and-search" powers before the rioting broke out. "For ages," he said, "I have been trying to point out [the eventual result of their provocative actions] to the police. They just regard you as a leftie ... if you mention community relations to the ordinary policeman he either falls about laughing or starts cursing. That is the attitude the poor bloke has been given."[13] Whatever the cause of the riots, the Reverend Hind had put his finger squarely on the fatal weakness of the reform notion of police autonomy: anyone who tries to influence the police is dismissed as politically motivated, in this case as a left-wing extremist. Much of value is thereby lost.

Lord Scarman, who ran the inquiry that followed the riots, suggested local consultative committees as one apparently sensible way the police could overcome their self-imposed distance from the public. The idea was later given the force of law (the Police and Criminal

Evidence Act, 1984), and local police commanders were obligated to attend their meetings.

The fact that community consultation was being imposed on the police, rather than instituted voluntarily, had two unfortunate side effects. First, it reinforced the perception that the police themselves did not want any greater local accountability and accepted it only as a necessary evil. Second, it heightened the police's feeling that they were beleaguered by unwanted external pressures.

Naturally many police officers presumed—and still do—that political opponents dominated local consultative committees and were reluctant to do any more than attend the meetings and proclaim their operational independence wherever necessary. In fact, a study of consultative committee meetings two years after their formal implementation suggests that, far from being hotbeds of political criticism, they operate more like elementary classes in policing.[14] The committee members are on the whole respectable and well disposed toward the police, while ignorant of their function; the committees are therefore unable and unwilling to examine police policies critically; any committee members who ask difficult questions are regarded as malevolent; the police tend to set the agenda and choose what information to present, portraying any failings as the inevitable result of personnel shortages; the committees are written off as "window dressing" by many who are genuinely concerned about policing issues. In short, serious public discussion and analysis of operational policy is no more a reality with the consultative committees than it was without them. This is largely the fault of the police, who have not opened up enough to allow—much less encourage—a meaningful conversation. Mechanisms of community consultation mean little without a corresponding police belief that public voices and concerns are legitimate, and this the police do not yet feel.

No doubt a few consultative committees are dominated by political opportunists, and senior police officers are politically astute enough to recognize that reality. But stonewalling is not a constructive defense against badly motivated or negative influences; erecting barriers (or hiding behind existing ones) simply prolongs the impasse. These reactions make no progress toward resolution of the issues or toward effective dialogue between police and public.

The police can perhaps be forgiven for some of their uneasiness about opening up to public and political influence. Policing has long been an easy mark for politicians eager to make their careers. It has sometimes, usually in periods of national unrest over social policy, become highly charged politically; this was true in the United States during the civil rights and antiwar movements and is true today in Britain, where policing has emerged as a key issue in the battle between left and right. Whatever the merits—and they are often great—of the critiques that emerge at such times, they are very difficult for the police, and many in the police have come to view their relations with the rest of the world in terms of long periods of political calm, when they are left alone to do as they see fit, interspersed with painful periods of politically inspired harassment. They have come to equate politics with trouble, tension, and interference. Inviting public review and consultation—that is, inviting politics—thus seems sheer lunacy.

What the police have failed to realize—with the exception of figures like John Avery, Kevin Tucker, and Sir Kenneth Newman—is that they do a great deal to set themselves up for being hammered in such debates. By keeping their distance from the public and its representatives, they often allow themselves to drift away from doing the things the public would like them to do. By not being honest about what they can and cannot accomplish, by keeping alive the myth of solitary and heroic crime fighting, they create unreasonable expectations that haunt them in times of trouble. By not being open about what they do and how they do it, they make credible the vilest accusations of official misconduct. The overwhelming majority of people simply have no framework for assessing the credibility of such allegations. (Ordinary citizens, when asked the simple question What do you think of the police? usually reply by immediately referring to the last incident in which they were personally involved. This will typically be a road accident that occurred several years earlier. Many people's abiding impression of the entire police service rests heavily on whether the officer who happened to attend their accident or incident was courteous or abrupt.)

Further, because the police have defined any deviation from their cherished autonomy as capitulation, even responding in any depth to criticisms is often ruled out of bounds. American police are extremely reluctant to explain even the most basic operational policies on the ground that they are professional matters not open to unqualified—meaning public—review. British police, who are subject to stringent legal restraints on what they can say regarding matters that end (or may end) in court, eschew public debate to a quite astonishing degree. Police executives seldom weigh in with anything more potent or persuasive than "No comment" or "This matter is sub judice" or the slightly more informative "We have set up an internal investigation: it would be improper of me to anticipate the findings of that inquiry." The public behavior of the police under attack has about it the habit of a mollusk: defense is a matter of retiring into a shell.

The Best Defense

As Avery, Tucker, and Newman have come to understand, there is a better method of protecting the police service from political winds, one that has the further virtue of ensuring that the voices of genuine community concerns do not get buried or disregarded along with those of "police bashers." Rather than retreating into their shell and guarding it at all costs, police have to emerge from it fully, with a policy of aggressive and deliberate openness. Police executives can protect themselves from unreasonable political voices by making sure that broad and legitimate community concerns are publicly framed, acknowledged, and served. That means, of course, that police will have to embrace community consultation processes rather than reluctantly submit to them. If accusations of inappropriate action or resource misallocation are hurled, a full and effective response will be available: police executives will be able to demonstrate a high level of broad community support for the policies in question. That will not mean that the policies are *right,* of course; the public, the police, municipal government, and the courts will still face that question at any number of levels and in any number of guises. It will mean that the police will have something more than their arcane and always questionable professional judgment to offer in their defense.

161

This approach, however, does not lend itself to partial or halfhearted implementation. It demands a firm commitment and a great deal of perseverance from chiefs. Opening up a police department that has been closed for decades (in practice if not in theory) will inevitably be painful. Chiefs will face the realization that the community, when forced to consider police priorities, may not arrive at the same decisions that the department would by itself. Practices in place for years may be overturned. Problems the police regarded as of no consequence may be put at the head of the agenda. Traditional ideas about what constitutes police effectiveness may have to be sacrificed.

Nor is such a policy compatible with the current police culture. Beliefs such as "The public is, on the whole, a nuisance" and "No one else really understands the nature of police work" do not fit with a policy of genuine and energetic community consultation. For a police executive, the task of opening up a department has to go hand in hand with the task of transforming its culture. To a certain extent the former can be used to expedite the latter, for chiefs can bring external pressure to bear on their officers by deliberately creating public expectations about their behavior.

Happily, however, as Kevin Tucker found, the challenge currently facing police executives—the obligation to improve policing—becomes a little lighter when it is shared with responsible elements of the community. The insularity of the reform model concentrates the whole burden on the police chief. Policing is most likely to be improved when improvement becomes a joint enterprise.

ORGANIZING FOR RESPONSIVENESS

This does not mean that the police cannot act on their own to make large improvements in their working relationship with the public. Already lurking in most major departments are three offices set up specifically to deal with certain aspects of the police relationship with the outside world. There is always a complaints and discipline department, often inappropriately called "Internal Affairs." Often there is a community-relations department. And there is normally a press and public relations office, or something similar. These units form something of a natural trilogy, each with a specific role in ensuring proper communication between the department and its public.

Unfortunately, the existence of these departments can easily provide police executives with false grounds for complacency. The fact that they have been set up does not necessarily mean that the department's orientation has been altered in any fundamental way. Nor does it necessarily mean that the public has been given an effective voice in shaping policing. Frequently the actual effect of such offices, rather than bringing the police and public closer together, is to protect the rest of the department from public reaction, enabling it to carry on with the "real police work." They therefore bear some scrutiny. We will look at each in turn, with an eye to how its mission should be framed in order to make an effective contribution to public accountability.

Complaints and Discipline

When asked to define the role of their unit, officers working in a complaints office customarily give a first reply like this: "To satisfy the requirements of the law relating to the investigation of complaints against the police."[15] (Frequently, procedures for dealing with such complaints are carefully prescribed by law, and they often obligate police departments to arrange the referral of serious cases to either outside agencies or some independent review body.*) It would be easy for a department to comply with the letter of the law while transgressing its spirit, so most chiefs expect their complaints departments to do more than simply satisfy the requirements of the law. They expect those offices to back up the publicly stated position that the chief is determined to deal swiftly and effectively with police officers who are corrupt, violent, disobedient, or neglectful. A more realistic view of the complaints department's role could therefore be summed up thus: "To discharge the obligations of public and political

---

*In England and Wales the procedure is now described in part 9 of the Police and Criminal Evidence Act, 1984. This act also set up an independent national review board, the Police Complaints Authority.

accountability for complaints against the police and police miscon-duct." There is a fair degree of consensus, both in complaints offices and throughout police departments, that this is the complaints office's proper role. The common perception, therefore, of the complaints department is that it exists to satisfy external demands, deal with external attacks, and protect the chief by providing evidence of a thorough and efficient complaints investigation system.

When a member of the public makes a formal complaint against any police officer it will, in the normal course of events, be referred to the central complaints department. The complainant will then be interviewed by a staff member, who will approach the interview with the express purpose of clarifying the complaint and explaining any relevant points of law or procedure that may have given rise to misunderstanding between the complainant and the officer against whom the complaint is being made. Then the complaints investiga-tion procedure will be spelled out to the complainant, who will be asked if, and how, he or she wants the complaint to be pursued.

A very high proportion of genuine complaints* are "withdrawn" at this early stage, for a variety of reasons.[16] Often complainants are happy to have found someone polite enough to listen to them for a while. Sometimes complainants decide not to pursue their complaints because they are persuaded that an elaborate formal investigation is not appropriate for an officer's small, albeit hurtful, misdemeanor or because their anger has dissipated. Sometimes complainants with-draw because they realize the futility of taking the matter further, often because they have no supporting witnesses and would simply pit their own account against that of the officer. Complainants learn that internal disciplinary hearings place the burden of proof on them, and they feel the weight of the odds.

Whatever the reason for a withdrawal, two important things have happened: the complaints department investigator has obtained a

---

Genuine complaints are those that were made out of sincere disappointment with an officer's behavior. Many complaints, perhaps as many as two-thirds, are motivated by something else—for example, a desire to exercise malice, obtain revenge, thwart or obstruct a prosecution, acquire some political gain, or get unmerited police attention. It is difficult to estimate the proportions of complaints falling into these categories, however, because that judgment is never recorded by police departments.

withdrawal, and has gained some information. Both are important, but for different reasons.

The withdrawal is important because the disposal of the complaint (proven, unproven, discontinued, withdrawn, informally resolved, and so on) is recorded for official statistics, which are required of the complaints department by either law or tradition and are periodically transmitted to the various watchdog agencies—police complaints authorities, local councils, central government, and so on. It is in part by these statistics that public dissatisfaction with the police service will be publicly monitored. In this context a withdrawal is positive, because it allows the assumption that the complaint had no foundation. (This is the retrospective public interpretation placed on withdrawals by police departments.)

The information gained by the investigating officer may tell a different story. He or she will have heard, in detail and at some length, why the complainant was dissatisfied. This information gives the complaints staff a very clear idea of what aspects of police activity or inactivity cause public concern. The complaints staff is thus in a unique position to build up a remarkably complete picture of the ways public and police expectations of police behavior differ.

In trying to understand the practical role of complaints departments, it is interesting to ask what they do with these two commodities—the withdrawal and the information. In practice, the withdrawal of the complaint is carefully recorded, and disseminated to all the relevant external agencies. The information regarding public dissatisfaction will, on the whole, go nowhere.

What really counts within the department is that one more complaint has been withdrawn—and that simple fact renders the complaint's motivation and content largely irrelevant. Officers posted to complaints departments soon learn that obtaining withdrawals on potentially troublesome complaints is a sure path to being accepted as a team player in the department. They learn, often subconsciously, to practice subtle forms of coercion to assist in the process. Any inclination to dwell on the shortcomings of police policy or practice, except when forced to do so by a complainant who refuses to go away, will be interpreted as disloyalty to the organization and colleagues. The practical aim of the complaints department is to "dispose effectively of all complaints, legally and properly."

This is not lost on many complainants, who discover that they become witnesses in a hearing conducted by the police, for the police. They are not normally allowed to see the statements of other police witnesses or to hear their testimony. They do not hear the officer's own account of what happened and are not allowed to cross-examine. They have no right of appeal against the hearing's judgment. The complaints system is simply an adjunct to the internal disciplinary system. Due to growing dissatisfaction with police complaints procedures, a steadily increasing proportion of the public is turning instead to civil litigation.[17] In the civil courts the burden of proof is less, the judgment is visibly independent, and compensation is available.

Meanwhile, much of what the complaints department learns is wasted. Without doubt the department's members can all identify the types of officers and behavior that provoke complaints and enumerate the motivations behind public complaints. They learn these things, though, by accident. They are not required to analyze cases in order to generate a coherent and reliable picture of the causes of dissatisfaction, the shifting pattern of complaints, or the way public perception of police duty changes. If such analysis is not expected, it will not get done; if it does not get done, its results cannot be effectively fed back to management and troops. It does not formally exist.

What does exist—statistical summaries—is of little help. These statistics say very little, if anything, about what police are doing wrong and how they might improve. They focus almost exclusively on the number of complaints and their formal outcomes. They also record the number of cases referred to outside investigative or supervisory bodies, with a breakdown of case disposals. They tell more about the routing of complaint files than about the failures of the police.

From the point of view of bringing police and public into a more harmonious relationship, the following might be more worthwhile questions:

1. How many complaints in a given period resulted from genuine disappointment with the conduct of police? How many of these were withdrawn? Why were they withdrawn?
2. Which precincts have unusually high levels of complaints regarding excessive use of force?
3. What kinds of complaints are most frequently made about officers recruited between ten and fifteen years ago? What kind of in-service training do they need?
4. What are the public's common misperceptions of the police role? In which areas do the police need more effective public communication?
5. What types of complaints are commonly made by store owners? by the elderly? by motorists?

All the information needed to answer these questions, and others like them, is available to the complaints department. Fed back into officer training and management, it would be an invaluable aid in narrowing the gap that separates police from public. Complaints departments have the opportunity to be dedicated "ears" for the police, but few have adopted that role energetically. Changing their traditional, defensive stance is something that police departments can do entirely on their own. More should do so.

Community-Relations Departments

The role of community-relations departments is generally seen as that of peacemaker. They are responsible for establishing rapport with minority or immigrant communities and are obliged to monitor levels of tension in different sections of the community.[18] They may be asked to defuse potentially explosive situations. They may well be called in to assist a serious crime inquiry in a neighborhood that, because of its racial or religious mix, is impervious to normal police approaches. They are supposed to have the keenest understanding of the causes of community disquiet.

One could reasonably, then, expect community-relations departments to be in very close contact with complaints departments;

the community-relations people would be hearing the same kinds of messages from communities and community leaders that the complaints offices hear from individuals. In reality, however, the two are poles apart. The reasons for this separation are a little obscure, but they throw light on the functions of both departments. A complaints investigator, asked why there was virtually no communication between his department and the community-relations department, had this to say: "I suppose because there is no need for [communication between us]. Our jobs don't really overlap at all. What they do is nothing to do with the mainstream of policing—it's all the nice, harmless stuff. You know, school programs, charity cycle rides, handing out badges for the kids at village fetes—that sort of stuff. No one complains about that kind of thing. It's the real police work—arrests, prosecutions, cracking down on villains—that sparks complaints."[19]

In reality community-relations officers hear complaints constantly, not usually about brutality or malfeasance but about local problems the police might help with and police practices and priorities community leaders take issue with. Such information usually goes nowhere for the sufficient reason that most departments are not organized and willing to act on it. Community-relations officers suffer from their "grin-and-wave" reputation because their departments will let them do nothing else. They, like the complaints office, are there to insulate, not to inform.

The view that community-relations work is specialized and disassociated from real police work is widespread among police. The majority of patrol officers acknowledge that the community-relations department probably generates a fair amount of good publicity for the force, and they are thankful for its existence because it leaves them free to carry on with their work, undisturbed by the need to make speeches to community groups or distribute crime-prevention literature to kids.

But this perception is ironic and unfortunate. Departments often set up community-relations offices as a deliberate demonstration of their progressive natures. Yet these offices often absolve the remainder of the force from its responsibility for establishing and maintaining closeness with the community. Police departments need to change that separation of purposes and to incorporate the information community-relations officers gather into the routine of setting priorities and allocating resources. The potential is there; policing must realize it.

Press and Public Relations

The third specialist department focused on handling a police department's community relationships is the press office, responsible for answering media inquiries and packaging and disseminating media statements. But this department's existence, and its professionalism, does not guarantee genuine openness. The scope for effective communication is still largely determined—meaning, usually, limited—by the senior managers of the police department.

Here is the complaint of one highly professional police press officer who had to endure a major departmental crisis: "I have always had good access to the chief, and his deputy, and all their assistants. Whenever there's a celebration of good service, or a passing-out parade, or some praise for the force, they are there, groomed to perfection, just itching to have their picture taken. And we do an awful lot of that, and I think it does the force a lot of good.

"But when this [scandal] hit the fan it was as if they didn't exist. No sign of them. Vanished. And I've got five national newspapers pestering me on the phone. And I'm supposed to sound reasonable and intelligent—but I can't say a thing because no one [at headquarters] is prepared to stick their head over the parapet, and the result is I get no guidance at all. Then, eventually, the chief said I should go on television. I asked if he thought I should be briefed first. He apparently didn't think that was necessary. I did it. It was awful. They screened a ten-minute interview and all I was allowed to say was that it was under investigation. I must have said that ten times. I really looked stupid. Talk about creating a bad impression."[20]

The press office can only be as open, and as responsive, as the senior managers of the force. Most such offices still work under reform-model chiefs who view outside inquiry as intrusion and public explanation as surrender. As a consequence, their public responses to criticisms are limited to "No comment" on the tough questions, press releases on major busts, and a soothing stream of reports about charitable achievements. They are inhibited from tackling the real issues. But press departments could do much to explain what the police do, how and why they set priorities and allocate resources, what they would like from the community: they could and should begin the process of opening up to and informing the public.

The Way Ahead

Current practices in complaints, community-relations, and press offices provide little evidence of police commitment to genuine openness and effective accountability. In the worst cases, the very offices that should be ensuring clear and effective communication with the community are instead being used as a shield behind which the remainder of the organization can operate as usual. The major danger in giving the bulk of responsibility for community relationships to specialist headquarters departments is that doing so makes community accountability and effective public communication the preserve of a small minority of officers rather than a fundamental axiom guiding every police action. This leads to a more general, and quite interesting, question. Under these arrangements, who in police agencies comes closest to being properly accountable to the public? Who has the greatest community contact?

The answer is rather strange but perhaps typical of large bureaucracies: it is the officers at the very top and the very bottom of the organization who have extensive contact with the public. The middle managers, for the most part, do not. The communities to which the very senior and very junior officers are accountable are relatively easy to identify. The chief and his or her deputies are responsible for the entire city, or county, or state. Patrol officers are responsible to the members of the public whose calls they answer, beat officers to the residents on their beats. In some cases district or area commanders have well-defined communities to serve as well.

The community contact experienced by the top and bottom ranks differs considerably. The contact at the top is largely political consultation and such hobnobbing as is commensurate with high office. The contact at the bottom is the business of serving the department's clients and hoping to satisfy them. The rest of the work tends to be internal to the department, and most middle managers spend much of their time in their offices.

The picture that begins to emerge from this division of labor matches very nicely the perception of operational police officers, patrol officers, and their immediate supervisors. They see themselves as the "front line" or as working "at the sharp end." They regard themselves as the only officers who know "what goes on out there." They see the whole of the police management structure, even with its politicking, as a comparatively cozy internal world. In their eyes one of the attractions of promotion is its offer of protection from a harsh and demanding external world. Patrol officers can therefore be forgiven for thinking that they insulate the rest of the organization from the public.

It would be unfortunate, though, if this pattern of community contact and concern continued. Middle managers should wherever possible interact as fully with the community as the most senior and most junior officers. Their jobs should be redefined wherever possible to promote responsibility for communities and their problems. Thus they would become a meaningful resource for patrol officers; they would be able to provide contextual frameworks, at successively higher levels, to assist subordinates in understanding and resolving community problems.

Perhaps more important, they could fill one gap in police accountability that frustrates the public enormously. It is relatively easy to criticize the chief for the management of the entire department, or to criticize an individual officer for his or her conduct of a particular case or inquiry. But it has been almost impossible for neighborhood groups, community groups, and community institutions of varying sizes to find appropriate police ears for their concerns. It is the ears of the middle managers that must become available if policing is to become truly flexible and responsive.

CHAPTER 7

■

Partnerships

THE PROMISING, sometimes startling, stories of Wilshire, New Briarfield, and Link Valley represent early, and positive, returns on one of the new policing's highest hopes: that what neither the police nor other parties can do alone, the police and neighborhood groups, the police and the parks and recreation department, even, as in New Briarfield, the police and the federal government, can accomplish together. These stories show the power of the pragmatic, focused, ambitious working partnerships between the police and the public, and the police and other government agencies, that hold so much hope for controlling crime, promoting public safety, and improving the quality of life.

It seems more and more apparent that the police cannot alone solve many of the problems of crime, fear, and public safety society faces today.[1] No conceivable infusion of strength or technology will do the job. If the police can make a major contribution, they can do so only in league with other parties who have resources—time, money, expertise, knowledge, ideas, energy, equipment, and more— of their own to offer. These resources, as many departments have found, are there: among parents and neighbors, in block clubs, in civic associations, in churches, in the schools, in businesses and business groups, in government, and elsewhere. And the experience of many departments, as we have seen, is that the police and such groups can join forces to remarkably good effect.[2]

They often do so, however, with difficulty, or at least with growing pains. Partnerships—in marriage, business, the arts, and not least policing a city—are notoriously tricky. The police and their new allies may want different things, have different understandings about what's negotiable and what's not, have different ideas about who owes what to whom. These difficulties are often exacerbated by differences in class and standing between the police and their various potential clients and partners. As one officer put it, "When you're an officer in the suburbs, you're a civil servant. When you're an officer in the ghetto, you're god."[3] Neither stance—minion or overlord—is consistent with the idea of a partnership among equals.

These difficulties can and should be overcome. In this chapter we explore the potential of working partnerships and the rules and arrangements that might regulate them. We believe that effective working partnerships cannot be formed, at least not successfully or for long, as isolated adjuncts to business as usual, grafts onto the body of reform policing. Police departments that do not allow their values to change, that do not truly believe that it is appropriate to seek outside help and accept outside guidance, that remain unwilling to trust or to speak truthfully to their new partners will falter and fail. The police cannot simply mobilize the public; the public has its own wants and needs, which must be respected. The police cannot simply demand help and support from other parts of government; they must persuade, negotiate, and compromise to get what they want. The police rarely have all the answers; if they are not willing to listen to and learn from their partners, much of the strength of the new coalitions will be lost. To make partnerships work, departments must be far more open, flexible, and responsive than they are accustomed to being.

But the openness and flexibility essential to forming partnerships bring with them a thorny new police responsibility, one that the reform model rendered essentially moot but that no new

173

policing can escape: how to decide which voices should be heard, which requests for police support and assistance honored. The problem of discriminating among political voices, solved by the reform model through the simple device of blocking them all out, must now be faced directly. The fruits of these new relationships must be not only bountiful but just. Ensuring that they are, that the police neither use nor are used for ill, is the new policing's greatest moral challenge.

WORKING WITH THE PUBLIC

To almost every police executive, the public presents itself as an enormous and tantalizing resource. What could the police not accomplish if they had the active aid of the great mass of ordinary people? Police visions of such a law-enforcement utopia almost invariably, at least at the outset, take the same form: the police do what they have always done—fight crime—more or less the way they have always done it, and the public helps: by keeping an eye on neighbors' property, watching for suspects, passing along important information, coming forward during investigations, and the like.[4] The Los Angeles Police Department started out this way when it began holding neighborhood meetings in 1970. The idea was purely to have officers "mobilize the community to help them," according to now chief of operations (then area captain) Robert Vernon. "It was, Here's what's happening in your neighborhood: we're having a lot of car clouts along this street, and this is what we need to do to attack that. It was us telling them what their problems were and giving them proposed solutions."[5]

The neighborhood meetings were often very successful on those terms. Local people frequently knew who was up to what, or saw crimes being committed, or simply saw something suspicious, and senior lead officers found that once they were known in their areas, through meetings or otherwise, they learned a surprising amount from residents. Neighborhood watch leaders confirm that result. "You ought to see it, once people get started and they get a little confidence," says one. (She, and apparently others like her, even get calls—often anonymous—with information to pass on to the department.)

Information was, from the very outset, what the department was chiefly after, and SLOs used the meetings in part to train residents in how to be effective eyes and ears. "I tell them all, I don't want you to be a hero, I don't want you to go out there and grab somebody by the arm," says one. "That's not your job; that's our job. We want you to be a good witness. If you see a car that doesn't belong there, is doing something suspicious, get the license number. Don't just call and say it's a blue car and hang up. If you can't get the license number, get the color of the plate. If you see a burglar, look at what they're wearing. It all helps." Sometimes it helped a lot. In one residential section of the city, an SLO recalls, "They were having such a bad burglary problem that the SLO's whole area up there was involved in it. The community had just had it; he had seventy and eighty people at his meetings. And they reduced their problem; we got flooded with calls about suspicious persons and vehicles and license numbers and some panned out. The people really do help."

Fighting serious crime this way is very important, and—as Wilshire, Link Valley, and the like suggest—very promising. When it works both sides are satisfied. But the wants and needs of police and public do not always line up so nicely, and when they do not, how to strike a proper balance in the partnership becomes a pressing issue.

Balancing Conflicting Priorities

One problem usually comes quite quickly to light: neighborhood groups and the police do not always agree on what problems deserve police attention. This came as something of a shock to the LAPD.[6] "What we found when we started getting very close to the community was that maybe some things that we thought were important to them really weren't that important, and other things we didn't think were important at all, were very important," Vernon recalls. "Like abandoned cars: in one of our areas, that was a very important thing. They were really bugged about all these abandoned cars, and they thought it was a bad police department that wouldn't take care of them. When we started removing the cars their opinion of us went up, even though because we'd changed priorities we were putting fewer drug addicts in jail."

Things are the same in Los Angeles today. When LAPD officers visited a neighborhood watch group recently to give a crime-prevention lecture, people listened closely. But when the floor was opened, they turned out to be on fire not about murder and mayhem but about someone down the street who was running an illegal autobody shop out of his garage: the noise and congestion were driving them crazy. Similar scenes play out all over the city.

As long as police do not make themselves easily available to the public, as long as people have to go out of their way to get the police's attention, this can remain a stable situation—unhealthy perhaps, because police feel unappreciated and the public feels ill served, but stable. If police put themselves forward, though, as they must in any kind of community policing, they suddenly face demands they would normally never have heard (or probably taken seriously if they had heard). When the London Met's Hackney Division began its neighborhood policing experiment in 1983, the whole tenor of its policing changed.[7] "As we made contacts—which we hadn't before— in the early days with local tenants' associations and various other groups, we went along to these people and explained what neighborhood policing was about and that we wanted to be involved in the community more," says a Hackney inspector. "And we did, but of course that has a knock-on effect. Once they realize that you are concerned with what's going on in their little bit of the community, they're likely to bring more problems to you, hoping that you can solve them. Whereas before they wouldn't have contacted the police regarding a small bit of rowdyism, or children playing football in a particular council estate, now they rung us up and said, Come and deal with this. It's not just that you get more burglary reports, or more rape reports, but you get more broken lavatory systems reported by old ladies to whom that is a real problem. And you can't walk away, once you go into an estate and say, Look, we are available, we are a caring organization."

Not only can police not afford to walk away if they want to maintain their credibility, very often they find that they don't *want* to walk away from the problems they encounter, even the apparently minor ones. Partly this is because the seemingly ordinary often turns out to conceal matters worth real police attention, even in reform-model terms. "Say you have a problem family on a large housing estate," says the Hackney inspector. "You might find from the initial call that you've got a fifteen- or sixteen-year-old suspected of doing a burglary. When you dig a bit deeper, as we started to do, you find that he in fact is doing drugs, and that's why he's doing the burglaries. And when you start digging around in there, you might find that there's a drugs problem in a school, or in a youth club, or somewhere on the estate. So you start digging in there. You're unwrapping a load of stuff which previous to trying to do this style of policing you wouldn't have attended to at all: you'd have come in and dealt with the initial burglary call, and arrested him, and away."

Partly, too, this engagement develops because police, once exposed to the public in a constructive fashion, often become extremely attached and committed. In Hackney, in Newport News, in Wilshire, officers who had more or less given up went to great lengths once they really got to know residents and understand their plight.[8]

In a variety of ways, then, the public's fear and order concerns, and the problems that give rise to incidents, force themselves on police attention as soon as departments abandon their focus on simply responding to calls. It is at this juncture that the nature of the police-public relationship reveals itself. If it is truly a partnership, if the public has some legitimate claim on police priorities and resources, then their needs will be taken seriously. If it is not a true partnership—if the police can accept help and guidance only on their own terms—then they will not.

The new policing will take the former path, for at least two good reasons. On the one hand, what bothers people—even if relatively trivial by traditional police standards—is worthy of at least some police consideration simply because people are bothered. On the other, if police expect people to help them on large matters—when a local person is sought for a major crime, for instance—then they'd best have laid a foundation of trust and goodwill on smaller matters. Principle and prudence alike counsel responsiveness.

This is not a matter the police can afford to ignore much longer. From their perspective the choice looks to be one of doing more or less as they have always done or forging new relationships with the public to do the old, and some new, things in new ways. The situation may, however, be much more dire than that. It may in fact be a choice between being responsive and delivering what the public wants and needs, and becoming increasingly unpopular and unimportant. Individuals, private institutions, the society as a whole can always turn to private security arrangements to allay their fears. And, as we noted in chapter 2, when the police do not satisfy, the public is increasingly turning elsewhere: to security guards, Guardian Angels, and even direct action.

To satisfy their clients and keep ahead of their competition, the police must be responsive enough to the public's concerns to seem the most attractive option, without sacrificing their defining principles. The only way to accomplish that is to do what is legitimately desired of them—even if that means considerable change—while reminding society of why it needs public rather than private policing: to sustain the quality, material, and moral of democratic society.

Handling Inappropriate Demands

Any new policing that seeks to forge close working relationships with the public will likely have no shortage of opportunities to furnish those reminders, for the public will surely demand things from the police that they cannot in good conscience deliver. Two interesting examples come from Seattle. In one, local merchants sought to use the police to move street people, whose aggressive panhandling they thought was bad for business, off the sidewalks near their stores.[9] In the other, a patrol officer responded to community concerns about drugs by making a large number of suspect house searches and evidence seizures.[10] The community appreciated his efforts so much that when the chief, Pat Fitzsimons, sought to discipline him for

misconduct he was pilloried in some of the local media for bureau-
cratic quibbling.

In both these cases the community wanted things that a democratic community should not ask for, and that a democratic police
force cannot allow itself to deliver. It would simply have been wrong,
for the police to sweep the streets of the homeless. It would have
been equally wrong for Fitzsimons to allow his eager patrol officer
to continue unchecked, for it is his constitutional duty to ensure that
his officers invoke the power of their offices properly. In both cases
if the police had acceded, they would have been attacking—however
popularly—rather than defending freedom.

A reform police department could have gotten away with simply
refusing to act on these demands, on the basis of law, professional
standards, or both. A police department that seeks productive partnerships with the public must do more: it must explain, educate, and
seek alternatives if it means to sustain public support and cooperation. In Seattle the police worked with the merchants to write an
ordinance that described specific acts sufficiently offensive to warrant
community control of panhandling and did so in language precise
enough that the law could be enforced reasonably equitably.[11] The
resolution honored both community sentiment and the Constitution.
It altered the framework of freedom in the city—expanding the
privileges of some while trimming those of others—in a way that
seemed fair to both the city and the courts.

Fitzsimons handled the problem of his renegade officer by visiting critical newspapers' editorial offices and reminding them of the
imperatives that shaped the department's internal disciplinary rules:
namely, the protection of citizens from arbitrary police action. He
explained that while it was easy to see drug dealers as today's major
threat, someday they would be gone, leaving behind—if rule bending
were allowed—a police force that had become less accountable to
its public.[12] Fitzsimons might have thought that the community would
not need a police chief to remind it of these key democratic values,
but in a world in which those values were about to be willingly
sacrificed, the job fell to him, and he did it. It will fall increasingly
to the police to play this role, a matter we will return to at the end
of the chapter.

Organizing for Partnership

At the opposite end of the spectrum from communities that want the police to do the wrong things are communities that need police help but seem unable, for various reasons, to voice those needs and help in filling them. In cities' poorest and most vulnerable neighborhoods, many lack the courage and self-confidence even to call 911, much less to organize cooperative partnerships and projects with the police. Not every Link Valley has a capable, vigorous middle-class community nearby. Too often there seems to be no partner with whom the police can join to try to turn things around.

Or so the police often believe. They may be right, but it could also be that they do not know how to look. Random patrol and emergency response make it difficult for the police to form an accurate idea of the strengths of the communities they serve. Personnel practices make it unlikely that many members of police departments will have come from the poor communities they police so intensively. Traditions of professional independence and autonomy make it hard for the police to acknowledge the potential usefulness of people who have long criticized and attacked them.

As a result the police may fail to see the community's capacity for self-defense because they see the community through undiscriminating eyes. They cannot see that the community seems so helpless because it feels abandoned, and would discover new strengths if only the police could make an effective alliance with important community elements. Overcoming these blinders is one of the principal justifications for seeking a closer, more thoughtful discriminating relationship with communities.

Departments that have taken early steps into community and problem-solving policing are full of stories of apparently lost neighborhoods that flowered under new police attention. New Briarfield and Wilshire are two. In another Los Angeles housing project battered by the drug trade, SLOs found the population so cowed that they were wary even of talking to their new foot-patrol officers and totally unwilling to organize against the dealers. The officers, figuring to attack the problem from the flanks, worked with residents to address a wide variety of local nuisances. The most important step turned out to be persuading the post office to install and service a mail drop, the lack of which residents found particularly irritating. After that, and some related successes, the SLOs found people willing to take on tougher issues. The place was still a no-man's-land, and both police and residents trod lightly, but there was no longer any question that the police had made their mark and found numerous allies.[13] The same might well be true in any number of other places where the police presume that they will not be welcome.

If this is so, and the police fail to understand and act on it, it is a tragedy, for it means that those most deserving of public protection and help will be unable to get them. An extraordinarily valuable potential will be lost—not as a result of overwhelming structural factors but instead because of failures of thought, organization, and strategy. That this loss will occur under the current model of policing is almost a given, for the reform model gives police no inclination to reach out to apparently lost communities. The new policing is developing the thoughts and tools to do so; it will have to keep ever before it the question of how they can be applied even in the face of the greatest demoralization and despair, for it is exactly there they can do the greatest good.

Allocating Resources and Control

Given that policing must be more responsive to public needs, even that investing resources in seemingly lost communities may be one of policing's most important tactics, handling resource constraints and making resource allocation decisions will take on new complexity and significance. Limited resources pose a very real challenge to new styles of policing.

Even in departments where there is now a strong official commitment to innovative approaches, the tension is constant. The LAPD's chief of operations, Robert Vernon, says, "I wouldn't like to say this to the troops, because I keep on saying, 'You can still do it'—you know, keep pushing them—but I don't think they have time to mobilize the community as we would like." Joe Ciancanelli, an LAPD SLO, explains that between calls, or on his way to answer a call, he tries to pass some of the trouble spots identified by local residents. "If you see something going on, you do what you got to do and the other call gets reassigned," he says. "It's like handling a call within a call; it's so busy sometimes you've just got to work them in in between." Any system that consistently demands that degree of dedication and initiative is destined for real trouble.

For most police executives, the temptation in the face of such demand is to trim the department's nontraditional activities. This eventually happened in Wilshire, where the Community Mobilization Project SLOs were put back on patrol part-time. They feared that the change struck at the heart of what they'd started to build. "We establish some credibility in the community when we go out and take care of some of these problems," one said. "Now we've got people pumped up, people on the bandwagon, people out involved in the community helping us clean up some of these problems. But when they allow you less time to go out and deal with these problems, you tend to lose your credibility with people. . . . Your people start to fall off."

The point here is not so much that the LAPD's command staff did the wrong thing, as they may well have done, but more that it regarded the decision as solely its province, a matter of professional police competence, and made it with a complete disregard for the opinions and concerns of both Wilshire's line officers and its residents. The department had shown itself willing to recruit residents to act on its behalf; it had not shown itself willing even to listen to them on a matter that they thought very important (judging by letters Wilshire area had on file). It took account of neither the pragmatic nor the moral imperatives for paying close heed to its public partners. It showed what was true: that it did not really regard itself as a partner to the people of Los Angeles but as a separate and autonomous power.

The LAPD's is an attitude that is still extremely common, perhaps more common than not, even among departments that think of themselves as committed to more responsive policing. Very few have been able to come to terms with the conflicts that can arise when the public takes a larger hand in police affairs. To change that, to make real partners of the public, the police must move to empower two groups: the public itself and the street officers who serve it most closely and regularly. Only when the public has a real voice in setting police priorities will its needs be taken seriously; only when street officers have the operational latitude to take on the problems they encounter with active departmental backing will those needs really be addressed (this is a matter to which we devote the next chapter). No department has fully figured out yet how to make these things happen, but there are some clues.

The Baltimore County Police Department's COPE fear-reduction experiment, for instance, was based from the very beginning on the idea that the public would have to tell the police where to direct their energies. COPE squads actually went door to door in neighborhood after neighborhood to get the most grass-roots picture possible of what was worrying people. The process turned the standard structure of police decision making on its head: local people raised a host of concerns, street officers sifted them and came up with solutions, and the department helped in any way it could with implementation. The reasons for this procedure were simple. As Baltimore County's Chief Neil Behan recognized all too well, neither his department nor any other knows much about fear or how to address it. Fear, almost by definition, is in the eye of the beholder, so the opinions of county residents deserved every bit as much weight as anything the police might have thought. Nor do police have established tactics for fighting fear, so there were no set approaches or policies to guide the COPE squads; they had to figure out for themselves how to get things done. (The department could have fixed this responsibility at a higher rank, but Behan was committed to making the most of his line officers.)

What made the approach work, as it seemed to, was the whole department's commitment to being guided from below. The public's concerns were automatically given great credence, and COPE officers were accorded considerable autonomy in addressing them. Higher levels of the department were content with support and oversight roles. The commitment came relatively easily because fear was a new area: no established institutional arrangements had to be upset, no operating authority lost or devolved as would have been necessary had the target been crime. All that was needed was a way to routinize public input—found in the neighborhood surveys—and an opportunity for line officers to tackle problems—provided in the largely autonomous COPE squads. With those essentials in place, the public's willingness to speak out and officers' considerable creativity drove the program along.

The LAPD's Wilshire Area Community Mobilization Project provides a similar model aimed much more closely at traditional crime-fighting goals. Here too the public's views were accorded more than usual weight from the beginning, as a result of the area's conversion to the broken-windows approach to policing. Public influence over the police was encouraged by devoting SLOs full-time to soliciting and responding to local concerns. Line officers' operational latitude was encouraged by the area's determination that those SLOs should use all legitimate means to handle the problems that came their way, whether painting out graffiti, organizing neighborhood watches, working with the city council, or running special police operations.

Here too the approach seemed very successful. A considerable number of Wilshire's residents proved ready to work with the police, and the police proved willing and able to respond to both the traditional and nontraditional issues those residents raised. The officers and the precinct were willing to be guided from below, and if LAPD headquarters had been similarly willing, it could have enhanced and expanded rather than curtailed the experiment. Public wants and needs must be allowed to shape departmental ends. Only then will policing be of help in nontraditional ways and the public be of help in traditional police areas.

WORKING WITH OTHER GOVERNMENT AGENCIES

The other key partnerships police departments can enter into are formed with other parts of government. The LAPD's Wilshire SLOs worked closely with their local city council to handle problems the police could not handle alone (or sometimes at all); Baltimore's COPE officers drew in a wide variety of local agencies to help with fear-reduction projects; the Newport News problem-solving experiment found officers making common cause with prosecutors, heads of city departments, even the federal Department of Housing and Urban Development. It is difficult for outsiders to grasp just how groundbreaking these sorts of alliances are. Traditional police departments are notorious for their willful isolation from the rest of local government. "Even though we're only a block from city hall, there is traditionally a chasm between the police bureau and the rest of city government," said Chief Richard Walker, when, after a career in the ranks, he took over the Portland, Oregon, police department in 1987. "Very frankly, we have not done our part in reducing that distance, that feeling of being aloof, of rumbling along in our own methodical way. . . . We should have the same camaraderie between ourselves and the commissioners that the Water Bureau does, or the Transportation Bureau does, or that neighborhood associations do. But it's not so."[14] The fierce autonomy of reform policing, the isolationist impulse of police culture, and a number of other factors have fed this distancing. Breaking it down is one of the most remarkable achievements of the new policing experiments.

This change, like most of the other changes a new policing will bring, is a result of different police conceptions of the job they are expected to do. Police, especially street officers, have always drawn on other parts of government, but traditionally they have done so largely by referrals. The homeless, the hungry, and the battered have been sent to Welfare; homeowners hemmed in by uncollected garbage and abandoned cars have been sent to Public Works; parents concerned about dim or damaged playgrounds have been sent to Parks and Recreation. The police emphasis on patrol and rapid response usually allowed time for little more, and officers who pursued such complaints further were usually saintly, workaholic, or both.

Things change, though, when forums such as neighborhood meetings establish a public expectation, or departments decide of their own accord, that problems will actually be *solved*. Solving problems, as opposed to merely registering them, requires the police to follow through. And because traditional police tactics are obviously often unsuitable—when all the lights in a park have been broken for months, the important thing is to get them replaced, not gear up

185

an investigation to catch the miscreants—following through often means dealing with the city authorities who can get things done.

The Benefits of Multiagency Involvement

Police follow-through can make a big difference to the people with problems. "Out of necessity," says Wilshire's Ernest Curtsinger, when the CMP program got under way and the SLOs started handling all sorts of local complaints, "they had to get in touch with elected officials, because people will call the police department for everything. Things that we have absolutely no responsibility for! As an example, if the streetlights went out, ten years ago to the police department that was only mildy interesting. Now, all of a sudden, people have a contact, and they say, 'I'll call Officer Hall to get those lights turned back on.' So by God they call Officer Hall, who now knows the system downtown, and he calls the field deputies for the city council—a lot of them have become very tight with the councilpeople themselves, and so they have very close working relationships—and he says, 'Hey, I've got a problem down here, I need the streetlights on.' They know how to get things done in the city, and guess what: we get the streetlights on!"[15] Police take on, in this guise, a role akin to that of municipal ombudsmen.[16] When municipal services fail to the point that residents can convince the police there's a risk to the public safety, and the police can in turn convince local government, things happen.

Tackling problems that *do* have a flavor of more traditional police business can lead just as directly to multiagency involvement. When COPE officers tackled run-down Garden Village by focusing local utilities' attention on safety problems and persuading the county to build new recreational facilities, they were after—and got—not just quality-of-life but crime-control improvements. The same was true in New Briarfield and, ultimately, in Wilshire. The police, acting in concert with other arms of government, can *focus and enhance the latent power of government to act in the interest of public safety*. No new municipal capacities are at work; Baltimore already had the ability to fix lights and roads, and Los Angeles the power to trim trees. In most cities and towns, however, no one body has or takes responsibility for bringing such capacities to bear as part of a coordinated attack on crime, fear, and order problems. It's natural, once the lack is recognized, that the police—as the arm of government closest to such problems—should take the lead. The result, as Link Valley shows, can be stunning.

Not even the criminal justice system itself routinely benefits from such coordination. When the Newport News police tried to rid a downtown red-light district of prostitutes as a step toward cutting down violent street crime in the area, the officer in charge of the project worked with both prosecutors and judges to make sure everybody along the criminal justice chain was pulling together. The strategy they worked out was considered and measured. Convicted streetwalkers were sentenced more heavily than before, but most of the sentence was suspended, to be served only if they reappeared in the red-light district or were caught soliciting elsewhere in town. Local bars and hotels were warned that antisoliciting statutes already on the books but not previously much applied would soon be enforced, and for the first time customers were arrested and prosecuted. It worked: robberies dropped more than 40 percent.[17] In most jurisdictions this kind of planning is almost unheard of; in almost none is it routine. A new style of policing could make it so.

The resources government has available include not only powers and services but also knowledge, contacts, and savvy, the majority of which are normally out of reach of the police. When Newport News's agency heads convened to consider what to do about New Briarfield, it was the first time in memory that such combined attention had been brought to bear on any kind of problem. The specialized competencies the group represented turned out to be crucial to the strategy that evolved: the fire department knew just how expensive it would be to bring the apartments up to specification, and the codes compliance department was central in making the case for foreclosure to HUD. The mayor's excellent contacts at HUD turned out to be essential to working out a smooth and mutually satisfactory solution. The more routinely the police and other public agencies work together, the more frequently such assets will be brought to bear.

Although we've focused here primarily on the help other parts of government can lend to attain police objectives, the police can themselves lend a great deal of help to other parts of government. The police cover ground, and have eyes and ears, like no one else in public life. Their work draws them inexorably to sites of trouble and failure, and their availability, day or night, attracts complainants of every description. Thus they have the potential to serve government in at least two important ways.

One is to help in the delivery of essential municipal services. The police do this now insofar as they make communities safe for garbage collectors to pick up the garbage, fire fighters to respond to alarms, and schoolteachers to stay after school. They could play an even more direct role by having officers become an integrated part of case intake systems, smoothing and routinizing the process of referral, which today in most places occurs only casually and capriciously. One of Baltimore County's COPE units, for instance, developed a form for patrol officers to use when they ran across elderly, indigent, or disabled residents in need of county help. Dropped into the county's internal mail system, it went directly to social-service agencies capable of providing a wide range of assistance: emergency food and fuel, shopping and home visiting, emergency door and window repairs, daily phone checks for the ill, and the like. The county already offered all those services, but it had no capacity to seek out those in need. The police provided the connection.[18] They could do the same, through a variety of mechanisms, for any number of crucial municipal functions.

The other way police can assist government is to serve as the eyes and ears of policymakers, particularly mayors and those in similar executive roles. Mayors must concern themselves with the entire life of their cities and towns. They get information from a bewildering variety of sources: the media, constituents, municipal departments and agencies, the police. What they normally get from the police is crime information, filtered through the chief: statistics, trouble spots, perhaps progress on a few particularly big cases or neighborhood concerns. They could, however, get a great deal more. Latent within the police department as a whole is a tremendous amount of knowledge and insight about the state of the city. The police know where the garbage is and isn't being collected, where streetlights do and don't work, which schools can and can't keep their students in class, how fast potholes get fixed, whether homelessness is on the rise, which neighborhoods seem particularly stressed, and a vast number of other things. Just as police departments routinely ignore the information about their own workings contained in their internal affairs offices, mayors rarely tap the fount of police information about the workings of their cities. If they could learn to do so, they would gain a considerable advantage.

Cooperation and Coercion

Police departments who ask discover that government agencies are often more than willing to lend their help. This is not necessarily due entirely to altruism and civic virtue. "What we've found is that normally, when you start to pull a problem apart, start to understand the situation that causes the police to spend a lot of time there, you often find that other governmental departments and agencies are spending just as much time and resources responding to a different aspect of that same problem," Darrel Stephens says. "The New Briarfield area, for example, was the highest area for calls to the fire department in Newport News, and it was one of the areas that was of greatest concern to the fire department because of the potential for loss of life because of the way the structures were constructed. We found that the people who were responsible for enforcing city codes were spending a tremendous amount of time trying to fix those sorts of problems. We found that people in the health and welfare area had lots and lots of clients there, were trying to get employment programs and training programs going, and they couldn't do that very effectively. It wasn't just New Briarfield: many times, where the police were having trouble, there were also large amounts of re-

189

sources going in from other departments. So as you begin to understand the problem, you begin to know who's affected, and there are your resources for helping deal with the problem, all the way from the community to the federal government."[19] Not everything always lines up so tidily, but often many agencies have a stake in the resolution of a troublesome situation.

Difficulties can arise, though, when agencies don't have that stake or have less of a stake than they think warrants the action police would like them to take. "I think the biggest danger in approaching these sorts of relationships is the police simply laying their problem on somebody's doorstep, pointing a finger, and saying, 'If you would fix this then that wouldn't happen,' " says Stephens. "That's where you run the risk of causing a lot of trouble, and very, very severely damaging relationships between agencies. But sometimes the police enjoy a greater level of visibility and influence over what happens in a city than a water department or some similar agency, and sometimes they can use political muscle to get things to happen. It's probably not healthy, but they can and do handle some things that way."[20]

The COPE program has run into this kind of trouble.[21] COPE teams were encouraged from the beginning to use any means they could to attack problems, and they have drawn heavily on a wide variety of city resources. The city has not always been as willing to give as COPE has been to take. The decision to build Garden Village's much celebrated basketball courts, for instance, was rammed through the county parks department despite the fact that a system of twenty-two volunteer-staffed county recreation councils had already decided how the money should be spent. This was a clash of populisms; Garden Village's advantage was that it had the police on its side, and the parks department blinked first. Their feathers were not the only ones ruffled as the experiment proceeded. COPE officers continued—as they were supposed to—to draw wherever they could on the resources of other departments, and "after a few years there was a hue and cry from the department heads that we were adversely affecting their schedules and priorities," says one of Chief Behan's aides.

In the short run, support from the county executive underscored

COPE's right to make sudden and unpredictable claims on county government. To deal with such problems in the long run, Baltimore County Executive Dennis Rasmussen established an executive office of community outreach.[22] Inspired by COPE, the new office's main job is to routinize COPE's problem-solving approach for a wide variety of municipal ills. It combines, in one place, under one administrator, representatives of all the key county agencies, so that citizens and neighborhoods with problems that cross agency boundaries can hope for a coordinated response. It's also, however, been designed to process COPE's major requests for city resources and, if necessary, refuse or pare them down. "So far, COPE's demands . . . have been fairly easily handled," says Regina Aris, the office's first director. "There will come a time . . . when we're going to have problems. The more effective COPE and the executive are at getting through to people and uncovering problems, the more demands we're going to have to balance. [O]ne of the reasons that this office was established was to do that when the time comes."[23]

Baltimore County's is one early attempt to manage the demands problem-solving and neighborhood-oriented policing can put on other parts of government. In other places, under different circumstances, other mechanisms will surely emerge. One can imagine, for instance, an office of public safety attached to every municipal agency, responsible for fielding and channeling police requests, or a central committee of agency heads to set overall policy on such matters and decide difficult issues as they arise. Whatever the structure, the imperative for police executives seems clear: to prepare themselves to play in a much larger arena than has been the case under reform policing. "They'll have to have a greater grasp of local government and services than many do at the current time," Darrel Stephens says. "And a much broader view of the role of the police than many do at the current time. They'll have to be comfortable dealing with a pretty wide range of people on some very specific sorts of issues."[24] Negotiation and coordination will carry at least as much weight as command. Such is the nature of alliances.

GOVERNING RESPONSIVENESS WITH
RESPONSIBILITY

None of this means that the police should behave exactly as the public it serves, or the municipalities it works with, might want. Just as no department *can* do everything asked of it—a matter of resources—no department *ought* to do everything asked of it. This is a matter of justice. Various parties in cities will, as they always have, seek the exercise of police power on their behalf, and not all their motives and ends will be proper. Policing must learn to govern responsiveness with responsibility. Police have always faced this question, although under the reform model they often did their best to avoid facing it directly: with fighting crime by enforcing the law fixed as their only acceptable job, police either acted correctly or they acted illegally. The job description was a fiction, but a sustainable one. In a new policing that description will be neither sustainable nor desirable. No clear set of legal standards governs fighting fear, maintaining order, solving problems; none even says what fear, order, a problem, *are*. The exercise of police discretion will be absolutely central.

This will be enough to make many cling to the reform model, and understandably so. The idea of a police department tied closely to outside parties but not held to any strict and objective standards of conduct can be frightening, the prospects for misbehavior and abuse easily all too high. Fear, disorder, problems are all in the eye of the beholder. Southern police who maintained segregation and allied themselves with the Klan, Chicago police who assaulted antiwar protesters, Brixton police who harassed West Indian immigrants all felt themselves to reflect—indeed probably did reflect—the positions and wishes of powerful majority communities. How are the police to be controlled if they are granted an authority whose application cannot be exactly prescribed?

There are several important things to be said on this subject. One is that it matters a great deal. Every democratic society should look carefully and with great skepticism at any program for the exercise of state power over its citizens and should feel quite sure that any abuses that might occur will be open to recognition and correction. A program for a new policing is no different from any other in this respect. It is precisely because a call for a new policing is a call for increased police discretion that new, open, and effective methods of ensuring police accountability must be developed and applied in tandem with other innovations. This pairing is not only right but prudent; no new model of policing, no matter how promising, will long withstand the taint of abuse.

Another important point is that discretion and the need to exercise it should not be taken, in and of themselves, as a strike against a new style of policing. Discretion is exercised throughout the criminal justice system: by prosecutors in prosecuting and plea bargaining, by judges in sentencing, by parole boards in releasing prisoners. The lack of discretion supposedly accorded police stands out as a relative rarity. And, as we have said before, there never was much truth in that supposition. Nobody ever thought that the police should wink at robberies or child molesting, but whether officers were put in every bank and schoolyard or devoted full-time to traffic regulation was pretty much left up to police authorities. Law simply does not offer that sure a guide to many of the choices police face. Discretion is an important and inescapable feature of the landscape of policing, and it will be to policing's benefit to recognize and try to make the most of it. Where it is acknowledged it can be faced, and where it can be faced it can be guided and, when necessary, constrained.

A final point is that policing is taking on most of its new domains—fear, order, problem solving, and the like—using tactics other than the application of criminal sanctions. Arrest is used only when it is appropriate, and very often it is not. When Wilshire's SLOs tackled the disintegration of their area by painting out graffiti and hauling away abandoned cars, the worst that could reasonably be thought was that their actions were a waste of time: nobody went to jail. When Baltimore County's COPE team found a neighborhood uneasy with racial tension between gangs of kids, it moved their bus stops rather than sweeping the streets. Any ordinary people could have done the same. The advantage the police hold over ordinary people in such situations lies in their special standing, access, and influence, but not usually in any ability to criminalize actions and situations that were not already criminal and at least nominally open to police attention.

The police certainly do have the means to *focus* on particular offenses, and particular offenders, in ways that they or the community desires. When a Baltimore COPE team found out that a community of elderly people felt terrorized by a young local villain, it not only made sure he was arrested and prosecuted but bused residents to the trial to provide moral support for those testifying against him. The accused no doubt felt that the rules of the game had been changed rather suddenly and unfairly. Although that charge seems unfounded, at least in this case, the power of particular segments of the community to rally police support against others is obvious. Abuse of this power would be reprehensible, and the police need to eschew and protect themselves against it: but it is not a new problem, or one in any way unique to new forms of policing. Any merchant who's offended a local power-that-be and suddenly found his delivery trucks sprouting parking tickets, any bookie who's woken up in jail because the mayor discovered crime on the eve of election day, knows that police priorities can be affected by any number of ignoble interests. This is not to be countenanced, but it's no reason to oppose the redistribution of influence over the police. Communities are unlikely to sin more often and more grievously than politicians, businesspeople, and other notables always have. The police, in fact, will probably find communities, as relatively diffuse groups, easier to stand up to when the need arises.

So, granting that the problem surely will arise, it will be the police's duty to withhold their cooperation and support when the communities they work with ask them to do something illegal, unfair, or discriminatory. Illegal requests will almost always be easy to identify and should present no real problem. Unfair and discriminatory requests will, we suspect, usually be almost as easy to identify. Sometimes they will not. Was the neighborhood watch complaint to the Los Angeles Police Department about an illegal body shop mentioned earlier really because of noise, or was it because of some old local feud, or because the proprietor was unpopular? There can obviously be no easy way to know, and police will not be able to avoid making mistakes. Three likely features of any new style of policing will help here. Because arrest is rarely the best solution to such problems, some less drastic solution will often be brought to bear, giving injured parties a chance to make their cases before too much harm is done. The problem-solving approach encourages police to look beyond the surface of incidents and complaints, making it more likely that hidden motives will be found out. Finally, a new openness, and the dialogue that results, will make both police and public more likely to learn from their mistakes.

Managing through values, and the values police executives choose to manage by, will play a crucial role here, as will breaking down the barriers police culture now imposes to revealing and correcting police misbehavior. Iron discipline and direct supervision cannot control racist or brutal officers; they will always find times and places to do what they will. Insisting on just and measured conduct, however, and rewarding and punishing on that basis, can create values that will guide police behavior even in the darkest alleys. If those values are bolstered by a sense that proper conduct is more important than collegial loyalties, if the code of silence is dissolved, then policing will go a long way toward policing itself, and discretion need not be so feared. As policing is today, opening up its scope and methods would often be very dicey indeed. If its culture can be changed in the ways we have described, the remaining risks will be worth taking.

This will be a major shift, both for policing and for society as a whole. For the most part, the United States has relied on the courts and groups like the American Civil Liberties Union to remind it of its long-term interests in preserving constitutional protections. These institutions, for their part, have been content to stand apart from society and play the role of conscience. They have not worked particularly hard to help society understand and adopt the values they are correctly pledged to defend; they have preferred the priestly role of constitutional guardian to the grubbier ones of educator or politician. It has been enough that they are there to defend threatened values and principles. The police have rarely shared, much less supported, the courts' and civil libertarians' sensitivity to playing the game cleanly and honestly; generally they have been content to complain loudly about court-ordered restrictions that cramp their style and hamper their effectiveness.[25]

But as policing seeks a more intimate engagement with the public and opens itself up to more demands, it will be particularly important that the police themselves do what Pat Fitzsimons did in Seattle: become defenders of democracy's commitment to the protection of individual rights. Otherwise the police will be dragged back into the dishonor of the political era, a disgrace that it has taken them two generations to overcome.

This absolute commitment to combining responsiveness with responsibility is perhaps the key distinction between the way the police were close to cities and communities in the political era of policing and the way they can be in the future. The core value of the intervening reform era—that policing must always hew to law and democratic values—must not and will not be lost. One can even imagine that as new styles of policing become more common, as close working relationships between police and the public increase, rejections of the public's improper requests—small but pointed lessons in the value society puts on fairness, lawfulness, and the sanctity of constitutional rights—might come to be seen as one of policing's most valuable civic contributions. The symbol of policing, to society's great discredit, has already moved from the sheriff in the door facing down the lynch mob to Dirty Harry. It is time to move it back.

CHAPTER 8

■

Managing for Progress

Promoting Innovation and Commissioning Officers

THROUGHOUT THIS BOOK we have called for changes in policing: in its ends, in its means, and, perhaps more important, in the structure of its working relationships, both external and internal. We have paid special attention to the organizational changes departments have essayed as they reach for a new and better policing. It is the new ways of doing business—new values, new deals with the community, the embrace of accountability, the effort to establish working partnerships with community groups and government agencies—that give real weight to the hope that policing can be better. We have singled out chiefs who have created the conditions under which these processes can thrive and departments that have grown and learned. These are chiefs and departments who have grasped the fundamental challenge now facing policing: that in the unknown terrain between the fading of the reform model and the wide acceptance of whatever will replace it, policing must orient itself toward, and learn to live with the stresses of, experimentation and innovation. The easy days of knowing just what policing is and does are over.

Insightful police chiefs are beginning to understand that their job is shifting from the caretaking role the field is accustomed to, with its emphasis on stewardship and efficiency, to the much different and more challenging task of introducing cultural, managerial, and operational innovations. Like Darrel Stephens charging his officers with solving problems, Neil Behan sending his officers out to fight fear, John Avery challenging his specialists to accept wide responsibility for the well-being of communities, and Kevin Tucker reaching for a new relationship of accountability to the community, chiefs are testing the abilities of their departments to do new jobs. The most ambitious are, with Sir Kenneth Newman and Lee Brown, testing their departments' capacity to handle change itself, to manage rapid and wholesale movement into many new areas at once.

We think more chiefs will soon be joining the few we have highlighted here. The environmental pressures on police departments are numerous, powerful, and shifting. Police executives are beginning to face a barrage of questions, previously unasked or unacknowledged, about the effectiveness of their current strategies. Change is coming, and promoting and managing it is going to be one of the main jobs facing police chiefs and departments.

We will look in this chapter at what we feel to be two essential elements of that job: understanding and promoting innovation and freeing up the creativity of ordinary officers, one of policing's great untapped resources. If policing can learn to promote innovation, it will be a long way toward winning the adaptability it so badly needs. If it can learn to learn from its officers, it will unleash a vast reservoir of energy and insight. Neither of these elements is far advanced in today's policing, but there is reason to hope for better.

INNOVATION IN POLICING

Ordinarily, when people think about innovations in policing, they think in terms of *program innovations*. Such innovations are broadly analogous to product or production process innovations in the private sector; they are policing's food processors and robot welders. Sometimes a police department is confronted by an inescapable operational challenge, like hostage takings or Uzi-toting youth gangs, and develops SWAT teams or gang squads to deal with it. Sometimes problems that the department has neglected—domestic assault, child abuse, drunk driving—are nominated for increased attention by political forces in the community, and the police respond with a new program. Sometimes a program to deal with a frustrating police problem such as drugs or domestic assault is shown to work, and other departments adopt it to remain on the cutting edge.

Typically, police departments introduce such innovations by writing out a new policy for the policy manual, or initiating a special training program, or establishing a special unit to highlight and incubate the idea. Typically, the innovations involve only a portion of the organization's activities and resources.

By contrast, a *strategic innovation* is meant to change the department as a whole. It involves a paradigm shift that redefines mission, operational methods, and basic organization. Such innovations are heralded by changed thinking about policing, both outside and inside police departments.

Such innovations are rare in policing. Looking back, one can see the reform model as a strategic innovation that began in the Progressive Era but did not really take root until 1940 to 1960. Looking ahead, one can see the outlines of a strategic innovation in the concepts of problem-solving and community policing. The bundle of programmatic and administrative changes in Scotland Yard and Houston might count as strategic innovations; they are organizationwide and challenge current conceptions of the proper ends, means, and working relationships of policing. Time will tell whether they offer real competition to the reform model.

A third kind of innovation is administrative. The most common *administrative innovations* are designed to produce efficiencies in the department's ordinary business: a better shift schedule or elimination of a redundant level of command. Other administrative innovations support particular program innovations, for example, when an organizational unit is created to manage a new program. Still other administrative innovations support a new strategy of policing, for instance, when a department is reorganized from a centralized, func-

199

tional form to a decentralized, geographic basis; or when a new personnel category, such as Los Angeles's senior lead officer, is created to give impetus and capacity to a new function.

A fourth kind is *street-level innovation:* individual officers taking advantage of their discretion to invent new responses to the problems before them. Sometimes their invention is a specific tailoring of the organization's standard response—generally enforcement—to recurring situations, for example, fighting public drinking by enforcing sanctions against liquor stores. Such a response might better be called an adaptation. But at other times the response is entirely novel and suggests to the individual officer and others a whole new way of dealing with a class of problems. This is properly called street-level innovation; Wilshire SLOs' discovery that they could win the cooperation of their residents by painting out graffiti and ridding the streets of drunks is an example.

Unlike most outside observers, the police have not been much interested in program, strategic, and street-level innovations over the last few decades. Once the strategic innovation of the reform model was in place, and its program innovations of radio cars, rapid response, and 911 systems invented and established, policing turned largely to administrative innovations. These have been concerned principally with establishing control (which cut deeply into street-level innovations), eliminating corruption, seeking productivity gains, and enhancing the appearance of professionalism. They have tended to build the power of administrative staffs over both line commanders and officers. They have also been seen as instruments of the chief's control over the department.

More recently policing has become interested in program innovations. This trend was the hard-won product of the federal Law Enforcement Assistance Administration, which succeeded at great cost during the 1970s in establishing a small tradition of experimentation with police methods.[1] That tradition has been kept alive in the United States by the Department of Justice's National Institute of Justice and by foundation-supported institutes such as the Police Foundation and the Police Executive Research Forum. It has been supported in England by a continuing research program carried out by the Home Office and in Australia by the National Police Research

Board. Now, in the United States and elsewhere, progressive police executives often initiate a program innovation to ornament their tenures.

More recently still policing has become interested in strategic innovations. The concepts of community and problem-solving policing, and the operational experience of departments such as Los Angeles, Houston, New South Wales, and Philadelphia, have put the issue of strategic innovations forcefully before the field. Indeed, many will read this book as an argument for a particular change in police strategy.

Actually, our purpose is a little different. We do think it is important that the police consider strategic innovations. We are attracted to many of the ideas associated with community and problem-solving policing and think that they point in interesting new directions. What is most important about these strategic innovations, however, is not that they give a definitive answer to the question of where policing should go. Instead, they do something quite different, and much more significant: they initiate the conditions under which the police *may continue to be adaptive and innovative*. They do not end with their own successful implementation but set the stage for continued innovation at all levels.

They do this in two ways. First, they bring the department as a whole into much closer contact with the range of problems that communities now face and to which the police might make an effective response if they took the time to think, analyze, and use their unique position to mobilize the community and other government agencies. Second, these strategic innovations make it easier for officers on the street to adapt and innovate, and for the department as a whole to learn from concrete operational experience.

Administrative innovations like geographic decentralization are required to produce that community contact, and strategic innovations like problem solving are required to allow the department—and society—to benefit from street-level innovations. Once implemented, however, these changes create conditions under which street-level and program innovations can occur far more easily and frequently. Strategic innovations that make the police more responsive and flexible not only make them better at fighting crime, reducing fear, and solving problems, they also set the police on a course toward becoming truly innovative and adaptive, ready to face new problems and changing public demands.

Obstacles to Innovation

Unfortunately, it is no easy task to introduce innovations to policing, and it is even harder to create innovative police organizations. It is difficult enough to accomplish these goals in private-sector organizations that know they must be innovative to survive and that are organized and staffed to promote innovation.[2] In public-sector organizations—where the visible pressures to innovate are much less and the organizations less designed to promote innovation—the problems are much greater.[3] In fact, the literature on private-sector innovation gives some clues about the obstacles facing those who want the police to innovate and become more innovative.

We know from private-sector experience that innovations occur messily, quickly, and experimentally.[4] They are difficult to produce but very easy to squash.[5] And we know that a company's ability to innovate depends more on organizational culture than on the effectiveness of management control; top managers can create an environment that promotes innovation, but they cannot command their companies to think and invent.[6]

Some private-sector companies have tried to expand their organizational tolerance of this messy process by creating special staff units that can act as advocates for both particular innovations and the process of innovation. Lewis Branscomb, chief scientist for IBM, was expected to play just such a role. His job, he says, was "to guide the scientific and technical activities of the company, to ensure that they met long-term needs. Specifically, it was my job to prevent the company from destroying itself by taking too short-term a view of its needs."[7] In other words, someone must look far enough ahead, prepare appropriate adaptations (in strategy, product line, market focus, advertising, and, most crucially, technologies), and preserve and foster the company's ability to adapt.

Texas Instruments sets aside a significant portion of its budget each year to fund new product and process ideas initiated by its midlevel managers.[8] The managers compete for these funds by submitting plans for bringing their ideas to market. If their plans go astray, money is reallocated to plans that seem more promising. The executives have to participate in this competition because they are evaluated not only on how well they manufacture and sell existing products but also on how many new products they bring to market.

In addition, private-sector firms often try to foster innovation and ensure its profitability by placing responsibility for developing new products and production processes with those who are closest to the customers.[9] The right and responsibility to innovate are pushed down and out in the organization.

Finally, private-sector organizations use the competitive pressures of their businesses to keep focused on innovation.[10] IBM and many private-sector firms in different businesses know that nothing is certain but change, and they count their ability to recognize and accommodate—even to create—change as one of their greatest competitive assets.

Public-sector organizations in general, and the police in particular, find it difficult to produce this focus on innovation. There are many powerful reasons why. Foremost is the widespread and understandable feeling that experimentation in the public sector is fundamentally irresponsible; that public service, instead, demands careful, cautious, and judicious management; and that proper stewardship of scarce public resources does not extend to playing around with unproven programs.

Even where the necessity for change is recognized, there is a strong tendency to reject the unpredictable, messy, and experimental way in which innovation takes place. The public trust, it seems, expects careful and thorough analysis proving the value of change and broad consensus that the proposed change is desirable before it can be implemented. Failure is often interpreted as evidence of inadequate prior analysis. As a consequence, the public sector is denied the luxury of altering and molding a program during its initial tests. Either it works, vindicating the analysis, or it doesn't, spelling failure. The rigidity of this approach militates against the kind of trial and error that proves so instrumental in private companies.

It is also hard to do controlled experiments in public service, so it is difficult to test the effects of any new idea properly.[11] It is both expensive and time consuming to measure the outcomes of important public-sector innovations. The complexities of social interactions make it extremely difficult to draw inferences from observed outcomes and hard to attribute apparent effects to a particular change. The strongest experimental designs, which require random assignment of people or geographic areas to different treatments, often seem (and, indeed, sometimes are) unethical in public contexts (this was a major hurdle for the extremely important Kansas City patrol experiment).

When the public sector does try something new, harsh political penalties await failure. There is little inclination, among politicians or the public, to recognize merit in having tried a public program that fails. The knowledge acquired is always valuable, but the stigma attached to failure invariably dominates. By contrast, consider IBM's abandonment, in the early 1970s, of the STRETCH computer system after an extremely expensive development effort. Lew Branscomb reports the obvious disappointment of many who had been involved but also says, "The loss of face associated with abandonment of that line of computers was reduced by the fact that decisions like that were being made all the time."[12] In the public sector, "decisions like that" are normally accompanied by scapegoating and recrimination. Heads must roll. The public sector in this sense is much less forgiving than the private sector.

Policing faces some extra problems imposed by its current culture. The police's strong self-image as the only true crime fighters inhibits them from talking about their inability to control crime and from consciously or explicitly accepting any limitations in that regard. Thus, it denies access to one of the strongest justifications for experimenting: a consensus that existing methodologies are inadequate. The police's belief that no one else understands their job prevents open discussion with the community about what police do well, do badly, could do differently, or don't need to do at all. Their steadfast fraternal loyalty fosters mutual protectiveness, which can include defense of the status quo precisely because it threatens one's colleagues least.

The police's belief that crime fighting requires breaking the rules—which, restated, implies unreasonable constraints imposed on police methods by forces outside their control—shifts attention first to the other parts of the criminal justice system (inadequate sentencing, incompetent juries, insufficient prison space) and subsequently to politicians, city management, housing planners, and the like. It perpetuates the myth that police have no room for maneuver, and that their apparent failings are all caused by insufficient support from other agencies and institutions. There is no incentive for innovation in policing when everybody agrees that what needs to change is the rest of the world.

Officers' belief that the public is basically unsupportive and unreasonable disclines them to acknowledge the seriousness of problems that members of the community face. Those who complain are complainers; those who call repeatedly are nuisances; those who write to senior officers are treacherous and untrustworthy. It is difficult with such beliefs to pay close attention to clients' problems or even to be sure who to regard as the client.

Finally, the belief that patrol work has the lowest status encourages creative and energetic officers to get out of patrol, siphoning talent to specialist squads. Although this trend may facilitate program innovations, it weakens the organization's capacity for street-level innovation. Patrol officers are discouraged from acknowledging their ability to solve substantial problems or to address substantial issues; they are, after all, only "woodentops," as they are sometimes referred to by detectives in Britain.

Collectively these beliefs promote organizational insularity, introspection, and detachment from the community. They protect the myths of the reform image of policing from both internal and external scrutiny. Police culture's debilitating effect on innovativeness and adaptability was observed by Mollie Weatheritt, who, as assistant director of the United Kingdom Police Foundation, was asked to review recent innovations (primarily program) in British policing. She noted,

> In asking me to carry out this review, the Police Foundation assumed that, by making information about particular innovations more widely

205

available, the review would alert forces to schemes which would otherwise remain unknown to them and thereby act as a spur to innovation. I now feel this assumption to have been misguided. Adequate sources are already available from which forces can find out what others are doing. The fact that they might not choose to implement innovative schemes is not for want of documented examples, but more to do with police attitudes (often entrenched) towards the need for and perceived purpose of change, and also the organisational impediments to implementing seemingly good ideas.[13]

Darrel Stephens—who, given his background as an officer in Kansas City during the patrol experiment, introducing problem-solving policing in Newport News, and as current head of the Police Executive Research Forum, is in a position to know—concurs. "I'd like to be able to say that the atmosphere towards innovation in policing is changing, but I really cannot," he says. "I'd like to say that people are now more willing to take things on, to take risks, to make progress, but that happens in relatively few places."[14] He notes that few departments try new things, that few value research enough even to have a library, and that police research and planning offices generally spend their time writing procedures, keeping statistics, and updating the force instruction manual.

It is the same in Britain. There most police forces have research and planning departments, but their functions tend to be administrative. They procure equipment, design new forms, institute paperwork efficiencies, occasionally test new "devices," and usually keep the policy manual up to date. Their daily output tends to be "more policy," which codifies existing but untested methods as proper professional practices. They seldom have the authorization, training, or time to examine the effectiveness of programs or think about new methods of policing. They are loaded down with all the jobs that don't fit neatly into any other headquarters department. Moreover, they are staffed almost exclusively by police officers, who have few or no research or analytic skills.

Nor are individual police departments supported effectively by national institutions that encourage and assume some of the financial and political burdens of innovation. As noted earlier, the United

States is reasonably well equipped with foundations and government agencies that support research and arrange meetings to discuss its results. Indeed, it seems safe to say that none of today's important changes in policing would have occurred without the contributions of institutions like the National Institute of Justice, the Police Foundation, and the Police Executive Research Forum. But even so, their support is limited. James K. Stewart, director of the National Institute of Justice, is fond of observing that the United States spends several times more on dental research than it does on criminal justice research.[15]

In England and Australia the problem is not only the level of support but also its focus. The research that is undertaken is largely technical.[16] It studies what bulletproof vests work best or what kinds of police batons should be issued. Matters of program effectiveness, let alone strategic issues, are rarely addressed.[17] In England the Home Office Research and Planning Branch was set up in 1963, charged with determining how the police service could use its personnel most productively and what to do about the grave problem of serious and unsolved crime. Initially the branch concentrated on central operational issues, such as Criminal Investigation Department (detective) methods and the effectiveness of foot patrol. Since expansion and reorganization—it is now called the Scientific Research and Development Branch—it spends over 90 percent of its research budget on technical research.[18]

This Home Office department, as well as its counterpart in Australia, has always regarded the police as its primary client and has consequently stayed close to police forces. The result has been a nonthreatening, uncritical research agenda that is compatible with police priorities. By contrast, another Home Office department, the Research and Planning Unit, stands generally apart from the police, has a wider mandate and a more public audience, and tackles broader issues. The price it pays is lack of access to police forces.[19]

The greatest obstacle to innovation in policing, however, may well be the view, widely held by both the public and the police, that none is required, that the current strategy of policing is working well or at least is the best that can be expected. Darrel Stephens emphasizes the limiting effect of common public perceptions of the police role: "Both the police and the public share a narrow view of what police are supposed to do—fight crime. When you talk to the public, they'll tell you that the police are just there to protect them from crime. But when you look at the calls they make, a wholly different picture emerges."[20] The public is all too ready to give back what it has been fed over the years by the police. This superficial agreement on the nature of the police role provides no incentive for innovation.

Ways to Encourage Innovation

Faced with such apparently overwhelming obstacles to police innovation, it may be tempting to conclude that pursuing innovation is next to fruitless. Things are not, however, so bleak. In fact, patrol officers are already remarkably inventive and creative. One of their aspirations is to be regarded by their peers as "streetwise." And being streetwise, for patrol officers, means being inventive, having developed a large vocabulary of nonobvious solutions to problems, being a lateral thinker, being mature, and knowing when to take risks, how to get the impossible done, how to use contacts, and how to get neatly out of potentially painful situations. In this respect patrol officers are not the problem. They are frequently highly creative, and they value creativity.

This is an even better sign than it might seem. Recent research into how successful public-sector innovation occurs has highlighted several key themes, all of which bode well for the police if they can learn to take advantage of the energy lurking in ordinary officers.[21]

First, it appears that the final form of successful innovative programs (those implemented operationally on a broad scale) is often substantially different from how they were conceived. A lot of progress seems to be made along the way. Making room, then, for trial and error—followed by constructive alteration rather than stark choices between acceptance and abandonment—seems to be of critical importance in preventing the premature ditching of potentially fruitful ideas. Few roles allow more opportunity for trial and error than that of patrol officer.

Second, most successful public-sector innovations arise when the innovators address problems that are important to their current clients (rather, say, than when they seek a new application for an existing technology). They arise when individuals or organizations acknowledge and focus on real-life problems. Few people see more real-life problems than patrol officers.

Third, many successful innovations display the key elements of a case management system: that is, the job of certain line workers (the "case managers") is defined relatively broadly, in terms of responsibility for solving clients' problems rather than for carrying out specific procedures.[22] Further, one of the most powerful spurs to innovation seems to be coupling the ability to solve problems with the opportunity to see them firsthand, which means finding a way to combine in one person (or team) three things: creativity, the ability to transform ideas into reality (the power to implement), and the opportunity and obligation to confront clients' problems directly. This is not now the definition or the conception of patrol work, but it could be.

Policing's problem, then, lies in how its organizational culture and management style deal with front-line creativity. Generally, policing stunts its growth. It is interesting that "streetwise" has quite a different meaning for low-level supervisors, such as sergeants and lieutenants, than it does for patrol officers. For supervisors, "streetwise" means knowing all the tricks one's officers are likely to be up to, being able to nip them in the bud, and, above all, never being fooled or deceived by one's own people. Thus, even the lowest supervisory ranks reflect the command and control, disciplinary style of management, and they feel the obligation to control far more strongly than the obligation to solve problems. They are not, after all, held accountable for the continued existence of community problems; they are certainly held accountable if one of their officers steps out of line.[23]

We believe, therefore, that a wealth of talent, resourcefulness, and initiative is being applied at the street level in microcosmic ways: but that its acknowledgment, encouragement, and diffusion are cramped by a management mentality that focuses on minimizing the risk of misconduct and criticism. Police departments must somehow find a way to bring that inventiveness to the fore.

One key to doing so may be to recognize two essential ingredients of innovation. First, there must be organizational acknowledgment that a problem exists, which means recognizing clients' concerns as serious. Second, there must be organizational acknowledgment of the capacity to solve a problem, which may mean forming appropriate new alliances or recognizing the value of particular knowledge (such as Officer Jones's familiarity with the juvenile problems on Thirty-seventh Street) in a manner hitherto foreign to the department's idea of relevant expertise. Certainly, if Officer Jones is to apply herself to solving some difficult problem, the department needs to help her believe that she has something relevant and worthwhile to offer. This is why the strategic and administrative innovations associated with problem-solving and community policing are so important.

Motivating officers to bring their own knowledge and creativity to bear on departmental problems is a major task. They have to be both empowered and confronted: empowered by having the department recognize the value of their knowledge and skills (rather than their obedience, mistake avoidance, or conformity) and confronted by being encouraged to tackle daunting community problems and being held accountable by both the community and the department for their performance.

And if low-ranking officers are to be encouraged or expected to take risks, to put forward their ideas, and to take on difficult problems, the department's management style and disciplinary system have to undergo radical transformations. In policing as it presently stands no officer in his or her right mind would take on such challenges, at least not with any visibility. The combination of visibility and risk taking is, for the most part, the short road to disaster.

Policing is currently so focused on immediate results and the avoidance of error that it often cannot even understand the idea of an experiment or important adaptation. "People won't look at the Kansas City patrol experiment as a way of answering a question; they look at it as a program," says Darrel Stephens. "So they regard it as a failure. I quite often get people talking to me about 'that patrol program in Kansas City that didn't work.' But that's not a failure. We got useful information from that experiment—so it's a success." But the fear of failure, or the fear that experiment and trial and error will be seen as such, is enough to chill the best-intentioned and most creative officer. "If police managers are in the business of chopping off heads, that's what people will remember; it doesn't matter whether it's operational or research," says Stephens. "The issue is the level of risk that officers see as being attached to the business of making decisions, whether it's operational or experimental."[24]

That level is currently very high indeed, but some departments are trying to reduce it. The San Diego police have recently written into their disciplinary procedures the recognition that mistakes happen and are essential to learning.[25] In June 1987 England's West Midlands force pared its instruction manual to the bone and issued a single laminated card to every officer entitled "Our Duties as West Midlands Police Officers." On it are eleven "commandments" laying out the department's new values. The first of these tenets goes straight to the heart of this problem:

1. Reasonableness of Action

Instead of relying on the written word and sanction of the Procedure Manual to identify and prove specific transgressions, conduct will be judged subjectively and in a broader context to determine whether disciplinary action should be taken in respect of deviations from the published procedures. If mistakes occur, as they inevitably will, the question of motive and reasonableness in the light of the known facts will be considered rather than non-compliance with the Procedure Manual.

What the San Diego and West Midlands departments have both realized is that they have to break the vicious circle of failure and recrimination, which operates like this:

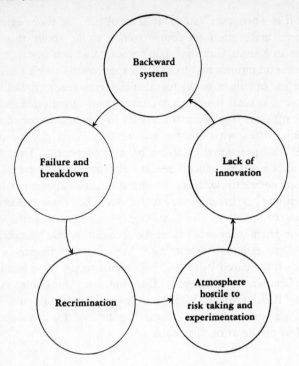

The system's backwardness, in the sense of not being adapted to a changing environment, produces failures. By tradition, after some kind of failure "heads roll." The allocation of blame and the recrimination that ensue preserve an atmosphere in which no one is prepared to take risks or try a new idea. That atmosphere in turn inhibits organizational innovation, the lack of which keeps the system backward.

Only one link in this circle can be severed: the one between failure and recrimination. Hence the explicit recognition, in San Diego, the West Midlands, and other forward-moving forces, that breakdown of operational plans or programs can have a multitude of causes not attributable to personnel. And breaking that link is, to a very great degree, the job of the largely unseen and unsung middle ranks of police departments.

The Role of Middle Management

Whatever the chief executive of a department says, or means, or intends, professional life should be like for the patrol officer, it is the sergeant, the lieutenant, and occasionally the captain who shape the patrol officer's professional environment. We have said much about the debilitating effects of rigid command and control, the prevalent style of these middle managers. But what aspects of their role need to change in an adaptive and innovative department?

First, middle managers separate knowledge from power in the department. Knowledge of the harsh realities of community problems has normally resided at the street level, and power over resources has been carefully preserved at the top. Middle managers must stop being a barrier between the two and start bringing them together. In particular they must encourage street-level officers to identify substantial community (or client) problems, help street officers win organizational acknowledgment of the importance of such problems, and bring appropriate organizational expertise and energy to bear.

Second, middle managers largely control the nature of a department's professional environment. They must understand the importance of coping constructively with failure, valuing ideas, and encouraging free and open communication, both positive and negative. It is only they who can break the link between failure and recrimination on an organizationwide scale. They must protect their officers from the political effects of legitimate failure.

Third, middle managers are the ones who can change the image of the procedure manual. Instead of an instrument of the disciplinary process, brought into play against wayward officers, it needs to become a fount of knowledge, guidance, and inspiration for patrol officers: a tool rather than a master. It is middle managers who invariably feel most threatened by any hint of diminished emphasis on manuals. Darrel Stephens notes wryly that "when you actually look at manuals' content you find it's not so much guidance for the street level as it is a focus on all the internal stuff—you know, where your collar brass has to be located, how you wear your hat, what you put in which box on what form—and so on ad infinitum about procedures. What it says most about is the internal management style."[26] Middle managers must sacrifice that security.

Fourth, it is principally middle managers who have routinely quashed new ideas; it is they who must embody the new organizational value "never kill an idea."

Fifth, midlevel managers must have a new role in defining work: to encourage their officers to tackle harder, broader problems and empower them by letting them know that the organization values their knowledge and expertise. They must identify deficiencies in capacity that their officers need help with and form the necessary partnerships to help solve problems. And they must change individual recognition of a problem into organizational acknowledgment and change individual recognition of a solution into organizational appreciation and education. In short, it falls to midlevel managers to harness their officers' creative abilities and from them fashion organizational adaptiveness.

Finally, middle managers control the extent to which discretion can be built explicitly into the value system rather than being hidden and denied. Thus they must tie the broad discretion granted to street officers to political support—through being tight on values and loose on methods and techniques.[27] Ultimately, middle managers have power to choose what they will do: tolerate yet another temporary change in the weather or lend their support to a change in the climate.

COMMISSIONING OFFICERS

Let us look at what all this might mean to the sort of police officers a new policing might call for. We will draw our two subjects, Norman Clarke and Nick Hollings, from England's resident beat system, under which officers still walk or ride beats in time-honored tradition.[28] Not all resident beat officers show the dedication to community service and the operational creativity Clarke and Hollings do, but all work in a style of policing that allows such qualities a chance to surface, and Clarke and Hollings took full advantage of that opportunity. We will see how they did their jobs and how their performance was managed and measured by their department. The picture that emerges gives clear pointers to the directions in which progressive police leaders will want to lead their departments.

Two Model Officers

In December 1980 Police Constable Norman Clarke, at the unusually young age of twenty-two, and with only 4 years' experience in police work, became resident constable on a residential estate of predominantly public housing in a market town close to London. He had always wanted to be a policeman. After secondary education (but no degree) he had joined the police service in 1977. After four years of patrol work (reactive policing on regular shifts), he had proved himself confident, capable, cheerful, and conscientious. He was enormously popular with his colleagues; he laughed a lot and made others laugh with a lively sense of mischief. He gained respect from colleagues and supervisors alike, mostly for his conscientiousness. If something needed doing, he would invariably do it, and from a sense that it needed to be done rather than to curry favor.

So it was that he was given responsibility for one of the most difficult estates in town. His "patch" (which also included an adjacent private estate) housed at least 15,000, including roughly 30 percent of the town's active criminals. From the point of view of a resident beat officer, it was huge.* PC Clarke relished his new challenge. "I held the resident's job to be the most important," he says. "I was looking for satisfaction in my work. It was the chance to really help the public—and that's what policing is really about. I felt I knew patrol policing—I'd done that, and I didn't think I could get any better at it. But the resident's job was different because you lived or fell by your own success or failure. It mattered how you got on with the public."

Clarke got on with them extremely well; in fact, to all appearances, they loved him. So did the media. Every holiday, every school festival, he was there, and week after week photos of this stocky, bearded policeman pedaling around the estate on his bicycle ap-

---

*The same area was covered by three beat officers in 1988.

peared in the local newspapers. "I never went out of my way to get publicity," he says. "I never asked the press to do a story or anything like that. Yes, they did keep on taking my picture. I don't really know why—maybe it's because they liked what they saw. The public certainly liked it. They used to come and tell me that they hadn't had a policeman of their own for at least ten years. I was approachable, I suppose—out in the street on my bicycle—they knew they could just flag me down and talk. Often it seemed that talking about their problem or fear was enough. I didn't actually need to do anything—just let them get it off their chest and they felt better.

"If I had been busy or on holiday and they hadn't seen me for a couple of weeks, they would complain next time they saw me. They'd say, 'Where have you been—we haven't seen you around the place for a while. We thought you'd deserted us.' Often when I wasn't there it wasn't my fault—but I'd get my ear bent about it all the same when I reappeared."

"Ownership" of a policeman in this way sounds like an expensive, and perhaps useless, luxury. But Clarke was under no illusion about the nature or magnitude of his task. It was certainly more than promoting good police-public relations. "My main aim was to have everyone living in perfect harmony on [the estate]," he says. "That sounds a bit idealistic, I suppose—but I saw my job was to deal with disharmony. Disharmony doesn't necessarily mean crime. I mean by it whatever bothers people. Their problems. Not ours. I found out what bothered people. At that time, on that estate, it was mostly kids. They'd hang around and be abusive, and drop litter, and walk over people's gardens. They would ride their bicycles and motorbikes up on the pavement [sidewalk]. That bothered lots of people—they thought of the danger for their own youngsters. Some kids would do wheel spins on the pavement in their cars. Then there were feuds between families—usually over stupid stuff. But they could get out of hand. They'd end up breaking each others' windows and hitting each other's kids if you didn't get a grip on it. I suppose my definition of disharmony was whatever affected people's peace of mind, or affected their family."

These are, in fact, exactly the problems that are most awkward for a reactive police service to deal with. They constantly recur as fleeting visit after fleeting visit fails to dent the underlying issues. So how was Clarke able to deal with such "disharmonies"?

"With the feuds," he says, "it was normally enough that I knew about it. Sometimes I'd have to spell out the facts of life to these people—but them knowing I knew was normally enough. And, of course, the fact that it would be me again next time. Not someone else. So I knew the whole picture. They couldn't have me over about the history of the thing. That was the difference—if another policeman turned up and dealt with a call he wouldn't know the background. They'd lie to him. He wouldn't know who to believe, and so he couldn't do much."

Continuity gave him an advantage with the youth as well. He says, "If a car rolls up after a complaint, the kids are anonymous. They know the police aren't going to arrest them, and they know they don't know who they are. So they push them close to the limit—abusive, disobedient, that sort of thing. Really they are laughing at them because they know the car is only going to be there for five minutes at the most. Then gone, and they can carry on. For the patrol car it's a nothing call, 'no offences disclosed' and that's the end of it. But what a difference when I nip round the corner on my bike. They never hear me coming, and they don't know when I'm about and when I'm not. And I say, 'Hallo, Sean,' or Micky, or whatever. I know them. So they're not anonymous anymore. I talk to them about the estate, about their behavior—how it affects people. And they know it's not a five-minute lecture, then gone. They know we will continue this discussion next time—with their parents and schoolteachers if necessary. I think they do begin to think about what responsible behavior is, what's OK for a lark and what isn't. I don't just 'move them on.' That accomplishes nothing. We talk about where it's OK to hang about, and where it isn't, and why.

"I talked to the people on the estate too, about the kids. I had to tell them I couldn't take the kids away. Some seemed to think I could. No—they were there, and had a right to use the streets, and my job was to make sure they didn't bother people. Sometimes that meant moving the kids; other times it meant telling the complainants to be more tolerant."

Because of the extent to which the estate's problems centered on youngsters, Clarke made it a point, with the local schools' blessing, to see every child in class at least once a term, talking about road safety, shoplifting, drugs, alcohol, and the police. He soon discovered that this made him known to the children's families as well. He also arranged quarterly meetings, in conjunction with the resident beat officer from an adjacent beat, with representatives of local institutions: headmasters, ministers, youth workers, doctors, store owners, teachers, probation officers, social workers, and the like (politicians were invited but rarely appeared). The sessions had no agenda; the idea was to allow any local concerns to surface and plan strategies to address them. On one occasion the group realized that glue sniffing was catching on and causing trouble not only for the young abusers but also for the schools and shops. Clarke and his fellow officer were able to mount an effective campaign to nip the trend in the bud.

Like officers in Wilshire and elsewhere, Clarke soon found that such closeness to the community meant information, not infrequently about crime and criminals. Neighbors, mothers, even wives passed on tips leading to arrests. Clarke usually arranged for other officers to make the pickups. Then, he says, "I used to visit the villains after they'd been released and say to them, 'I hear those CID [Criminal Investigation Department] bastards nicked you again. What's it about?' Chances are they'd tell me what someone else was up to. It worked pretty well." Most of his time, nonetheless, was spent on noncriminal matters. "Most of the people on my beat," he says dryly, "were noncriminals."

Clarke counts his three years as a resident beat officer as invaluable experience—and the most satisfying job he has done. He does not, however, think that his department understood what he was trying to do there, or how to measure or reward it. Part of the evidence came from his formal evaluations. "They couldn't measure how well I did the job, because they had no idea what it was," he says. "The only thing they could measure was my paperwork; the inquiries and my process [paperwork, specifically on prosecutions that do not involve arrests]. So that's what they measured, I suppose. Actually, what the governors thought seemed to depend entirely on the occasional letters which they'd receive from people on my patch. My sergeant knew that I was out there—because, as luck would have it, he used to cycle across the lower part of my beat on his way to and from work. He saw me out chatting to people often enough to know I wasn't skiving.

"I remember one staff appraisal with the superintendent. Half the time we spent talking about one man who had written in about kids riding on the pavement. Why hadn't I dealt with it? As soon as he mentioned the problem I was able to tell him the name of the man, his address, the nature of all his disabilities, and the name of his dog. And I told him the history of the man's problem. I think he was taken aback."

Other evidence came from what the department really seemed to value, which was not community work. "A lot of sergeants saw the resident officers as being available for anything. They obviously didn't regard our being on our patches as important," he says. Clarke was forever being reassigned to take statements for road accidents or from witnesses for other police forces, pursue delinquent car taxes, transport prisoners, or fill in for missing officers at the station. "What I regard as the important work—the real police work—I ended up doing on my way from one bit of paperwork to the next," he says. "The good thing is that once people knew who I was, and I was well established, just cycling down the road a couple of times seemed to do a lot of good."

As far as Clarke was aware, none of his supervisors made any attempt to discover what the public thought of his work. "Most of the time I don't think the governors knew who I was," he says. "I'm sure the superintendent didn't recognize my face. The trouble was I was always out of the station. Out of sight, out of mind."

Out of sight, out of mind eventually brought Clarke back into the mainstream of reactive policing. He wanted to be promoted, knowing that he was well motivated and highly capable. He had already proved his ability as a reactive patrol officer but felt that he would never "get noticed" as a resident beat officer. He asked for a posting back onto regular shift work in January 1984, having failed to be recommended for promotion each time he had applied as a beat officer. After working patrol cars for three years, he was promoted to sergeant in 1988.

This is not a particularly happy story. Officers as conscientious and resourceful as Clarke should not have to abandon what they're best at, and where they do the most good, in order to be noticed and promoted. Still, many of his troubles might reasonably be chalked up to growing pains in his department. Clarke was one of the first few officers to be assigned to a resident beat in his town, and one might expect that his role took a little sorting out, that the organization as a whole needed time to accommodate it properly. Many of his frustrations could be seen as natural for a pioneer. Some were alleviated; for example, a special "process section" was set up to take the bulk of routine inquiries away from resident beat officers.

By 1987, though, the resident beat system in Clarke's town was well established and had been expanded to the whole subdivision. There were twelve resident beat officers, each with a specific area and reporting to one sergeant. Such schemes are now commonplace throughout the Home Counties, as police managers take note of public pressure for a new style of policing. Chief constables are eager to portray their forces as progressive. Invariably forces now have active community-services departments based at headquarters and point to the growing number of resident beat officers as a measure of their commitment to partnership with the community.

That is the theory, but what about the practice? Are beat officers now appropriately trained, clear about the nature of their task, sure that good performance is properly defined, measured, and rewarded? Has the police culture changed? Do resident beat officers receive appropriate organizational support for their work? To what extent has the mainstream of policing altered its style?

In 1988 PC Nick Hollings found himself a resident beat officer in the same town. Among his colleagues (both resident beat officers and patrol officers) he is widely respected for his reassuring earthiness, initiative, and wisdom. He shares many of Norman Clarke's values. Hollings, like Clarke, defines his task in terms of "whatever bothers people, whatever affects their quality of life" and recognizes that this extends far beyond the prevention and detection of crime. He cares about the people in his area. "Any problem on that patch is my problem—whether I'm on or off [duty]," he says. "If incidents aren't dealt with properly, they'll only reoccur. If I can't deal with the problem, then I'm a buffoon. It's my reputation at stake."

Hollings also has his own definition of "serious crime." "I measure it in terms of people's ability to recover—to bounce back," he says. "So an expensive break [burglary] in a fancy detached house may not bother the occupants much. They're well insured, and the dog scared the burglars off, and they can fit alarms. But an old-age pensioner who has her purse taken the day after she collected her week's pension—that destroys them. Stuff like that I go back and see them time and time again to try and build them up. An old lady's purse has got to be more serious than a Securicor van robbery."

With those criteria in mind, Hollings often puts his energy into problems the rest of the force never took very seriously or had any hope of solving. One of his first challenges was a chronic alcoholic with a stormy home life who had a long history of causing scenes in his neighborhood. "The [police] station has had hundreds of calls on him," Hollings says. "When patrols are sent up there, they don't know what to make of him. But now he reacts superbly to me, because I pop in there from time to time and give him a quid for a coffee, and I sometimes give his wife a cigarette. I buy sweets for the kids. Then when there's a flare-up I take Johnny off to the park and dump him right in the middle of it—it gives him time to cool off on the way home. He knows it's fair. That way he doesn't upset anyone."

What Hollings was not able to correct, he was to a large extent able to alleviate. "There's a sweet young couple next door who bought their house in complete ignorance. When they found out what they had for neighbors they were mortified. I sat down with them and talked through the history, persuaded them that there was nothing dangerous or malicious about him, and tried to get them to see the comical side of it. Eventually, they believed me."

Like his fellows in Wilshire and Baltimore County, Hollings's different sense of what matters and what should be done about it often leads him to call in other social-service agencies. "I had the local shopkeeper tell me about an old boy who, in the middle of a harsh winter, had wandered into the shop in his pajamas and slippers. He had three hundred pounds in his hand, and he bought a can of baked beans and a tin of sardines. That's all. The shopkeeper thought I ought to know. We got that old boy a daily visit from a welfare visitor—an hour every day. He just needed some help looking after himself. I made a point of going back later and telling the shopkeeper what I'd done, so he didn't think he had wasted his time. He was really pleased something had been done, and that he had been able to help."

Hollings gets no more support for his work, however, than Clarke did before him, from either his peers or his superiors. "I get all this gung ho crap from the patrol car drivers about 'we're the superheroes on section,'" he says. "Well, I've done thirteen years of that, and it means hardly anything to the public. My supervisors just have no idea what I'm up to. A day's work, for a resident, is not quantifiable. Most of the work I do is not subject to 'incident logging.' So it doesn't get recorded. After a year they could go around and ask—then they'd find out. But they don't. The sergeant really only judges us by the paperwork, and I don't do much of that."

Some of Hollings's biggest problems, in fact, come when the department *does* notice what he and some of the other resident beat officers have done. Clarke's school-visiting scheme, for instance, which he had done informally and with his own area's problems in mind, attracted official attention and was made mandatory departmentwide. Hollings found such uniformity ridiculous. "It was probably great for his estate—it was a council estate, and the problem was kids," he says. "Now we have got the schools program—you know—all official. Sanctioned by the chief constable, so we all have to do it. All the lectures are prepared up at headquarters and we have to go and deliver them. A lot of it's really embarrassing. We have slide shows that are hand-drawn cartoons. We have to teach them the history of the police—they don't want to know that. It is really tough to make some of the lessons interesting. Some are OK, but I really don't need that on my patch. I don't have a problem with kids in the same way. For me it's not a high priority, but we all have to do it."

All in all, then, as much as he loves his job and endorses the direction the police are taking with resident beat officers, Hollings feels, as Clarke did, that his department is not with him. "They are only playing at it," he says. "I think my beat is four times the size it should be. But then there are only 12 of us out of 180 officers working in the town. They could find another 12 easily—another

30 if they really took it seriously. I'm on my beat at most 25 percent of the time, and that's more than most. But it's nothing like enough. I get absolutely no support from the [police station], because they don't know what I'm doing. And I get complained at all the time by the residents, because they want to see more of me. I think there is still no will within the police to take this seriously. It's still seen as the soft option."

Clarke and Hollings are exceptional police officers: highly motivated, sensible, responsive, caring. They are also inventive and courageous in living out their own vision of what it means to police the community. Their stories, however, do not reveal a police department that has shaped and guided their views or that actively encourages and supports what they stand for.

Rather, the picture that emerges from this particular, but perhaps typical, shire county town is that policing remains stolidly traditional and reactive. The management structure continues to be inflexible, the culture essentially hostile to the new philosophy. Dedication to community partnership and energetic local accountability remains on the periphery of policing; the core remains insular and highly protective of its image as a professional crime-fighting unit.

That Clarke and Hollings maintain their convictions in the face of organizational indifference is remarkable. It reflects well on the qualities of these police officers—their strength of character and their ideological commitment to valuable public service.

Perhaps we should conclude that, in this case at least, policing has not escaped the powerful clutches of the reform model—even though the public statements and theoretical commitments of some police chiefs would suggest otherwise.

A Prescription

The remaining problem is to prescribe an institutional environment that will actually support and promote the kind of humane, responsive, problem-solving policing that Norman Clarke and Nick Hollings so ably exemplify. The whole body of the police department has to be able to see management's commitment to such a style, and that visibility requires that all formal and informal aspects of the working environment reflect that commitment. The informal, cultural features, which take longer to change, we have discussed in chapters 2 and 5. Here we will concentrate on the formal aspects of the work environment: the systems, structures, and technologies.

1. High Status for Patrol Officers

Departmental commitment to a new style of policing can only be credible if appropriate status is accorded to patrol officers. The relative status of a job is most clearly revealed by its rate of pay and benefits, its degree of autonomy, the level of training provided in preparation, its associated privileges, the provision of resources, and its career prospects. At present nearly all these status indicators point to the detective as being the high-status role in policing. In many cities detectives receive higher pay than patrol officers. Almost universally they receive extra, specialized training. They operate over wide areas in plain clothes and have greater flexibility in their working hours, along with plenty of opportunity for overtime and expenses. A high proportion of senior officers have risen through the ranks in the investigations structure. There is extensive administrative backup for detectives that is often not available to patrol officers. All these features make good sense in the conceptual framework of a "crime-fighting" professionalism and provides a good illustration of an organization providing credible support to its high-priority functions.

They also give a clear insight into how the patrol officer's role can be professionalized:

- Pay them more, if possible.
- Allow them discretion over their use of plain clothes or uniform.
- Provide each with a dedicated telephone line or extension. Equip each line with an answering machine so callers can leave messages for "their" police.
- Allow them flexibility in setting their hours.
- Give them business cards.
- Provide them with an administrative backup team (which could

include their immediate manager) capable of helping them perform meaningful analyses of problems and design and use of questionnaires, newsletters, and other forms of research and communication.

- Make special training available to them to cover topics such as
  a. Juveniles and juvenile delinquency
  b. Liaison and cooperation with other public agencies
  c. Analysis techniques, basic statistics, and the use of microcomputers
  d. Public speaking
  e. Crime prevention and analysis
  f. Problem-solving methods
  g. Community institutions and their roles, capabilities, and resources
  h. Effective community consultation
- Give them small enough beats to enable them to make an impact.*
- Begin with officers who have credibility with their peers.
- Discontinue the present practice of regarding them as "available" for any other task.
- Give them primary responsibility for investigating crime in their areas, thus integrating the basic detective function with the problem-solving approach on a geographic basis. (Leave it up to patrol officers to call in specialist assistance when they consider it necessary.)

2. Master Patrol Officers

Many departments have no means for officers to gain status or recognition other than promotion. Pay scales are related first to rank and second to length of service. Frequently these are the only formal pay-dependent factors. Informally some extra financial reward has been available for detectives (and even more for those who work on

---

*There is a widespread tendency to "cover the whole town," however few the neighborhood beat officers. We feel this practice is often counterproductive. It frustrates the officers, provides inadequate service, and ultimately discredits the concept of neighborhood policing. By keeping beats small enough (however few beat officers there are), departments allow their effect to be more quickly seen, and the public in other areas may well demand similar service, thus providing external support for even greater commitment to this style of policing.

central squads) through enhanced opportunities for working overtime and claiming expenses.

Such a system means that in virtually all departments there is
no way a first-class patrol officer can be rewarded or recognized
without being removed from patrol. The natural consequence of this
situation is that ambitious and capable officers are not, on the whole,
attracted to patrol work. Worse, police managers have tended to
regard foot beat assignments in particular as suitable for officers who
are old, tired, and approaching the end of their service without any
hope of promotion. This assumption takes reassurance from the mistaken belief that the community will appreciate a mature face even
if its bearer lacks motivation and initiative. It grossly devalues the
potential and standing of beat work.

There are, as other forms of recognition, the occasional com-
mendations and unscheduled "reports of good work." But, as Norman Clarke comments, these customarily relate to "heroic policing"
rather than "good policing." They are essentially irrelevant to the
broader question of motivation.

There needs to be some career structure for patrol officers, some
new method of granting them higher status and recognition. Some
departments have considered ranks such as master patrol officer,
which would carry a significant pay increase as proper recognition
for officers who have mastered the complexities and subtleties of
effective beat policing.[29] (Such status could also include some responsibility for training other beat officers, but such commitments
would have to be carefully limited. Los Angeles's senior lead officer
rank brings both training responsibility and pay increases, although
the extra pay is minimal.)

The overriding objective of such a scheme would be to lengthen
the time successful beat officers can be kept on their beats without
slowing their career progress.

3. Relevant Performance Measures

The comments of Clarke and Hollings clearly reveal their feelings of isolation from the main body of the service. In large part
these arose from their belief that their supervisors were not aware

of their work and did not bother, or were not able, to measure crucial aspects of their performance.[30]

A meaningful monitoring and appraisal system for beat officers could exhibit features such as the following:

- It could measure their knowledge about their area, its residents and their problems, and its community institutions.
- It could log problems, not just incidents.
- It could record the process of problem solving through steps like:
  1. Problem identification
  2. Analysis of causes
  3. Design and implementation of action
  4. Monitoring of the action's effectiveness and subsequent reassessment.[31]
- It could emphasize initiative and avoid penalizing officers for trying solutions that fail.
- It could formally measure community satisfaction with the officer's work.[32] This assessment inevitably involves some kind of public canvassing—either random or representative. Specific focus on the views of other community institutions might also be appropriate.*
- It could provide a regular opportunity for the community to highlight any problems that, in its view, are receiving inadequate or unsuitable police attention.

It may even be possible to construct some meaningful performance measure for beat officers that specifically relates to the decrease in demand on emergency-response patrol cars as a result of their work. If a beat officer is effective in identifying and addressing community concerns, then the calls that continue to come in on the 911 system from that beat increasingly should be isolated, unpredictable emergencies. Repeat calls from the same complainant or about the same problem should tail off as the underlying problems are dealt with. And nonurgent calls should go to the beat officer's telephone rather than to central control.

*The system has to do this with sufficient intelligence to allow for the general antipolice feeling in some neighborhoods, so officers who take on "tough beats" are not penalized.

Imagine what would happen if a beat officer, during his or her first week on the beat, could be presented with an analysis of all the calls for service received from the area in the previous six months. And imagine he or she was then told that a significant performance measure would be the *decrease* in such calls over the next six months. Naturally there would still be occasional emergencies out of the beat officer's control. But the officer's attention would immediately be focused on repeat callers, sources of danger and anxiety in the community, and the identification and solution of underlying problems— exactly the commission a beat officer needs.

4. Learning from Street Officers

The isolation beat officers feel might also be overcome by creating professional forums in which they could discuss their work with one another and with their superiors. Currently these discussions occur in the locker room, with all the accompanying implications of snickering and secrecy. The alternative would be some sort of formal meeting in which patrol officers involved in a community forum, a neighborhood or municipal partnership, a problem-solving effort, or the like could review them with their peers and superiors. At the outset, such meetings might prove a valuable way of introducing new methods to a department. In the longer run, they would provide a basis for sharing knowledge and building an operationally based understanding of what works and what doesn't in dealing with various kinds of problems. Once the tradition of candor had been established, these meetings and case reviews might provide the basis for quality assurance in a truly professionalized police department, just as professional standard-review organizations now do for hospitals and other medical institutions.

It will also be important to provide opportunities in the department's planning and resource-allocation processes for individual officers who invent a new response to a problem to develop it further. If the problem on which they are working becomes larger, more complex, or more time consuming than anticipated, the officers ought to be able to ask for additional resources without surrendering their control over the effort, much as general practitioners can command the many resources of a hospital to help them deal with difficult health problems. If a problem is small but common, and their response to it is judged effective, the innovative officers might be encouraged to train others in their method or to test the method more systematically and across a broader range of circumstances than they could by themselves.

All these ideas have in common the awareness that police departments can learn from the experience of operational officers, and that they should construct methods to allow these officers to share their knowledge. Officers with this sort of increased standing and latitude can become the department's teachers and guides.

Perhaps the most striking fact about Norman Clarke's and Nick Hollings's thoughtful and creative approach to policing is that they were able to carry it off at all, despite the apparent lack of departmental support. They offer a salutary, and perhaps elementary, lesson for executives who aim to implement much broader and more radical changes in policing. Those chiefs would do well to remember that there are, in their own departments, officers who—through their own experience and creativity—have already developed images of what policing could and should be: images that differ significantly from the established norm, often in ways that promise both effectiveness and substantial public support.

In many departments, then, the first essential step toward new and better policing may well be for chiefs to set about creating an environment that nurtures and encourages good ideas. That means finding the Clarkes and the Hollingses, and giving them voice in the debate about what constitutes progress. Just to do that—simply to give creative officers a chance to do good work—remains, given the managerial styles and organizational cultures of most departments, a major challenge.

And, of course, it is only the beginning. Most of what Clarke and Hollings did could be classed as street-level innovation. Their good ideas were constrained by inflexible departmental prescriptions for resource allocation, supervision, and performance evaluation.

229

They were for the most part able to make only those changes that would remain invisible to, or squeeze into the cracks of, the rest of their department.

More ambitious and ultimately more promising developments—major program, administrative, and strategic innovations like COPE, decentralization, and problem-solving policing—will never take root without much deeper and more fundamental changes in departments' constitutions. The longer-term, and truly substantial, challenge for today's police chiefs is to produce the kind of adaptability, thoughtfulness, creativity, and democratic purpose that these two officers embody: *but to do so for the whole department,* not just for individual officers.

So, changing a police department demands flexibility and openness at every level. It requires programmatic changes like COPE, Wilshire's community mobilization project, and Newport News's problem-oriented policing that empower the department to take on bigger, more intractable, and more geographically dispersed problems than Clarke and Hollings were able to handle. It requires administrative changes, like the London Met's desquadding, John Avery's geographical organization, and Kevin Tucker's new political relationships, sufficient to make the whole department flexible, responsive, and responsible. And it requires, perhaps most important of all, a basic openness to creative strategic thought: a persistent and energetic dedication of the whole department—not just the chief—continually to revisit the questions "who are the police?" "what can we do?" and "where should we fit in the life of our city?"

This is a commitment of the highest order, and the sustained labor it will demand is clearly enormous. It is a challenge, however, that the police must take up. The old ways, as the streets of our cities so often make so clear, are no longer enough. The promise of a policing fired by new values, new openness, new partnerships, and new creativity is also enormous, as the residents of Link Valley, New Briarfield, and more and more places like them can attest. It is a promise that must be kept.

Conclusion

■

$\mathbf{D}$URING THE TIME we have spent researching and writing this book, we have occasionally been asked if we could identify the one police department that in our opinion has made the most progress; or is closest to our ideal in its strategies, organization, and methods; or is in some way the best.

The answer is no. We understand the appeal of the question: if there were one model department, the rest of us could stop thinking and simply follow its lead. But the reality is that very few departments, despite some heroic attempts, have made much progress at all in escaping the allure of the reform, or professional, model of policing. We have tried to describe in some detail the bonds that restrain policing and inhibit open and honest contemplation of its future. We have tried to outline the first essential steps of the way ahead. But we have not claimed that these steps, or any subsequent ones, will be easy or fast. Nor do we do so now. We expect progress, but we expect it to come slowly and painfully.

But what of our champions? Are their departments not in some senses models worthy of imitation? Perhaps they are. But John Avery, Kevin Tucker, Sir Kenneth Newman, Lee Brown, and the other eminent figures whose experiences we've drawn on so heavily are unanimous as to the extent of their progress; each feels he has only just begun, and each was astonished to discover the magnitude of the task. They have taken important steps, in some cases steps that felt like "stepping off a cliff." They have made great and fundamental progress, but they remain uncertain of the terrain ahead and of their departments' capacities to accommodate and commit to change. For Tucker, Newman, and Brown it came time to leave their departments before the job was finished, even the relatively small piece of the job they could then see clearly.

We should not underestimate the kinds of changes we have been discussing in these pages: they are not administrative changes, or methodological ones, or even predominantly organizational ones. We have been talking of transforming police culture, restructuring police's and society's most deeply ingrained attitudes toward each other and expectations of each other. If we can liken such a realignment to turning a ship, then it is a huge ship, with a great deal of momentum. But we remain optimistic, or we would not have written this book. Big ships can be turned, and by comparatively small rudders. It just takes a long time and a lot of patience, and it requires the rudder to remain firmly set throughout.

There is a lesson here for police executives. Consider what makes for a comfortable life. All the time a vessel goes straight ahead, there is no pressure on and no need for the rudder. But try to turn the ship and constant turbulence surrounds it. Constant turbulence will surround those chiefs who set out to transform the style and nature of their departments. That task will demand perseverance, stamina, farsightedness, and a readiness for substantial buffeting from within and without.

We salute those police chiefs, and all those police officers, who dare to ask uncomfortable questions about their own and their colleagues' convictions, about their agencies, and about their policing heritage; who are prepared to sweep aside the traditional defenses of insularity; who find the courage to begin to rethink their basic mission, operational methods, and organizational structures; who are ready to ask of a demanding, difficult, and diverse public, What do you want of us? And to listen to all the answers.

Afterword

■

PERHAPS WE SHOULD say just a few words about how this book came to be written, and that means a few words about who we are and why we care about policing.

The book itself is one product of a most rewarding partnership—and each of the three authors is quite convinced that no one of us, and no two of us, could have produced it. Of course, writing together has not always been easy. It never is. We have very different backgrounds and came to the project with very different intentions and agendas. But working out, over three years, how our perspectives fit together has taught us all a great deal. It is the fruit of that integrative process that we expect to be most useful.

David M. Kennedy is the senior case writer at the Kennedy School of Government, Harvard University. He has nearly a decade's experience, much of it spent in the field, researching and writing about the workings of the public sector; he has in particular spent a great deal of time studying developments in policing in a variety of cities, both at home and abroad. Through his own observation, of both police and public, and with his eye for the telling detail, he brought to this partnership both a wealth of information and insight and a conviction that police could and should have a far greater impact on the quality of life in cities than anyone—either police or public— seems generally to recognize. He has also taken on the task of putting the finish of a professional writer on the text.

Mark Moore is the Daniel and Florence Guggenheim Professor of Criminal Justice at the Kennedy School of Government, Harvard, where he teaches a range of public management courses. He is also faculty chair of the Research Center of Criminal Justice Policy and Management at the school and is an acknowledged expert on many aspects of the criminal justice system, including drug policy and juvenile justice. He has many years' experience as a teacher of police executives and as a consultant to police departments. He brought to this project not only extensive specialist knowledge but also a new and exciting perspective on the role of public managers and executives in developing their institutions.

Malcolm Sparrow worked for ten years in the British Police Service, rising to the rank of detective chief inspector before resigning to accept a faculty position at Harvard. He has experience in patrol work at four different ranks as well as in criminal investigation, complaints and discipline investigation (internal affairs), research and planning, tactical firearms, and, most recently, as head of the Kent County Constabulary Fraud Squad. At the Kennedy School of Government he teaches statistics, probability theory, decision theory, financial management, and information systems. He is also a patent-holding inventor in computerized fingerprint comparison and is currently researching applications of network analysis techniques to computerized criminal intelligence analysis. Despite his apparent technical bent, he brought to this project a conviction, borne through his own professional experience, that police attitudes and culture are absolutely central to progress, or any lack thereof, in policing. He also brought, through his concern for police and the quality of policing, an insistence that all our criticisms of police be constructive.

Acknowledgments

∎

WE CONFESS TO having lost count of the people who have contributed to this volume, so we are not going to attempt to recall all their names here. Even if we could, we suspect our publisher would object to the length of the list. But we should at least mention them all by category.

First there are the police officers, hundreds of them (some chiefs, many not), who have been so generous with their time. They have shared their experiences as well as their feelings, and they have been willing to work hard with us to interpret their personal observations in the context of broader trends in policing. We have never found any shortage of thoughtfulness or sincerity, or concern to make policing better, among these men and women.

Second, we want to thank all the members of the National Executive Session on Policing, a panel of distinguished leaders in the field who have convened regularly at Harvard over the last five years to grapple with exactly the issues we have tried to address in this book. These members include many of the nation's most prominent police chiefs; some of its most thoughtful mayors, city managers, and police union executives; and the leaders of other concerned institutions, such as the Police Executive Research Forum and the Police Foundation; as well as just a few academics. This panel has also imported some invaluable international experience in the persons of Sir Kenneth Newman (ex-commissioner of the London Metropolitan Police) and John Avery (commissioner of the New South Wales Police).

What's so impressive about this group, and what has helped us so much in developing our thinking about policing, is that none of them has succumbed to the temptation to rest on laurels. All of them were entitled to do so, given their exalted positions and considerable career successes. But they all have been faithful and energetic in pressing ahead, in airing their frustrations and failures as well as their successes, in seeking advice and guidance as well as giving it, and in thrashing out their differences. The intellectual work done collectively by this group seems to us quite astonishing. We have been privileged to watch it and absorb it, as well as to make some modest contribution to it.

Given the final form and content of this book, we should single out from this group James "Chips" Stewart (director of the National Institute of Justice), Darrel Stephens (director of the Police Executive Research Forum), Professor Herman Goldstein (of the University of Wisconsin at Madison), and Hubert Williams (president of the Police Foundation): Chips Stewart for having reminded us countless times of the importance of the police as a democratic institution; Darrel Stephens not only for his extensive contributions to the material we have used (through both his actions and his words) but also for his generous encouragement; Herman Goldstein, whom we have come to regard as the father of "problem-oriented policing," for his extraordinary wisdom in these matters, so carefully thought out but always so eminently practical; and Hubert Williams for his constant attention to the special concerns of minorities and minority urban communities.

Many of the police chiefs whose innovations we have described in this book are known to us through these executive sessions. It would be quite wrong for us to claim either that these are the only pioneering executives in policing or that they are necessarily the furthest ahead in the kinds of progress we discuss. They are, quite simply, the ones we happen to know best. We are sure that there are many other equally compelling stories—which we hope one day to hear—from other places and departments.

Closer to home, we must thank our colleagues at the Kennedy School of Government's Criminal Justice Research Center—particularly Bob Trojanowitz, George Kelling, and Bob Wasserman. They have all profoundly shaped our views about policing, through both their writing and the unending supply of observations they bring home from their travels around the policing world.

Lee Brown falls in many categories—member of the executive session, pioneering police chief, research colleague, and friend. We wish him well as commissioner in New York City and could not hope anything better for this book than that it help to produce more like him.

Financial support for the executive sessions has come from the National Institute of Justice, the Charles Stewart Mott Foundation, the Daniel and Florence Guggenheim Foundation, and the Smith-Richardson Foundation. Support for development of the material in chapter 8 came partly from the Ford Foundation, through the Program on Innovations in the Public Sector, which is a joint enterprise of the Ford Foundation and the John F. Kennedy School of Government.

Notes

■

CHAPTER 1

1. For a description of the problems of American cities, see Michael C. D. MacDonald, *America's Cities* (New York: Simon and Schuster, 1984). For more analytic accounts, see Katherine L. Bradbury, Anthony Downs, and Kenneth A. Small, *Urban Decline and the Future of American Cities* (Washington, DC: Brookings, 1982), or Paul E. Peterson, ed., *The New Urban Reality* (Washington, DC: Brookings, 1985).
2. Wesley G. Skogan, "Fear of Crime and Neighborhood Change," 203–29, and Richard M. McGahey, "Economic Conditions, Neighborhood Organizations, and Urban Crime," 231–70, both in *Communities and Crime,* ed. Albert J. Reiss, Jr.; and Michael Tonry, vol. 8 of *Crime and Justice: A Review of Research* (Chicago: University of Chicago Press, 1986); James K. Stewart, "The Urban Strangler: How Crime Causes Poverty in the Inner City," *Policy Review* 37 (Summer 1986): 2–6; Charles E. Silberman, "Fear," in his *Criminal Violence, Criminal Justice* (New York: Random House, 1978), 3–20.
3. Bradbury, Downs, and Small, *Urban Decline,* 24–26.
4. Skogan, "Fear of Crime," 210.
5. Peter Kerr, "Citizen Anti-Crack Drive: Vigilance or Vigilantism?" *New*

York Times, 23 May 1988, B1; Patrice Gaines-Carter and Sari Horwitz, "Drug Patrol Turns Violent: Muslims Beat Man in NE Narcotics Market," *Washington Post,* 19 Apr. 1988, A1; Isabel Wilkerson, " 'Crack House' Fire: Justice or Vigilantism?" *New York Times,* 22 Oct. 1988, A1.

6. Jerome H. Skolnick and David H. Bayley, *The New Blue Line: Police Innovation in Six American Cities* (New York: Free Press, 1986); Jerome H. Skolnick and David H. Bayley, "Theme and Variation in Community Policing," pp. 1–37 in *Crime and Justice: A Review of Research,* vol. 10, ed. Michael Tonry and Norval Morris (Chicago: University of Chicago Press, 1988); James Q. Wilson and George L. Kelling, "Making Neighborhoods Safe," *Atlantic Monthly,* Feb. 1989, 46–52; David M. Kennedy, *Neighborhood Policing in Los Angeles,* Kennedy School of Government case C16-87-717.0 (Cambridge, MA: Harvard University, 1987); David M. Kennedy, *Neighborhood Policing: The London Metropolitan Police Force,* Kennedy School of Government case C15-87-770.0 (Cambridge, MA: Harvard University, 1986); David M. Kennedy, *Fighting Fear in Baltimore County,* Kennedy School of Government case C16-90-938.0 (Cambridge, MA: Harvard University, 1990); David M. Kennedy, *Fighting the Drug Trade in Link Valley,* Kennedy School of Government case C16-90-935.0 (Cambridge, MA: Harvard University, 1990).

7. This account of community policing in Wilshire is based heavily on Kennedy, *Neighborhood Policing in Los Angeles.* The research assistance of Detective Inspector P. E. C. Doone, New Zealand Police, is gratefully acknowledged.

8. Ibid. For a more complete account of the origin and operations of SLOs, see chapter 3.

9. James Q. Wilson and George L. Kelling, "Police and Neighborhood Safety: Broken Windows," *Atlantic Monthly,* Mar. 1982, 29–38.

10. Wesley G. Skogan and George E. Antunes, "Information, Apprehension, and Deterrence: Exploring the Limits of Police Productivity," *Journal of Criminal Justice* 7 (1979): 217–41.

11. This account of problem-solving policing in Newport News is drawn heavily from John E. Eck et al., *Problem Solving: Problem-oriented Policing in Newport News* (Washington, DC: National Institute of Justice, Police Executive Research Forum, 1987). We are also indebted to Darrel Stephens for frequent discussions on this case.

12. George L. Kelling et al., *The Kansas City Preventive Patrol Experiment: A Summary Report* (Washington, DC: Police Foundation, 1974).

13. Wickersham Commission Reports, no. 14, "Report on Police," Publication no. 6: *Patterson Smith Reprint Series in Criminology, Law Enforcement, and Social Problems* (Montclair, NJ: Patterson Smith, 1968), 5.

14. We are indebted to George L. Kelling for this telling detail.

15. Kansas City Police Department, *Response Time Analysis,* 3 vols. (Kansas City, MO: Board of Commissioners 1977–1979); William G. Spelman and Dale K. Brown, *Calling the Police: Citizen Reporting of Serious Crime* (Washington, DC: National Institute of Justice, 1984). For an alternative view, see Richard C. Larson and Michael F. Cahn, *Synthesizing and Extending the Results of Police Patrol Studies* (Washington, DC: National Institute of Justice, 1985), 85.

16. Eck et al., *Problem Solving,* 14.

17. Eric J. Scott, *Calls for Service: Citizen Demand and Initial Police Response* (Washington, DC: National Institute of Justice, 1981); Spelman and Brown, *Calling the Police;* William Spelman, Michael Oshima, and George Kelling, *On the Competitive Enterprise of Ferreting Out Crime: The Nature of the Problem, the Capacity of the Police, and the Assessments of Victims,* Program in Criminal Justice Policy and Management, Kennedy School of Government, Working Paper 87-05-01 (Cambridge, MA: Harvard University, June 1987).

18. Herman Goldstein, "Improving Policing: A Problem-oriented Approach," *Crime and Delinquency,* Apr. 1979, 236–58.

19. Eck et al., *Problem Solving,* 72.

20. This account of drug control in Link Valley is based heavily on David M. Kennedy, *Fighting the Drug Trade in Link Valley,* Kennedy School of Government case C16-90-935.0 (Cambridge, MA: Harvard University, 1990).

21. Ibid.

CHAPTER 2

1. George L. Kelling and Mark H. Moore, "The Evolving Strategy of Policing," *Perspectives on Policing,* no. 4 (Washington, DC: National Institute of Justice and Harvard University, Nov. 1988); Hubert Williams and Patrick V. Murphy, "The Evolving Strategy of Policing: A Minority View," *Perspectives on Policing,* no. 13 (Washington, DC: National Institute of Justice and Harvard University, Jan. 1990); George L. Kelling and James K. Stewart, "The Evolution of Contemporary

Policing," in *Municipal Police Administration* (Washington, DC: International City Management Association, forthcoming); Robert M. Fogelson, *Big-City Police: An Urban Institute Study* (Cambridge, MA: Harvard University Press, 1977); Leon Radzinowicz, *A History of English Criminal Law and Its Administration from 1750,* 5 vols. (London: Stevens and Sons, 1948–1986).

2. For a review of the evidence on the effectiveness of police tactics, see Mark H. Moore, Robert C. Trojanowicz, and George L. Kelling, "Crime and Policing," *Perspectives on Policing,* no. 2 (Washington, DC: National Institute of Justice and Harvard University, June 1988). For further discussion of these points, see chapter 4.

3. Allan Silver, "The Demand for Order in Civil Society: A Review of Some Themes in the History of Urban Crime, Police, and Riot," in *The Police: Six Sociological Essays,* ed. David J. Bordua (New York: John Wiley, 1967), 1–24; Charles Reith, *A New Study of Police History* (Edinburgh: Oliver and Boyd, 1956); Radzinowicz, *History of English Criminal Law.*

4. Metropolitan Police Act, 1829. See also *First Report of the Commissioner Appointed as to the Best Means of Establishing an Efficient Constabulary Force in the Counties of England and Wales* (London, 1829); Radzinowicz, *History of English Criminal Law,* 158–207.

5. Kelling and Stewart, "Evolution of Contemporary Policing."

6. Jonathan Rubenstein, *City Police* (New York: Farrar, Straus and Giroux, 1973).

7. Ibid., 11.

8. Fogelson, *Big-City Police,* 13–39.

9. Ibid., ch. 1, 17.

10. *Picturesque Expressions: A Thematic Dictionary* (Detroit, MI: Gale Research Co., 1985), 423.

11. Fogelson, *Big-City Police,* 16.

12. Ibid., prologue, 1–11.

13. Ibid., 89–90.

14. Ibid., prologue, 2.

15. Ibid., 5.

16. Ibid.

17. Ibid., 76–84.

18. Personal observation by Malcolm K. Sparrow.

19. Gene E. Carte and Elaine H. Carte, *Police Reform in the United States: The Era of August Vollmer, 1905–1932* (Berkeley: University of California Press, 1975); Orlando W. Wilson and Roy C. McLaren, *Police*

Administration, 4th ed. (New York: McGraw-Hill, 1977). William H. Parker's innovations in Los Angeles are chronicled in William A. Bopp, *A Short History of American Law Enforcement* (Springfield, IL: Charles C. Thomas, 1972).

20. Wilson and McLaren, *Police Administration.*

21. Fogelson, *Big-City Police,* 78.

22. George L. Kelling and James Stewart, *Municipal Police Administration* (forthcoming).

23. Eugene C. Peggio, *Blueprint for the Future of the Uniform Crime Reporting Program: Final Report of the UCR Study* (Washington, DC: U.S. Department of Justice, Bureau of Justice Statistics, May 1985).

24. Ibid.

25. National Crime Prevention Institute, *Operation Identification—Special Information Package* (Rockville, MD: National Criminal Justice Reference Service, 1977); William DeJong, *Arresting the Demand for Drugs: Police and School Partnerships to Prevent Drug Abuse,* National Institute of Justice Issues and Practices Report (Washington, DC: U.S. Department of Justice, Nov. 1987).

26. Personal communications to the authors during Executive Session in Community Policing, Program in Criminal Justice Policy and Management, John F. Kennedy School of Government, Harvard University, Cambridge, MA, 1985. This represents aggregate views of a number of police chiefs as expressed over a period of years.

27. Kent W. Colton, ed., *Police Computer Technology,* vol. 3 of *Urban Public Safety Systems* (Lexington, MA: D. C. Heath, 1978).

28. Ted Robert Gurr, ed., *The History of Crime,* vol. 1 of *Violence in America* (Newbury Park, CA: Sage, 1989).

29. "Offenses Known to Police and Percent Cleared by Arrest," table 4.18, p. 510, and "Estimated Percent Distribution of Personal and Household Victimizations," table 3.4, p. 285, in *Sourcebook of Criminal Justice Statistics, 1988,* ed. Katherine M. Jamieson and Timothy J. Flanagan (Washington, DC: U.S. Department of Justice, 1989).

30. Darrell Steffensmeier, Cathy Strieffel, and Miles D. Harer, "Relative Cohort Size and Youth Crime in the United States, 1953–1984," *American Sociological Review* 52 (Oct. 1987): 702–10; David Cantor and Kenneth C. Land, "Unemployment and Crime Rates in the Post World War II U.S.: A Theoretical and Empirical Analysis," *American Sociological Review* 50 (June 1985): 317–32; Terrence P. Thornberry and R. L. Christenson, "Unemployment and Criminal Involvement," *American Sociological Review* 49 (June 1984): 398–411.

31. See Barbara Boland et al., *The Prosecution of Felony Arrests, 1986,* Bureau of Justice Statistics Report (Washington, DC: U.S. Department of Justice, June 1989). See also Jamieson and Flanagan, eds., *Sourcebook of Criminal Justice Statistics, 1988.*

32. Mark A. R. Kleiman et al., *Imprisonment-to-Offense Ratios,* Bureau of Justice Statistics Discussion Paper (Washington, DC: U.S. Department of Justice, 15 Nov. 1988).

33. George L. Kelling et al., *The Kansas City Preventive Patrol Experiment: A Summary Report* (Washington, DC: Police Foundation, 1974).

34. Kansas City Police Department, *Response Time Analysis,* 3 vols. (Kansas City, MO: Board of Commissioners, 1977–1979); Eric J. Scott, *Calls for Service: Citizen Demand and Initial Police Response* (Washington, DC: National Institute of Justice, 1981); William G. Spelman and Dale K. Brown, *Calling the Police: Citizen Reporting of Serious Crime* (Washington, DC: National Institute of Justice, 1984). For an alternative view, see Richard C. Larson and Michael F. Cahn, *Synthesizing and Extending the Results of Police Patrol Studies,* National Institute of Justice Research Report (Washington, DC: U.S. Department of Justice, Apr. 1985).

35. David M. Kennedy, *Neighborhood Policing in Los Angeles,* Kennedy School of Government case C16-87-717.0 (Cambridge, MA: Harvard University, 1987).

36. "Comparison of Differences in Proportion of Call-for-Service Assignments to Study Units by Classifications of Incidents and Significance," table 18, p. 28, in John E. Boydstun, Michael E. Sherry, and Nicholas P. Moelter, *Patrol Staffing in San Diego: One-or-Two-Officer Units* (Washington, DC: Police Foundation, 1977); "Officers Activity Summary," table 3, p. 25, in John E. Boydstun and Michael E. Sherry, *San Diego Community Profile: Final Report* (Washington, DC: Police Foundation, 1975).

37. Peter W. Greenwood, Jan M. Chaiken, and Joan Petersilia, *The Criminal Investigation Process* (Lexington, MA: D. C. Heath, 1977); John Eck, *Solving Crimes: The Investigation of Burglary and Robbery* (Washington, DC: Police Executive Research Forum, 1984).

38. For a description of private reactions to crime, see Wesley G. Skogan and Michael G. Maxfield, *Coping with Crime; Individual and Neighborhood Reactions,* vol. 124 of Sage Library of Social Research (Beverly Hills, CA: Sage, 1981).

39. Wesley G. Skogan, "Community Organizations and Crime," in *Crime and Justice: An Annual Review of Research,* vol. 10, ed. Michael Tonry and orval Morris (Chicago: University of Chicago Press, 1988), 39–

78. For the results of recent surveys on what citizens do to defend themselves, see Catherine J. Whitaker, *Crime Prevention Measures*, Bureau of Justice Statistics Special Report NCJ-100438 (Washington, DC: U.S. Department of Justice, Mar. 1986).

40. William C. Cunningham and Todd H. Taylor, *The Hallcrest Report: Private Security and Police in America* (Portland, OR: Chancellor, 1985), 39–52.

41. Albert J. Reiss, Jr., *Policing a City's Central District: The Oakland Story* (Washington, DC: National Institute of Justice, 1985), 7; Albert J. Reiss, Jr., *Private Employment of Public Police*, National Institute of Justice Issues and Practices Report, (Washington, DC: U.S. Department of Justice, Feb. 1988).

42. Clifford D. Shearing and Philip C. Stenning, "Modern Private Security: Its Growth and Implications," in *An Annual Review of Research, Crime and Justice*, vol. 3, ed. Michael Tonry and Norval Morris (Chicago: University of Chicago Press), 1981, 193–245.

43. Cunningham and Taylor, *Hallcrest Report*, table 8-3, p. 108.

44. William Blackstone, *Commentaries on the Laws of England Book IV*, 249, 270 (Oxford: Clarendon, 1765. First ed., reprinted London: Dawson, 1966).

45. For an excellent discussion of the current state of the law of self-defense, see George P. Fletcher, *A Crime of Self-Defense: Bernhard Goetz and the Law on Trial* (New York: Free Press, 1988).

46. Isabel Wilkerson, " 'Crack House' Fire: Justice or Vigilantism?" *New York Times*, 22 Oct. 1988, A1.

47. Patrice Gaines-Carter, "Behind the Muslim Patrols: They Use Tough Tactics but They Bring Pride to the Streets," *Washington Post*, 24 Apr. 1988, D5.

48. For a description and explanation of the current police culture, see Arthur Niederhoffer, *Behind the Shield: The Police in Urban Society* (Garden City, NY: Doubleday, 1967); Rubenstein, *City Police*; Egon Bittner, *The Functions of the Police in Modern Society: A Review of Background Factors, Current Practices, and Possible Role Models* (Cambridge, MA: Oelgeschlager, Gunn and Hain, 1980), 15–21, 31–35, 52–61, and 63–71. For a vision of an alternative culture for police, see Edwin J. Delattre, *Character and Cops: Ethics in Policing* (Washington, DC: American Ethics Institute, 1989).

49. For a discussion of the role of the police culture in both encouraging corruption and preventing its effective investigation, see Commission to Investigate Allegations of Police Corruption and the City's Anti-

Corruption Procedures, *Commission Report* (New York: Knapp Commission, 1972). For a more systematic treatment, see Lawrence W. Sherman, *Scandal and Reform: Controlling Police Corruption* (Berkeley: University of California Press, 1978).

50. George L. Kelling and Mary Ann Wycoff, *Organizational Reform,* vol. 1 of *The Dallas Experience* (Washington, DC: Police Foundation, 1978).

51. See, for example, Stanley Vanagunas and James F. Elliott, *Administration of Police Organizations* (Boston: Allyn and Bacon, 1980), 37–64.

52. Personal testimony to Malcolm K. Sparrow, July 1986.

53. Mary Manolias, *Stress in the Police Service,* Home Office Scientific Research and Development Branch, Human Factors Group, Workshop Study Report, 1983.

CHAPTER 3

1. Cornelius Behan, personal communication to David M. Kennedy.

2. Sir Kenneth Newman, personal communication to David M. Kennedy.

3. David M. Kennedy, *Neighborhood Policing in Los Angeles,* Kennedy School of Government case C16-87-717.0 (Cambridge, MA: Harvard University, 1987).

4. *1984 Summer Olympic Games After Action Report* (Los Angeles: Los Angeles Police Department, 1 Aug. 1985).

5. For a more complete account, see Kennedy, *Neighborhood Policing in Los Angeles.*

6. *An Invitation to Project DARE: Drug Abuse Resistance Education,* Program Brief (Washington, DC: U.S. Department of Justice, Bureau of Justice Assistance, June 1988).

7. For a detailed description of the Watts riot, see Robert Conot, *Rivers of Blood, Years of Darkness* (New York: Bantam, 1967).

8. "Drugs Are Everyone's Problem," Project DARE Juvenile Division. Unpublished pamphlet, Los Angeles Police Department [n.d.].

9. Unpublished DARE factsheet, Los Angeles Police Department, 19 Jan. 1990.

10. William DeJong, *Project DARE: Teaching Kids to Say "No" to Drugs and Alcohol,* National Institute of Justice Report SNI 196 (Washington, DC: U.S. Department of Justice, Mar. 1986).

11. Ibid., 3.

12. Joseph Wambaugh, *The Blue Knight* (Boston: Little, Brown, 1972).

13. "Drugs Are Everyone's Problem."

14. For a more complete description of Behan's actions in Baltimore County, see David M. Kennedy, *Fighting Fear in Baltimore County,* Kennedy School of Government case C16-90-938.0 (Cambridge, MA: Harvard University, 1990). See also Philip B. Taft, Jr., *Fighting Fear: The Baltimore County COPE Project* (Washington, DC: Police Executive Research Forum, 1986).

15. For more details on Newport News, see John Eck et al., *Problem Solving: Problem-oriented Policing in Newport News* (Washington, DC: National Institute of Justice, Police Executive Research Forum, 1987). This report has been embellished by interviews with Darrel Stephens.

16. Personal communication to David M. Kennedy.

17. John K. Avery, *The Police: Force or Service?* (Sydney: Butterworth, 1981).

18. Much of this information is based on the personal observations and consulting experience of Mark H. Moore. It has been reviewed by John Avery.

19. Commission of Inquiry into the New South Wales Police Administration, Report of the Commission of Inquiry into the New South Wales Police Administration. Sydney: The Commission, April 1981. Commission report in New South Wales that discovered corruption and proposed a remedy.

20. This account is based heavily on the observations and experience of Mark H. Moore, who was a member of the Philadelphia Study Task Force, a consultant to the department, and an instructor in programs for Philadelphia midlevel managers. For a journalistic account, see Christopher Hepp, "The Man Who's Rebuilding the Philadelphia Police Department," *Philadelphia Inquirer Magazine,* 8 Feb. 1987, 12–19. See also *Philadelphia and Its Police: Toward a New Partnership* (Philadelphia: Police Study Task Force, Mar. 1987).

21. *Philadelphia and Its Police: Progress toward a New Partnership* (Philadelphia: Police Commissioner's Council, Dec. 1987), 14.

22. For a more complete description, see David M. Kennedy, *Neighborhood Policing: The London Metropolitan Police Force,* Kennedy School of Government case C15-87-770.0 (Cambridge, MA: Harvard University, 1987).

23. Ibid.

24. Ibid. Personal observation by David M. Kennedy.

25. Kennedy, *Neighborhood Policing.*

26. Ibid.

27. Ibid.

28. Ibid.

29. For a more detailed description of the changes in Houston, see Zachary Tumin, "Lee Brown: Community Policing in Houston," unpublished manuscript, from which this chapter draws, with permission. See also Lee P. Brown, "Community Policing: A Practical Guide for Police Officials," *Perspectives on Policing,* no. 12

30. Lee P. Brown, "Community Policing: A Practical Guide for Police Officials," *Perspectives on Policing,* no. 12, 4.

31. Interview with Assistant Chief Thomas G. Koby, by Peter C. Dodenhoff, *Law Enforcement News,* 31 Mar. 1989, 12.

CHAPTER 4

1. For a discussion of these and other emerging strategic conceptions of policing, see Mark H. Moore and Robert C. Trojanowicz, "Corporate Strategies for Policing," *Perspectives on Policing,* no. 6 (Washington, DC: National Institute of Justice and Harvard University, Nov. 1988).

2. For a discussion of the concept of groping and its importance to public-sector managers, see Robert D. Behn, "Management by Groping Along," *Journal of Policy Analysis and Management* 7, no. 4 (Fall 1988): 643–63.

3. For a more detailed discussion of the sorts of offenses that elude the reactive strategy, see Mark H. Moore, "Invisible Offenses," in *Abscam Ethics,* ed. Gerald M. Caplan (Washington, DC: Police Foundation, 1983), 17–42.

4. For an evaluation of the effectiveness of these techniques see Tony Pate, Robert A. Bowers, and Ron Parks, *Three Approaches to Criminal Apprehensions in Kansas City: An Evaluation Report* (Washington, DC: Police Foundation, 1976).

5. Steven Schack, Theodore Schell, and William G. Gay, *Specialized Patrol,* vol. 2 of *Improving Patrol Productivity* (Washington, DC: National Institute of Law Enforcement and Criminal Justice, 1977), 88–93. See also Andrew Halper and Richard Ku, *An Exemplary Project: New York City Street Crime Unit* (Washington, DC: National Institute of Law Enforcement and Criminal Justice, n.d.).

6. For a description and evaluation of such operations, see R. A. Bowers and J. W. McCullough, "Assessing the 'Sting'—An Evaluation of the LEAA Property Crime Program" (Washington, DC: National Institute of Justice, 1983).

7. For a general discussion of these programs, see Mark H. Moore, Susan R. Estrich, Daniel McGillis, and William Spelman, *Dangerous Offenders: The Elusive Target of Justice* (Cambridge, MA: Harvard University Press, 1985), 151–69. For a more particular evaluation, see John E. Boydstun, Richard L. Mekemson, Margaret E. Minton, and Ward Keesling, *Evaluation of the San Diego Police Department's Career Criminal Program* (San Diego: Systems Development Corp., 1981). See also Susan Martin and Lawrence Sherman, "Selective Apprehension: A Police Strategy for Repeat Offenders," *Criminology* 24, no. 1 (Feb. 1986): 155–73.

8. For an analysis of these opportunities, see Ronald V. Clarke, "Situational Crime Prevention: Its Theoretical Basis and Practical Scope," in *Crime and Justice: An Annual Review of Research,* vol. 4, ed. Michael Tonry and Norval Morris (Chicago: University of Chicago Press, 1983), 225–56. For a vivid set of examples describing the approach in operation, see "CPOP: Community Policing in Practice" (New York: Vera Institute of Justice, 1988).

9. Lawrence W. Sherman, "Policing Communities: What Works?" in *Communities and Crime,* ed. Albert J. Reiss, Jr., and Michael Tonry, vol. 8 of *Crime and Justice: A Review of Research* (Chicago: University of Chicago Press, 1986), 343–79. For a general review, see Dennis P. Rosenbaum, ed., *Community Crime Prevention: Does It Work?* (Beverly Hills: Sage, 1986).

10. Leonard Bickman et al., *Citizen Crime Reporting Projects, National Evaluation Program—Phase 1: Summary Report* (Washington, DC: National Institute of Law Enforcement and Criminal Justice, 1976). See also D. E. Frinell, E. Dahlstrom III, and D. A. Johnson, "Public Education Program Designed to Increase the Accuracy and Incidence of Citizens' Reports of Suspicious and Criminal Activities," *Journal of Police Science and Administration* 8, no. 1 (Mar. 1980): 221–30.

11. A. D. Gill, R. A. Kolde, and S. R. Schimerman, *Evaluation of Operation Identification—Phase 1* (Washington, DC: National Institute of Law Enforcement and Criminal Justice, 1975).

12. For an example of an intervention combining various elements, see Floyd J. Fowler, Jr., and Thomas W. Mangione, *Reducing Residential Crime and Fear: The Hartford Neighborhood Crime Prevention Program* (Washington, DC: U.S. Department of Justice, 1979).

13. David M. Kennedy, *Fighting the Drug Trade in Link Valley,* Kennedy School of Government case C16-90-935.0 (Cambridge, MA: Harvard University, 1990).

14. See, for example, John E. Boydstun and Michael E. Sherry, *San Diego*

Community Profile: Final Report (Washington, DC: Police Foundation, 1975), 25.

15. G. Marie Wilt, James D. Bannon, Ronald K. Breedlove, John W. Kennish, Donald M. Sandker, Robert K. Sawtell, Susan Michaelson, and Patricia B. Fox, *Domestic Violence and the Police: Studies in Detroit and Kansas City* (Washington, DC: Police Foundation, 1977).

16. An important exception to this statement was an effort to train New York City police officers in mediation techniques to resolve domestic disputes. For a description, see Morton Bard, "Family Intervention Police Teams as a Community Mental Health Resource," *Journal of Criminal Law, Criminology, and Police Science* 60, no. 2 (1969): 247–50. Now that approach has been eclipsed by a return to law enforcement approaches. See Lawrence W. Sherman and Richard A. Berk, "The Minneapolis Domestic Violence Experiment," *Police Foundation Reports* (Washington, DC: Police Foundation, 1984), 8 ff. For an interpretation of the changing approaches to domestic violence, see Saul N. Weingart, "Adding Insult to Injury: Domestic Violence and Public Policy" (Ph.D. dissertation, Harvard University, 1989).

17. For a more detailed description of these events, see the following articles in the *Boston Globe:* "Witness Says He Called Police Three Times about Rape," 15 July 1985, 17; "Editorial on Boston Police Department's 911 Emergency Phone Service," 18 July 1985, 20; "Boston Council Holds Hearing on 911 Emergency Service," 23 July 1985, 1. For the outcome, see *Boston's 911 System: Recommendations for Improvements in the Emergency Public Safety Response System* (Boston: Mayor's Committee on 911, 1985).

18. Personal communication to the authors during Executive Session in Community Policing, Program in Criminal Justice Policy and Management, John F. Kennedy School of Government, Harvard University, Cambridge, Mass., 1985.

19. For examples of two departments that faced these problems, see *Annual Report—1978* (Phoenix: Phoenix Police Department, 1978); and *Simi Valley, California, Police Department—Patrol Workload Study* (Simi Valley: Simi Valley Police Department, 1977).

20. Lawrence W. Sherman, P. R. Garten, and M. E. Buerger, "Hot Spots of Predatory Crime: Routine Activities and the Criminology of Place," *Criminology* 27, no. 1 (Feb. 1989): 27–55. See also Lawrence W. Sherman, *Repeat Calls to Police in Minneapolis* (Washington, DC: Crime Control Institute, 1987).

21. Kent W. Colton, ed., *Police Computer Technology,* vol. 3 of *Urban Public*

Safety Systems (Lexington, MA: D. C. Heath, 1978). For an account of how such efforts can hinder departments' attempts to use new strategies, see David M. Kennedy, *Computer-Aided Dispatching in Houston, Texas,* Kennedy School of Government case C16-90-985.0 (Cambridge, MA: Harvard University, 1990).

22. David M. Kennedy, *Patrol Allocation in Portland, Oregon (B), PCAM in the City,* Kennedy School of Government case C15-88-819.0 (Cambridge, MA: Harvard University, 1988).

23. J. T. McEwen, E. F. Conners, and M. I. Cohen, *Evaluation of the Differential Police Response Field Test: Final Report* (Washington, DC: National Institute of Justice, 1984).

24. Robert C. Trojanowicz et al., *An Evaluation of the Neighborhood Foot Patrol Program in Flint, Michigan* (East Lansing: Michigan State University, 1982), 86.

25. Egon Bittner, *The Functions of the Police in Modern Society: A Review of Background Factors, Current Practices, and Possible Role Models* (Cambridge, MA: Oelgeschlager, Gunn and Hain, 1980), 31–35.

26. For a discussion of the ultimate accountability of police executives to the political system and the unimportance of civil service protection, see Donald C. Witham, *The American Law Enforcement Chief Executive: A Management Profile* (Washington, DC: Police Executive Research Forum, 1985), 67–68.

27. Stephen D. Mastrofski, "Community Policing as Reform: A Cautionary Tale," in *Community Policing: Rhetoric or Reality,* ed. Jack R. Greene and Stephen D. Mastrofski (New York: Praeger, 1988), 47–68.

28. Based largely on personal communication to Mark H. Moore. For newspaper treatment, see Christopher Hepp, "Control of Police at Issue in Council-Tucker Clash," *Philadelphia Inquirer,* 25 Jan. 1987, 1.

29. Table 14 in Michael T. Farmer, *Survey of Police Operational and Administrative Practices: 1977* (Washington, DC: Police Executive Research Forum, 1978), 29, 30.

30. Personal communication with David M. Kennedy.

31. Bittner, *Functions of the Police,* 52–62; Jonathan Rubenstein, *City Police* (New York: Farrar, Straus and Giroux, 1973), 26–68, 434–55.

32. Mary Manolias, *Stress in the Police Service,* Home Office, Scientific Research and Development Branch, Human Factors Group, Workshop Study Report, 1983.

33. *Philadelphia and Its Police: Toward a New Partnership* (Philadelphia: Police Study Task Force, Mar. 1987), 60–61.

34. See "Our Duties as West Midlands Police Officers," issued by the Chief Constable's Office, West Midlands Police Force, June 1987.

CHAPTER 5

1. This story is based on the experience of Mark H. Moore, who was a member of the Philadelphia Police Study Task Force and, along with Gerard Caplan, a consultant to Kevin Tucker.
2. *Survey of Community Attitudes toward Philadelphia Police: Final Report,* prepared for the Philadelphia Police Study Task Force by National Analysts (Sept. 1986), 13.
3. Ibid., 22, 24.
4. Comment by a Philadelphia police officer at an executive development program conducted by Mark H. Moore.
5. *Statement of Ethical Principles* (Philadelphia: Philadelphia Police Department, 1987).
6. Hubert Williams and Patrick Murphy, "The Evolving Strategy of Policing: A Minority View," *Perspectives on Policing,* no. 13 (Washington, DC: National Institute of Justice, 1990).
7. Saul N. Weingart, "Values in Community Policing" (unpublished manuscript prepared for the Executive Session on Policing, Kennedy School of Government, Harvard University, 20–22 Nov. 1986); used with permission.
8. James Q. Wilson, *Varieties of Police Behavior: The Management of Law and Order in Eight Communities* (Cambridge, MA: Harvard University Press, 1968). See also Albert J. Reiss, Jr., *The Police and the Public* (New Haven: Yale University Press, 1971), and Donald Black, *The Manners and Customs of the Police* (New York: Academic Press, 1980).
9. Richard Elmore, "Organizational Models of Social Program Implementation," *Public Policy* 26, no. 2 (Spring 1978): 185–228.
10. Wilson, *Varieties of Police Behavior,* 49.
11. For a thorough description of how the police behave in encounters with the public and an analysis of the reasons, see Reiss, *Police and the Public.* See also Black, *Manners and Customs.*
12. Robert Wasserman and Mark H. Moore, "Values in Policing," *Perspectives on Policing,* no. 8 (Washington, DC: National Institute of Justice and Harvard University, Nov. 1988).
13. Jonathan Rubenstein, "Cop's Rules," in his *City Police* (New York: Farrar, Straus and Giroux, 1973), 37–41.

14. Mary Manolias, *Stress in the Police Service,* Home Office, Scientific Research and Development Branch, Human Factors Group, Workshop Study Report, 1983.

15. Edwin J. Delattre, *Character and Cops: Ethics in Policing* (Washington, DC: American Ethics Institute, 1989).

16. Arthur Niederhoffer, *Behind the Shield: The Police in Urban Society* (Garden City, NY: Doubleday, 1967). See also Rubenstein, *City Police,* 32–43, 63–68.

17. See *Accident Facts—1989 Edition* (Chicago: National Safety Council, 1989), 44–45.

18. The novels of Joseph Wambaugh offer a powerful description of these experiences. See, for example, *The Blue Knight* (Boston: Little, Brown, 1972) or *The New Centurions* (Boston: Little, Brown, 1970.) For a journalistic view, see James McClure, *Cop World: Policing the Streets of San Diego* (New York: Macmillan, 1984).

19. Thomas J. Peters and Robert H. Waterman, Jr., *In Search of Excellence: Lessons from America's Best-Run Companies* (New York: Harper and Row, 1982), 279–91, 318–25.

20. Ibid., 15.

21. John E. Eck et al., *Problem Solving: Problem-oriented Policing in Newport News* (Washington, DC: National Institute of Justice, Police Executive Research Forum, 1987, 45; see also 41–52.

22. Point of view expressed by a Philadelphia police captain at an executive training session run by the Police Executive Research Forum, Andover, MA, Feb. 1987. The good news is that he was saying this to his new commissioner, Kevin Tucker.

23. The statement of ethics for the Metropolitan Police, published under Commissioner Kenneth Newman in April 1985, "The Principles of Policing and Guidance for Professional Behaviour," ran to sixty pages. That is probably about as much as most officers will read. The longer the statement, the stronger the inclination to regard it as yet another manual.

CHAPTER 6

1. This discussion of the need for police accountability follows closely, sometimes exactly, a treatment of the same subject in Mark H. Moore and Darrel Stephens, *Police Organization and Management: Towards a*

New Managerial Orthodoxy (Washington, DC: Police Executive Research Forum, forthcoming).

2. Jeremy Schmalz, "Uneasy Miami Watches and Waits for Verdict in Officer's Trial," *New York Times,* 4 Dec. 1989, A15; Sean Murphy, "Five File Lawsuits Challenging Boston Police on Search Policy," *Boston Globe,* 22 Nov. 1989, 7.

3. Samuel Walker, "Setting the Standards: The Efforts and Impact of Blue-Ribbon Commissions on the Police," in *Police Leadership in America: Crisis and Opportunity,* ed. William A. Geller (New York: Praeger, 1985), 354–70.

4. Wayne A. Kerstetter, "Who Disciplines the Police? Who Should?" in Geller, ed., *Police Leadership in America,*149–82.

5. Michael Avery and David Rudovsky, *Police Misconduct—Law and Litigation,* 2nd ed. (New York: Clark Boardman, 1981).

6. See, for example, Francis B. Looney, "Rights to Privacy and Police Effectiveness," *The Police Chief,* June 1974, 6; or Don R. Derning, "Judicial Law and the Police," *The Police Chief,* Jan. 1973, 6. While the tone of these editorials is moderate, one can sense the underlying stubbornness about accommodating these values. This attitude may well be reasonable given that courts are imposing these rules with little understanding of the practicalities (and variety) of police work.

7. For a discussion of the impact of civilian review boards, see *Civilian Review of the Police—The Experiences of American Cities* (Hartford: Hartford Institute of Criminal and Social Justice, 1980). See also D. C. Brown, *Civilian Review of Complaints Against the Police—A Survey of the United States Literature* (London: Home Office Research and Planning Unit, 1983).

8. Filmmaker Roger Graef, interview by Malcolm K. Sparrow, London, 28 Apr. 1988.

9. Ibid.

10. Robert Trojanowicz and Bonnie Bucqueroux, "The Flint Experience," in their *Community Policing: A Contemporary Perspective* (Cincinnati, OH: Anderson, 1990), 195–228.

11. Mark H. Moore et al., "The Fourth Platoon, Police Deployment: General Considerations and Particular Problems in New York City," Kennedy School of Government case C14-75-13.0 (Cambridge, MA: Harvard University, 1975).

12. For a discussion of civil liability and its impact on policing, see W. W. Schmidt, "Recent Developments in Civil Liability," *Journal of Police Science and Administration* 4, no. 2 (June 1976): 197–202; Avery and

Rudovsky, *Police Misconduct;* Candace McCoy, "Lawsuits Against the Police: What Impact Do They Really Have?" in *Police Management Today: Issues and Case Studies,* ed. James J. Fyfe (Washington, DC: ICMA, 1985); "Project: Suing the Police in Federal Court," *Yale Law Journal* 88 (1979): 781, 814; Wayne W. Schmidt, "Section 1983 and the Changing Face of Police Management," in Geller, ed., *Police Leadership in America,* 226–40.

13. David M. Kennedy, *Neighborhood Policing: The London Metropolitan Police Force,* Kennedy School of Government case C15-87-770.0 (Cambridge, MA: Harvard University, 1987).

14. *Policing and the Community,* ed. Peter Willmott (London: London Policy Studies Institute, 1987).

15. These analyses are based on the experiences of Malcolm K. Sparrow and Mark H. Moore, who worked independently on revising internal disciplinary procedures. For views of others, see Wayne A. Kerstetter et al., "Who Disciplines the Police? Who Should?" in Geller, ed., *Police Leadership in America,* 147–98.

16. These conclusions are based on Malcolm K. Sparrow's study of disciplinary procedures in the United Kingdom.

17. Schmidt, "Section 1983."

18. Egon Bittner, "Community Relations," 114–118, in his *The Functions of the Police in Modern Society: A Review of Background Factors, Current Practices, and Possible Role Models* (Cambridge, MA: Oelgeschlager, Gunn and Hain, 1980); Louis A. Radelet, *The Police and the Community: Studies* (Beverly Hills: Glencoe, 1973).

19. A complaint investigator in the British Police Service, interview by Malcolm K. Sparrow, 18 Dec. 1986.

20. Head of a British police force's press and public liaison department, interview by Malcolm K. Sparrow, 12 Nov. 1986.

CHAPTER 7

1. See generally Jerome H. Skolnick and David H. Bayley, *The New Blue Line: Police Innovation in Six American Cities* (New York: Free Press, 1986). See also Herman Goldstein, *Policing a Free Society* (Cambridge, MA: Ballinger, 1977), 62–64; and Gerald F. Caiden, *Police Revitalization* (Lexington, MA: D.C. Heath, 1977), 335.

2. Dennis P. Rosenbaum, "Community Crime Prevention: A Review and Synthesis of the Literature," *Justice Quarterly* 5 (1988): 323–95. See also

Mary Ann Wycoff, "The Benefits of Community Policing: Evidence and Conjecture," in *Community Policing: Rhetoric or Reality,* ed. Jack R. Greene and Stephen D. Mostrofski (New York: Praeger, 1988), 103–20.

3. Personal communication to Mark H. Moore from a participant in the Police Executive Research Forum's Senior Managers in Policing Program.

4. One of the most popular of these is the "Crime Stoppers" program, which offers rewards to citizens who call the police. For a description and evaluation, see Dennis P. Rosenbaum, Arthur J. Lurigio, and Paul J. Lavrakas, "Crime Stoppers—A National Evaluation," Research in Brief (Washington, DC: National Institute of Justice, 1986). For survey data on how citizens cooperate with the police, see Catherine J. Whittaker, "Crime Prevention Measures," Bureau of Justice Statistics Special Report (Washington, DC: U.S. Department of Justice, 1986). For a description and evaluation of early efforts to encourage citizen reporting, see Leonard Bickman et al., *Citizen Crime Reporting Projects, National Evaluation Program—Phase 1: Summary Report* (Washington, DC: National Institute of Law Enforcement and Criminal Justice, 1976).

5. David M. Kennedy, *Neighborhood Policing in Los Angeles,* Kennedy School of Government case C16-87-717.0 (Cambridge, MA: Harvard University, 1987).

6. Ibid.

7. David M. Kennedy, *Neighborhood Policing: The London Metropolitan Police Force,* Kennedy School of Government case C15-87-770.0 (Cambridge, MA: Harvard University, 1987).

8. For evidence that this style of policing increases the commitment and morale of officers, see Wycoff, "Benefits of Community Policing," 111–14. For more anecdotal evidence, see "Contemporary Policing: The Officers' View," a videotape produced by the Program on Criminal Justice Policy and Management, John F. Kennedy School of Government, Harvard University, Cambridge, MA, November 1986. This videotape presents community policing officers from Houston, Los Angeles, and other cities talking about their experiences. Their enthusiasm is evident.

9. "Seattle Law on Aggressive Panhandling Wins Cautious Praise," *New York Times,* 26 Dec. 1987, 10.

10. Personal communication to Mark H. Moore.

11. "Seattle Law."

12. Personal communication to Mark H. Moore.

13. Personal communication to David M. Kennedy.

14. Richard Walker, personal communication to David M. Kennedy. The good news, Walker notes, is that when the Portland bureau reached out to municipal agencies, neighborhood organizations, the business community, and the press—as it did in beginning community policing—it found all parties willing to strike new, cooperative relationships.
15. Kennedy, *Neighborhood Policing in Los Angeles*.
16. For general description of this function, see Ulf Lundvik, *The Ombudsman as a Watchdog of Legality and Equity in Administration*, Occasional Paper 9 (S.L. [Edmonton]: International Ombudsman Institute, 1980); Sam Zagarin, *The Ombudsman: How Good Governments Handle Citizens' Grievances* (Cabin John, MD: Seven Locks Press, 1988).
17. John E. Eck et al., *Problem Solving: Problem-oriented Policing in Newport News* (Washington, DC: National Institute of Justice, Police Executive Research Forum, 1987), 80.
18. Personal communication to David M. Kennedy.
19. Personal communication to David M. Kennedy.
20. Ibid.
21. Kennedy, *Fighting Fear in Baltimore County*.
22. Ibid.
23. Ibid.
24. Darrel Stephens, personal communication to David M. Kennedy.
25. See, for example, Francis B. Looney, "Rights to Privacy and Police Effectiveness," *The Police Chief*, June 1974, 6; or Don R. Derning, "Judicial Law and the Police," *The Police Chief*, Jan. 1973, 8.

CHAPTER 8

1. Susan O. White and Samuel Krislov, eds., *Understanding Crime: An Evaluation of the National Institute of Law Enforcement and Criminal Justice* (Washington, DC: National Academy of Sciences, 1977). For a review of the Law Enforcement Assistance Administration's experience that emphasizes the costs, see Thomas E. Cronin, Tania Z. Cronin, and Michael Milakovich, *U.S. v. Crime in the Streets* (Bloomington: Indiana University Press, 1981), 134–69. For a slightly more favorable view, see Malcolm M. Feely and Austin D. Sarat, *The Policy Dilemma: Federal Crime Policy and the Law Enforcement Assistance Administration, 1968–1978* (Minneapolis: University of Minnesota Press, 1980).
2. Rosabeth Moss Kanter, *The Changemaster: Innovating for Productivity*

in the American Corporation (New York: Simon and Schuster, 1983), 69–101.

3. Victor A. Thompson, "Bureaucracy and Innovation," *Administrative Science Quarterly* 10 (1965): 1–20.

4. James Brian Quinn, "Managing Innovation: Controlled Chaos," *Harvard Business Review*, May–June 1985, 73–84.

5. Robert H. Hayes and Ramchandran Jaikumar, "Manufacturing Crisis: New Technologies, Obsolete Organization," *Harvard Business Review*, Sept.–Oct. 1988, 77–85.

6. Kanter, *Changemaster*, 278–306.

7. Personal communication to Malcolm K. Sparrow.

8. Richard C. Vancil, *Texas Instruments Inc., Management Systems: 1972*, Harvard Business School case 172-054 (Cambridge, MA: Harvard University, 1972).

9. Thomas J. Peters and Robert H. Waterman, Jr., *In Search of Excellence: Lessons from America's Best-Run Companies* (New York: Harper and Row, 1982), 193–99.

10. William J. Abernathy and James M. Utterback, "Patterns of Industrial Innovation," *Technology Review*, June–July 1978, 41–47.

11. Eleanor Chelimsky, ed., *Program Evaluation: Patterns and Directions* (Washington, DC: American Society for Public Administration, 1985). See also Jeremiah T. Murphy, *Getting the Facts: A Field Work Guide for Evaluators and Policy Analysts* (Santa Monica, CA: Goodyear Publishing, 1980).

12. Lewis Branscomb, interview with Malcolm K. Sparrow and David M. Kennedy, Cambridge, MA, 18 Oct. 1988.

13. Mollie Weatheritt, *Innovations in Policing* (London: Croom Helm, 1986).

14. Darrel Stephens, interview with Malcolm K. Sparrow and David M. Kennedy, 21 Oct. 1988, Cambridge, MA and Washington, DC.

15. James K. Stewart, Speech to the Panel on the Causes and Prevention of Violence, Committee on Law Enforcement and the Administration of Justice, National Academy of Sciences, June 15, 1989. Mark H. Moore was in the audience.

16. Weatheritt, *Innovations in Policing*, 12–14.

17. Excessive focus on technology was also a criticism of America's Law Enforcement Assistance Administration. For an explanation of why technology was pushed, see Cronin, Cronin, and Milakovich, *U.S. v. Crime*, 149.

18. Weatheritt, *Innovations in Policing*, 12.

19. Ibid., 13–14.
20. Stephens interview.
21. See, for instance, Mary Jo Bane and Olivia Golden, "Managing and Sustaining Innovation in Human Services: Innovation in State and Local Government" (paper presented at the annual meeting of the American Political Science Association, Washington, DC, 3 Sept. 1988).
22. Ibid., 23.
23. Some discipline investigation officers have worked to the maxim "every time an officer gets disciplined, his supervisor should be too." Personal experience of Malcolm K. Sparrow.
24. Stephens interview.
25. Lieutenant Dennis A. Gibson, Internal Affairs Department, San Diego Police, personal communication to Malcolm K. Sparrow. A narrative description of the new disciplinary philosophy adopted by the command staff during fall 1987 appears in the *City of San Diego Police Discipline Manual.*
26. Stephens interview.
27. Peters and Waterman, *In Search of Excellence,* 318–25.
28. Both of these are pseudonyms. The officers were concerned that the views they expressed might not be well received by their senior officers. The authors regret this state of affairs but are bound to honor the officers' wishes. These portraits are based on extensive personal interviewing by Malcolm K. Sparrow.
29. For a preliminary discussion of this concept, see J. Kretz, *Exploratory Interviews Concerning an Alternate Set of Rank Titles for the Washington Metropolitan Police Department—Report* (Washington, DC: Bureau of Social Science Research, 1974).
30. For a review of the field's experience with performance appraisals, see Pennsylvania State University, *Police Performance Appraisal—Final Report* (Washington, DC: National Institute of Law Enforcement and Criminal Justice, n.d.).
31. For a more detailed discussion of the problem-solving process, we recommend John E. Eck et al., *Problem Solving: Problem-oriented Policing in Newport News* (Washington, DC: National Institute of Justice, Police Executive Research Forum, 1987).
32. For an example of a department that did this, see *Police Services: A Survey of Citizen Satisfaction* (Peoria, IL: Advisory Committee on Police-Community Relations, 1982).

INDEX

■

Index

Attitudes, police (*continued*)
service role, 53, 63, 66; toward creativity, 209; toward "nuisance" calls,
101–2; toward patrols, 51, 53, 205;
toward public, 160–61

Attitudes, public: toward police autonomy, 151–52; police violence and,
152–53; Stephens on, 208–9

Australia, police innovation in, 207. *See
also* New South Wales Police Department

Automobiles, abandoned, police and,
175–76

Autonomy of police: as key strategic
issue, 108–12; in London Met, 87–
88; as mixed blessing, 77–78; operational, community involvement vs.,
112–14; public attitude toward, 151–
52; as stonewalling mechanism, 158

Avery, John, 114, 198; appointment as
reformer, 73–74; balance of geographic and specialized units in
NSWPD, 118; policing philosophy of,
72

Baltimore County, innovations in po-
licing in, 67–70, 191. *See also* Garden
Village housing project (Baltimore
County)

Beat patrol: emergency telephone system and, 227–28; as means of crime
prevention, 32–33; motorized, in Los
Angeles, 62; performance measures for,
226–28; resident (U.K.), 220; size of,
225. *See also* Clarke, Norman (pseud.);
Foot patrol; Hollings, Nick (pseud.)

Behan, Neil, 71, 96, 198; COPE program of, 67–70; on dealing with community fears, 183

Bond, Pappy, deregulation of police
force, 91

Boston Police Department, foot patrol
vs. rapid response, 104

Branscomb, Lewis, on innovation at
IBM, 202, 204

Brixton, riots against police, 83–84,
158–59

"Broken Windows," 10, 14

Brown, Lee, 198; community collaboration and, 113; neighborhood policing reforms of, 90–94

Bunker mentality of police, 144. *See also*
Values of police

Burglary: community cooperation
against, 175; in New Briarfield Apartments, 18–19

Caldwell, Harry, Houston Police Department and, 91

Career structure for patrol officers, 225–
26

Centralization: strategic choices regarding, 118–23; of London Met, 87; of
police department administration,
119–21; of police departments, 36, 43

Chiefs of police: changing nature of job,
197–98; innovations by, 58–59; values held by, 136. *See also* Behan, Neil;
Bond, Pappy; Brown, Lee; Davis, Ed;
Dyson, Frank; Fitzsimons, Pat; Gates,
Daryl; Short, Herman; Stephens, Darrel; Walker, Richard

Ciancanelli, Joe, 9, 181–82

Cities, crime in, 5–8, 23–24

Citizen-Oriented Police Enforcement.
See COPE teams

Civilian review boards, limited effectiveness of, 153

Civil liberties: courts and, 195; police as
defenders of, 136, 179, 195–96

Clarke, Norman (pseud.), 214–20, 229,
258n28

260

Clearance rates, 44

Colleagues, loyalty to, 51, 52

Collins, J.W., 21–22, 23–24

Commissioners of police, creation as reform agent, 35, 36

Communication: barriers to, in police departments, 146–47; of police values, 146–48

Community: collaboration, 113; cooperation against burglary, 175; COPE and fears of, 183–84; crime prevention and, 46–47, 100, 112–14, 174; isolation of police from, 52; police attitudes toward, 51, 53; Senior Lead Officer and, 175, 180–81

Community attitudes: complaints against police and, 165–67; inappropriate requests of police and, 178–80, 194–96; need for change in, 131; in Philadelphia, 133–34; toward police, 102–3, 207–8; police failures and, 151–53; in poor communities, 180–81; problem-solving policing and, 185–86

Community consultation: advantages of, 161–62; imposed after Brixton riots, 159

Community Mobilization Project, 9, 12; community relations, 184; police priorities and, 64; rapid response and, 107; reduction in resources for, 182; successes of, 129–30. *See also* Wilshire Area, L.A.

Community organizations: crime prevention and, 21, 28, 63, 64; for oversight of police, 159

Community policing: effects of, 129; theory of (Avery), 74; in Wilshire Area, 8–14. *See also* Neighborhood policing

Community-relations departments, 167–69; complaints departments and, 168; police attitude toward, 168. *See also* Community attitudes

Community service role, 101–3; of early police departments, 34; of London Met, 86–87; of Newport News police, 70–71; of NSWPD, 74; police attitude toward, 53, 63, 66; of Senior Lead Officer, 9–12, 61, 193, 200. *See also* DARE

Complaints against police, 163–67; characteristics of, 164*n*; community attitudes and, 165–67; law governing, 163; withdrawal of, 164–65

Consultation, community, 159, 161–62

Cooperation, interagency, 185, 186, 189–91, 256*n*14

COPE teams: in Baltimore County, 67–70; fear and, 183–84, 194; interagency cooperation and, 190–91; other local agencies and, 184–85; racial incidents resolved, 100, 193; social service agency and, 188

Cordons (roadblocks), 24, 25–27

Corruption: in early police forces, 32; in New York City police force, 34, 35; reform of, 36–37

Courts, civil liberties and, 195

Creativity: management styles and, 209–10; police departments' attitudes toward, 209. *See also* Innovation(s)

Crime: in cities, 5–8, 23–24; housing deterioration and, 4, 18–19, 22; in nineteenth-century England, 32; public perceptions of, 62–63, 175–76, 177–78; retrospective investigation of, 47

Crime control: community assistance in, 46–47, 100, 112–14; dispute resolution and, 102; LAPD, 174–75; as major goal of policing, 41; means of, 42–43; problem-oriented policing and, 99–100; reactive vs. preventive, 42–43, 97–100; as source of police legitimacy, 151

Crime prevention: communities and,